Notorious

Also by John Pearson

Non-fiction
Bluebird and the Dead Lake
The Persuasion Industry (with Graham Turner)
The Life of Ian Fleming
Arena: The Story of the Colosseum
The Profession of Violence
Edward the Rake
Barbara Cartland: The Crusader in Pink
Facades: Edith, Osbert and Sacheverell Sitwell
Stags and Serpents: The Cavendish Dukes of Devonshire
The Ultimate Family: The Making of the House of Windsor
Citadel of the Heart: Winston and the Churchill Dynasty
Painfully Rich: J. Paul Getty and His Heirs
Blood Royal: The Story of the Spencers and the Royals
The Cult of Violence
One of the Family: The Englishman and the Mafia
The Gamblers: Aspinall, Goldsmsith and the Murder of Lord Lucan

Fiction
Gone to Timbuctoo
The Life of James Bond
The Kindness of Dr Avicenna
The Authorised Life of Biggles
The Bellamy Saga

Notorious

How the Kray Twins Made
Themselves Immortal

John Pearson

Published by Century in 2010

First published in the United Kingdom in 2010 by
Century
Random House, 20 Vauxhall Bridge Road,
London, SW1V 2SA

www.randomhouse.co.uk

Addresses for companies within The Random House Group Limited can be
found at: www.randomhouse.co.uk

The Random House Group Limited Reg. No. 954009

A CIP catalogue record for this book
is available from the British Library

ISBN 9781846051524

The Random House Group Limited supports The Forest Stewardship
Council (FSC), the leading international forest certification organisation.
All our titles that are printed on Greenpeace approved FSC certified paper carry
the FSC logo. Our paper procurement policy can be found at
www.rbooks.co.uk/environment

Mixed Sources
Product group from well-managed
forests and other controlled sources
www.fsc.org Cert no. TT-COC-2139
© 1996 Forest Stewardship Council

Typeset by SX Composing DTP, Rayleigh, Essex
Printed and bound in the United Kingdom by
CPI Mackays, Chatham, ME5 8TD

For Mark Booth

Praise for *The Profession of Violence* by John Pearson

'The most famous biography of criminal life to have been published in Britain . . . it has become something of a cult among the young.'
Time Out

'The person who best understood what made the Kray industry tick and the Kray fascination blossom remains John Pearson whose book *The Profession of Violence* summed the two men up.'
Deborah Orr, the *Independent*

'All credit to Mr Pearson for a brave and disturbing book.'
Daily Express

'The biography is brave and well-written . . . an exciting read.'
The Times

'Mr Pearson has produced a scrupulous dossier of the Krays' weird career.'
Daily Telegraph

'The book is extremely well-written and is fitting deadpan.'
New Statesman

Contents

1	Introduction	1
2	The Trial: April 1969	6
3	Birth: 1934	11
4	Twins: 1937	15
5	East End	20
6	Crime as Destiny: 1954–48	27
7	God Bless the Royal Fusiliers: 1952–54	39
8	The Billiard Hall: 1954–59	47
9	Twins Apart	58
10	Esmerelda's and After: 1960–64	79
11	Enter Boothby: 1964	100
12	Cover-up: August–September 1964	121
13	Blackmail: 1964–65	138
14	Sing, Fuck You, Sing!	164
15	Killing Cornell	177
16	Exit the Axeman	193
17	Invitation to a Sacrifice	218
18	The American Connection	251
19	Murder for Two	265
20	The Kingdom of the Krays	277
21	Showdown in New York	297
22	Remand	315
23	The Trial of the Century	325
24	End Game	342
	Appendix	363

'From an early age Ron and I had taken it for granted that whatever path we took we'd end up being famous'

1

Introduction

I SUPPOSE FEW THINGS in life are more disturbing for a writer than the awareness of unfinished business, and having to accept that something you wrote about many years ago is unresolved – worse still, when you stumble on the truth that has eluded you for so long and it starts to haunt you. Which is what has recently been happening to me over the whole strange story of the Krays.

Back in 1967 when I first met them in the house which is now the stately home of former Rolling Stone Bill Wyman, I genuinely lacked the faintest notion of what I was in for, which was just as well. In some ways I was fortunate. It's not every day that a pair of celebrated murderers invite a biographer to share their reminiscences, meet their family and friends, and write the story of their lives. Later I learned that, before asking me, their first choice had been Truman Capote who had declined – which showed that Truman wasn't quite as silly as he seemed.

Time moved on. By the time my book was finished, nearly four years later, the Twins had been sent to prison for the rest of their natural lives, and I had spent six months of mine sitting through their remand hearing at the Old Street Magistrates' Court, followed by their trial at the Old Bailey. By then I probably knew more about them than they knew themselves, and when my book was published in 1972 under the title *The*

Profession of Violence they hated it – though later, when they saw what it was inadvertently doing for their prestige in jail, they changed their minds

Apart from the fact that, for reasons which I will explain later in this book, the project had all but bankrupted me, I was rather pleased with it. It has been in print ever since, and I'm told that it kicked-started a genre of so-called 'true crime' books, as well as a cottage industry of memoirs by almost anyone who believes that he can write and can claim the faintest contact with the Twins. At the last count there were over thirty of them. So when I heard that, after the Bible, *The Profession* had become the most widely read book in HM Prisons, and *Time Out* magazine was hailing it as 'the most famous biography of criminal life to have been published in Britain', I felt I'd said all that needed to be said about the Krays, and that was that.

I had not reckoned with the Twins. Throughout their time in captivity I'd kept in touch with them, and by the time of their deaths – Ron in 1995, Reg six years later – and the grandiose East End funerals that followed, something very odd indeed had happened. It seemed that, having been celebrity criminals for years, they had finally achieved something more. There had been a film about them. Every London taxi driver over fifty seemed to have some story to tell about them, and their former bitter gangland enemy 'Mad' Frankie Fraser was currently conducting gobsmacked tourists round The Blind Beggar, the unlovely East End hostelry where Ron had gunned down his fellow villain, George Cornell. David Bailey's photographs had, as the phrase goes, 'iconised' them, and when sociologists started writing learned papers about them it was clear that they had assumed their place in the social history of the Sixties. They were also something of a national obsession, and just as James Bond epitomises everything we take for granted in a secret agent and Sherlock Holmes is our ultimate detective, so the one word 'Kray' is embedded in our collective memory as accepted shorthand for the quintessential British gangster.

But who really were these two strange criminals whom I thought I knew so well? Why and how, out of all the variegated villains who have filled our newspapers and television screens during the last half-century, did it have to be the Krays, and they alone, who took their place beside Jack the Ripper as 'iconic' criminals of enduring fascination?

It was at their trial that I first sensed that something very strange indeed was going on, although, as so often with the Twins, it was hard to grasp exactly what it was. One thing I realised was how utterly unique they were, and that their role in the mythology of crime was nowhere near as simple as it seemed. There were certain things that both the Krays and the Establishment were determined to keep secret. But one thing and one alone stood out as the Everest point in their whole bizarre career, the scandal that for four long years before they were arrested had rendered them invulnerable. In fact, as I also finally discovered, there were actually not one but two quite separate scandals involving the Krays and the Establishment.

It was only in 1984, after the death of Baron Robert John Graham Boothby KBE, that I was able to outline the story of the scandal involving him and Ronnie Kray. Since then, papers recently released at the Public Record Office not only confirmed everything I wrote but revealed irrefutably the involvement of so many senior politicians on both sides of Parliament in suppressing the truth behind this whole unusual business that the cover-up must count as a separate scandal of vertiginous cynicism by both sides of the political establishment. Whenever I think of it and of what ensued, it is the sheer cynicism of the Establishment that somehow still offends me.

Perhaps it barely matters if our rulers lie to us in public – as long as their colleagues are willing to protect them. Still less may it matter if politicians take their sexual pleasures in the company of criminals, provided that the media and members of the judiciary are prepared to hush it up. And if gangsters thrive and men get murdered as a consequence, perhaps that doesn't really matter either, as long as the police have been warned off and the press are stopped from mentioning the truth. But if things like this *do* matter, then the story that I have to tell simply cannot be ignored.

In relating it I have been fortunate to find much new material, and I make no apologies for allowing it to form so large a part of my narrative. For not only are the Boothby scandal and the subsequent cover-up crucial to an understanding of the rise and ultimate destruction of the Krays, they also form an all-important segment of the history of the Sixties. Above all they offer us an unparalleled cautionary tale on the perils of corruption and complacency in our democratic body politic.

Apart from which, for me at any rate, the enduring fascination of the weird story of the Twins will always end where it began – with them, and with that whole doomed twin relationship which locked them so disastrously together, making them, both biologically and criminally, utterly unique. Because of this, there is for me something else in their story which gets overlooked – a twisted tragedy, which I hope I also manage to convey and so complete the task that I accepted so light-heartedly more than forty years ago.

I would like to thank Mike Abrahams, Frank Kurylo, Leon Morgan, Stewart Grimshaw, Pam Hirsch, Chris Jenks, Ben Hytner, Ian Sinclair, Nick Lloyd, Wilf Pine, Anke Lueddeke, Steve Wraithe, Michael Thornton, Julian Bell, Nick Davies, Dick Hobbs, Stan Frankland, Derek Jameson, Harriet Vyner, Jacqueline Williams, Justin de Villeneuve and Edda Tasiemka of the incomparable Hans Tasiemka Archive. I would also like to thank Neal and Harry Dickinson, and Edward Fry, who saved my sanity over my computer, and Penny Thomas, Mike Brooks and Tim Doyle for helping me to keep on walking. Ted Green and Ellie Grey were always there for me – so were my family and my wife Lynette who has been so wonderful that words fail me. Finally I must thank my saintly editor Katie Duce who ultimately made this book possible.

2

The Trial: April 1969

WHEN THE TRIAL was over, the judge, Sir Melford
Stevenson, hung up his wig and scarlet robes, knowing
that his greatest period of fame was over. The longest-running
legal show in town, which had started with the remand hearings
eleven months earlier, was concluding before him at the Old
Bailey and like any impresario at the end of a successful run Sir
Melford couldn't help a certain feeling of regret. One by one he
had dismissed his cast to the limbo of imprisonment. He had
despised the lot of them, as he despised all criminals, but the
truth was that he would miss them, especially the Twins.

He was only sorry that he couldn't hang them. The ritual
donning of the black cap, followed by the ancient litany
condemning a murderer to death had always fascinated him.
'You shall be taken hence to a place of execution and hanged
by the neck until you are dead, and may God have mercy on
your soul.' What finer culmination to this monstrous trial could
there have been? But his government had recently put capital
punishment on hold and would soon abolish it for ever.

Still, what a trial it had been, with witness after witness betraying
one another and relating tales of wickedness and cruelty from
across what seemed at times to be the whole gamut of criminal
humanity. It could all have gone very wrong indeed, and it was
largely thanks to Sir Melford that it hadn't. At the beginning of the
trial when he had tried to make the ten defendants in the dock

wear numbers round their necks (in order, so he said, to make it easier for the jury to identify them) and when all of them had angrily refused, Sir Melford had managed to control his temper and had accepted that his bright idea would never work. After a short recess to recover his dignity he had succeeded in continuing with the trial as if nothing untoward had happened. Even at the climax of the trial, when Reg Kray called the prosecuting counsel Kenneth Jones QC 'a fat slob', he took no notice. There had been just one curiously revealing moment, when Ron Kray had been giving his disjointed 'evidence' from the witness box and had made a passing reference to Lord Boothby. Having been carefully forewarned that this might happen, and what the consequences might be, Sir Melford had immediately blocked that dangerous line of reminiscence and the witness swiftly got the message.

And so, in spite of various distractions, everything had turned out as intended. The witnesses had been dismissed, the murderers and their accomplices found guilty, and despite the accounts of violence and betrayal, of sadism and sodomy, of bleeding hearts and bleeding faces, and the whole farrago of suffering humanity which Sir Melford had fairly patiently endured, nothing remotely like the truth about the Twins had actually emerged. But then, the last thing the Kray Twins wanted either was for the truth about themselves to be revealed in open court – nor, for that matter, had the prosecution wanted it. And nor, emphatically, had Sir Melford Stevenson.

So what had everyone been up to in this long and long-winded trial? Why all the huffing and puffing from so many turncoats, victims, senior policemen and half-baked gangsters, not to mention the hot air from so many sleek young barristers paid for by a grateful government? And what had happened to those fearsome allegations made against the Krays so many months before, when the trial began? Had they really been hand in glove with the American Mafia over their gambling rackets and the sale of stolen bearer bonds in Europe? Had one of the main prosecution witnesses been working, as he had claimed, for the US Secret Service? And what about the branding and the mutilation of their wretched victims, the bodies supposedly concreted into the pillars of the Chiswick flyover, not to mention the perversions, the hidden wealth, and the plans to kidnap the Pope and release President Tshombe of the Congo, fascinating stories which the prosecution had mentioned at the remand proceedings but subsequently had found no time to answer. And nor had anybody else.

Instead, the trial had finally boiled down to the fairly humdrum murders by the Twins of two fellow East End villains, one of them while sitting in a pub and armed with nothing more lethal than a pint of bitter, the other butchered while attempting to scramble through a window in a basement flat in Stoke Newington.

Was that meant to have the whole of Middle England shaking in its socks? Had that really been enough to turn the Kray Twins into the most feared and famous felons of the century? Forgive me, but did old Melford know something that we didn't?

Of course he did. But, as is the privilege of the judiciary, he wasn't letting on and one can only guess at why he felt such deep distaste for the principal defendants in this case. If he couldn't top them, he didn't hide the relish with which he did the next best thing, effectively condemning them to spend the remainder of their lives in prison. 'I think society has earned a break from your activities. Accordingly I condemn you to thirty years in prison with a recommendation that in your case thirty years are a minimum of thirty years – no less. Jailer, take them down.'

After which the old boy briskly thanked the jury and dismissed them. He commended the police and had a special word of praise for Detective Superintendent 'Nipper' Read who had 'masterminded' the investigation. And that was that. By the time the bulletproof police vans with their heavily armed escorts had rumbled off to the first of many prisons which would be the nearest thing to home the Twins would know until they died – Ron Kray to the so-called 'mini-Alcatraz', of the maximum security unit in Durham, his twin brother Reg to a similar set-up in Parkhurst on the Isle of Wight – the little judge was in a taxi heading for the Garrick Club, where he was known as something of a wit and enjoyed lunching with a few old legal cronies at the long table under the portraits of those other actors, Olivier and Kean and the great Garrick himself in the role of Macbeth – who, come to think of it, was another famous murderer.

The judge was greeted warmly by his friends, and over the Garrick's claret and kidney, steak and oyster pie they began to quiz him on the trial.

'Well, Melford, you were pretty tough on them. Now it's over, tell us what you really thought of them.'

'What did I think? To be honest, I've never had such an unsavoury pair to deal with in my life. But, you know, they did say two things that were true.'

'Like what?'

'In the first place, one of them called our portly friend Kenneth Jones a fat slob.'

'I'd not object to that. And what other nugget of truth did they offer?'

'When one of them claimed that the judge was prejudiced against them, I fear he was.'

'So you admit it, Melford. But would you really have been so happy to have topped them?'

Sir Melford nodded. 'Certainly. They were the most suitable candidates for capital punishment I have ever encountered.'

'Because they were unusually evil?'

'All murderers are evil, but with the Kray Twins that was not the point. They were a profound danger to society, as I said.

Society needs to see the back of Ronald and Reginald, and dead murderers can't talk.'

'Would it matter if they did? They had their chance to say anything they wished to at their trial. Why didn't they?'

'Because it didn't suit them. But they could always change their minds, and if they ever do they could cause an awful lot of damage. Still, thirty years in maximum security should keep them quiet and help everybody to forget them. But with any luck I think you'll find we've heard the last of Reginald and Ronald, and the rest of their unpleasant hangers-on.'

But Sir Melford Stevenson was wrong. Despite his verdict, prison life would not destroy them, and their extraordinary careers as criminal celebrities were far from over.

3

Birth: 1934

T HE STORY OF the Twins began in February 1934 in the womb of Violet Kray, wife to a Hoxton rag-and-bone man called Charles Kray.

In spite of the rate of infant mortality in the old East End, buxom Violet had had no problem producing one good-looking healthy son already. He was born in 1931 and was christened Charles, in honour of his father – this despite the fact that there really wasn't all that much to honour in the life of Charles Kray Sr. A lifelong boozer who, in the old phrase, 'kept low company', he would supplement his earnings by buying old gold brooches, wedding rings, and gold-mounted false teeth from needy widows he encountered on his buying expeditions through the south of England. In 1939 when war broke out and he was invited to defend his King and Country he would decline that honour too, instantly desert, and stay on the run for more than fifteen years. But Charlie was a wily bird, and thanks to the trade in second-hand false teeth and second-hand clothes he could always make a living and stay clear of the police, which was the most important thing a married man could do for his nearest and dearest in those hungry years.

Unfortunately for Violet, her parents were a pair of strong-willed Cockney puritans whose experience of the demon drink had made them lifelong teetotallers. So they had not been impressed by the prospect of Charles Kray Sr as a son-in-law.

But Charles was obstinate: the marriage went ahead, and the young pair started married life in a two-roomed flat in Hoxton and had lived there ever since.

Then, two years later, when Violet discovered she was once more pregnant, she sensed that things were not the same as when she'd been carrying young Charlie. She did not know it then, but for reasons of its own the fertilised egg inside her had decided to divide and the two segments were producing two identical but separate human beings. A few weeks later, when she went along for her check-up at the Mare Street clinic, Violet was told that she was having twins.

This was the moment when the world of Violet Kray was changed for ever, as was that of her family, although at this stage none of them realised what they were in for. This included Charles Kray Sr who, when he heard the news, put aside some money which would normally have gone on booze and started saving for a double pram. His in-laws were so impressed by this that they felt the time had come to finally accept him as a member of the family. They began to make arrangements for Violet and family to move into an empty house two doors away from theirs in Vallance Road, Bethnal Green. Since her married sisters May and Rose were already living opposite, this meant that Violet would soon be back among her own, with everything more or less forgiven. So it was that before they were even born the Twins had made their presence felt and helped to bring the family together. And this was only the beginning.

For a married woman in the tough disease-prone world of the old East End, the birth of a pair of healthy twins was regarded as something of an achievement and Violet made the most of it. As she pushed that small impassive pair of agate-eyed monsters out in Charlie's brand new pram, she knew that she was special too. To make the most of this, she did everything she could to show the world that they were twins and to emphasise the difference between them and all the other kids in Bethnal

Green. She dressed them identically in smart blue coats and white angora berets, 'so that they looked just like two little bunny rabbits in their pram'. She chose the names Reginald and Ronald for them, 'because the two names went so well together'. And when she wanted them to come to her, she always called out 'Twins', rather than 'Reggie and Ronnie,' as if they were one person with a single name. This was how the Twins grew up, in their private little world at the centre of the village-like community of Bethnal Green, where everyone knew everyone else and all the other children knew that Violet's twins were special. Even brother Charlie knew it and reluctantly accepted it, which was tough on Charlie, and he never quite got over it. But now that the Twins had started life as miniature celebrities they would go on being special when they were miniature no longer.

There was more to it than that. If the Twins were special, so was Violet, which meant that, like it or not, all three of them were joined in a more or less unconscious conspiracy, and as the years went by Violet was going to depend upon the twins for any self-esteem she had. Without them, she would have been Mrs Nobody, like May and Rose or any mother from Bethnal Green with a humdrum life and a wayward husband. Similarly, without Violet's devotion, in the rough, tough world of the old East End the Twins would have been two weird and isolated small boys, with no one to rely on or support them. But as long as the bond between the three of them endured, so would the special status that underpinned the trio's mutual self-respect.

This had its drawbacks. Being special meant being different, and there always would be something strange about the Twins. 'It's hard to say exactly what it was, but they weren't like other children,' said their cousin Billy Wilshire, and people who knew them still remember how self-contained they seemed to be within the little world that they inhabited. As Ron himself put it when he talked to me about this many years later: 'We had our mother, and we had each other, so we never needed no one else.'

4

Twins: 1937

IT DIDN'T TAKE the doctors long to discover that the Twins were even more remarkable than their mother thought they were. The most common sort of twins are so-called binovular twins, which occur when two eggs become fertilised within the womb. For all intents and purposes such twins usually turn out like ordinary siblings, each with a separate genetic make-up, physique and personality. Identical twins are different. In their case, when the single fertilised egg divides within the womb it produces twins who are literally identical, with the same genetic make-up, the same psychology and physique, and – as with Ron and Reg until they were well into their early twenties – they can be facially indistinguishable. Such twins are, in fact, one of the stranger quirks of human physiology.

Until you get accustomed to identical twins it can be disconcerting to be faced with what appears to be a human being in duplicate, often showing the same mannerisms, the same gestures, and with each twin's face an exact image of the other's. One theory has it that because we're not accustomed to seeing double versions of the same person, our first reaction is to feel baffled and uneasy in their presence. In the past this often caused identical twins to be treated with both fear and fascination. In some primitive societies they were regarded as ill-omened, and were sometimes even put to death at birth to avert divine displeasure, while others found something supernatural in their make-up. The ancient Greeks, who detected gods or demigods in almost everything, gave identical twins a special place in their mythology. Thus, when Zeus – who as father of the gods should have known better – tricked Queen Leda into having sex with him by disguising himself as a swan, the sacred nature of the copulation resulted in the birth of the heavenly twins, Castor and Pollux, whose immortality lives on in the twin stars still named after them.

In medieval England twins were sometimes found in freak shows and were shown at circuses. But in modern times scientists have started to take identical twins more seriously and, realising the importance of having two individuals with an identical genetic make-up, have begun studying their behaviour in depth.

In the 1930s one such scientist, the Austrian criminologist Lange, made a fascinating study of identical-twin criminals who had become separated at birth. Lange ended up convinced of the crucial role of heredity in criminal personality. If he was right, since Ron and Reg shared an identical set of genes, then if one twin showed a tendency to crime the other would be inclined to follow.

Normally, inherited similarities between identical twins tend to taper off with adolescence and can vanish completely with the advent of maturity as genetic similarities get overshadowed by environmental differences. But here again, the Kray Twins would be different and this disengaging process would not occur, thanks to another untoward event which was going to affect them both profoundly. At the age of three the bonds of twinship tightened so dramatically that the Twins would effectively stay locked together for the rest of their lives.

Until now the two boys had been extremely healthy and only Violet could tell the two of them apart. When Reggie was taken ill and the doctor diagnosed diphtheria, their mother knew that Ronnie would almost certainly succumb as well. He did so three days later.

This was serious. Diphtheria is an acute infectious disease in which a membrane sometimes forms within the throat, which can cause death by suffocation. The disease can also produce dangerous neurotoxins that damage the central nervous system. Today diphtheria is virtually a disease of the past, almost totally eradicated by immunisation; but in those days it was highly contagious and potentially deadly, particularly in the deprived conditions of pre-war Bethnal Green. So for the first time in their lives the Twins were separated and sent to different isolation hospitals, Ron to the Homerton Fever Hospital and Reg to one in Hackney. Both of them were seriously ill but within a few weeks Reg had started to recover and was soon sent home. Ron, though, showed no improvement. He remained painfully weak and seemed to lack the will to live. By now all hope for him was fading fast.

I remember the pride with which Violet described every detail of her starring role in the crisis that ensued. This was obviously one of the great moments of her life and it provides a key to her future relationship with the Twins. She described how she realised at once that the doctors had given up on Ronnie, and she knew the time had come to assert herself if her precious child was going to survive. So she refused to listen to the doctors and against their advice insisted on bringing Ronnie home to Vallance Road. 'The doctors didn't understand him but I did. It stands to reason. As his mother, I knew exactly what was wrong with him. He was simply pining for me and for little Reggie, and once he was back with us he started to recover. But he seemed so precious to me now that I couldn't bear to let him out of my sight, and I had him sleeping with me in my bed for the next six months or so.'

Violet was never going to forget how she had saved Ronnie's

life. But this period of the little boy's convalescence would also have a most profound effect upon the natural balance previously maintained between the Twins. Until then, as the first-born twin Reg had been the dominant one and during the months following their return from hospital it seemed as if this was going to continue, for Ron was slower now and seemed less energetic than his brother. But gradually Ron discovered how to compensate for this through bouts of bad behaviour, and by involving Reg in any devilment going. Sudden tiffs and outbursts of temper are common between identical twins and are usually followed by sunny periods as the balance between them is restored. With the Kray twins, this balance seemed to have become fatally upset after Ronnie's illness.

The twin relationship had become what is technically known as 'discordant', which can happen when one member of a pair of twins has been damaged or impaired. When this happens and the balance between them is destroyed their whole relationship can be at risk. This can become serious. Sometimes one of the twins can fail to survive, or both of them can end their lives in institutions for the emotionally retarded. But with Ron and Reg the outcome was different. Although it seemed that Ron's nervous system had definitely been damaged by his illness he fought against the situation, gaining strength from Violet who was always there to love him and to back him up against his brighter, quicker brother.

Throughout the Twins' childhood it would often be a no-holds-barred situation as backward Ron discovered different ways to assert himself and hold on tight to Reg. After involving him in some wickedness or other he would end by staging an emotional appeal. At other times the Twins would fight each other furiously. They were becoming more violent with every year that passed and sometimes seemed to fight each other almost to the death.

By now, violence seemed to play a crucial role in their

relationship as twins, with Ron always goading Reg until he lost his temper, and the fighting would go on until they seemed united in their rage against each other. At this point the fight would stop as quickly as it had started, and somehow Violet always forgave them because she loved them – especially Ronnie, who needed her affection so much more than Reggie.

At times Reg made determined efforts of his own to escape from the situation. But Ron was always there, and just when Reg seemed on the point of asserting his independence a sense of pity or responsibility for the dependent twin he was abandoning would bring him back. Thus Ron, although originally the weaker and younger of the two, discovered ways to use his weakness to arouse his mother's love and make Reg do his bidding. This suited Ron, of course, but for Reg this situation came to dominate their adolescence, especially as Ron's strength steadily increased. Thus Ron's childhood diphtheria ended up by robbing both the Twins of any chance of living separate lives. And slowly, inexorably, this closeness came to rule their whole existence.

5

East End

ONCE THEY WERE over their diphtheria it was time for an altogether different influence to home in upon this locked-together pair of twins. In pre-war Bethnal Green they were growing up within a world unlike any other.

Somewhere in the distant past, when Bethnal Green still had its village green and there was a white chapel in Whitechapel, the country bordering the Thames to the east of London was not unlike the country to the west, with the same green fields and farms and riverside villages. But as London expanded and the City and the country to the west grew in prosperity, the east was left to fester on its own, becoming in the process the dumping ground for everything that the wealthiest city in the world wanted to ignore. What better spot to place London's antisocial industries, not to mention its surplus human beings, with its acres of cheap slum dwellings being thrown up to house the casual labour needed in the sweatshops and the foundries and the miles of dockland bordering the river.

The East End's first immigrants were French Huguenot Protestants who arrived at the end of the seventeenth century, fleeing Catholic persecution in their native land. They prospered, creating a flourishing silk industry in Spitalfields and building fine houses, some of which survive in Fournier Street off Brick Lane. They even built a chapel of their own, which later became a synagogue and today is a temple for the local

Bengali community. For the Huguenots were followed by waves of poorer immigrants: Jews from the pogroms of Eastern Europe, Irish escaping from the potato famine who couldn't make it to America, gypsies who settled among them to look after the horses, all of them crammed together in what rapidly became some of the worst slums in Europe and struggling to exist upon what little was on offer.

This meant that London had become a divided city, with all the power and wealth and splendour on one side and just down the road beyond Bishopsgate the start of grinding poverty and human degradation. The East End criminologist Dick Hobbs called it 'a forgotten country, the land of the living dead.'

By the time the Twins were born in 1934 poverty had been grinding on for so long that it had produced its own culture of survival. A government report published two years before the twins were born concluded that sixty per cent of the children in Bethnal Green were malnourished and eighty-five per cent of the housing was unsatisfactory.

It had also produced its own morality. Few could afford the luxury of passing moral judgements on anybody else and if crime, petty or otherwise, was the only way to put food in the bellies of their children, it was better than the alternative. It was also a deviant society in which poverty, hopelessness and rejection produced an inverted image of the prosperous world outside.

The one activity that did flourish here was crime, and each separate quarter of the old East End had its criminal speciality. Around King's Cross there were the burglars, living off the rich houses in nearby Regent's Park, Hoxton had its pickpockets and the notorious 'whizz mob' who worked the crowds at football matches, Hackney traditionally had its forgers, Limehouse its pimps and their prostitutes servicing the sailors from the docks, while con men and cheats were supposedly south of the river. This left Bethnal Green, Whitechapel and parts of Hackney at the bottom of the heap. This was where the greatest poverty existed, together with the poorest and most hopeless criminals – the so-called villains, whose one time speciality was violence.

Since life in Bethnal Green was cheap, the local heroes were the desperate chancers you find in Dickens, like Bill Sykes and the Artful Dodger. The odds were against them and the best they could hope for was a memorable funeral. When the time came the Twins would not forget those funerals with black-plumed horses that they had seen as children, for they were growing up in a world that, as the criminologist Chris Jenks puts it, 'had lionised its most ostentatious villains and scoundrels'.

Before they were arrested the Twins introduced me to one of them, an octogenarian called Arthur Tresaden who had once been the 'Guv'nor' of Bethnal Green and whose memories went back to the grim years of the late nineteenth century.

'The truth about old East End villainy was that it was no more than the senseless criminality of poverty and despair. The old-style tearaway died young and never made much money. He lived like an animal and he died like one. Take *Dodger Mullins*, the last of the old Guv'nors of Bethnal Green. He really was like Bill Sykes. Dodger was strong and game as anyone alive, but any brains he ever had had been knocked out of him by the time I knew him. He was lazy and drunken, with a bashed-in face. Today you'd say he was a brute, but then it was a brutal world. Once when he was drunk he threw the woman he lived with out of an upstairs window. The police issued a warrant for his arrest and caught him at the Epsom races. They saw no point in sending him to prison, so they took him to the police station underneath the grandstand, and one of the coppers, a big bloke called Sergeant Rainer, took a knuckleduster and sploshed him on the face. It broke his nose, and didn't do anything to improve his looks, but Dodger didn't take the blindest bit of notice.'

'So what was the ordinary East Ender's attitude to the police?' I asked.

'Make no mistake, in the old days when I was in Bethnal Green the police were hated and despised throughout the whole East End. At best the police were indifferent to what was going on, and at worst they were corrupt. Their general attitude was to let villains like us get on with fighting one another, if that was what we wanted, "and so keep the numbers down", as I remember a copper saying to me once. They simply didn't want to get involved with the likes of us. They saw no point in it. You'd be surprised how often I've seen men stabbed in front of a policeman who just walked away. Life was cheap, and in those days all the Law was really bothered with was property.

'But there was one thing that we all kept clear of – killing, except for real loonies, like Spud Murphy, who had a tattoo on his forehead and killed two police and then shouted he'd be back later with a machine gun. And there was Rudge Martin out of Bethnal Green, who killed three coppers up at Carlisle. Rudge and Spud both swung for it, and the truth was that the rest of us were always fearful of ending up on the nine o'clock walk. Before we got into a fight I'd always check my boys beforehand for guns and knives. Guns were forbidden. So were knives as far as I was concerned, and I told them to confine themselves to glasses and bottles in a fight if they didn't trust their fists.'

But all of this was really over by the time the Twins were growing up and, like the old-timer that he was, Arthur Tresaden made it clear that the Bethnal Green he remembered was far tougher and more brutalised than anything the Twins encountered. What was odd about the Twins was that these old villains from the past made such a powerful impression on them both just as their world was about to vanish entirely, together with so much of the old East End itself, as the bulldozers completed the destruction started by the German bombs.

The reason for this almost certainly began with their father, old Charlie and all the years he spent as a deserter on the run from the authorities. Not long before he died he actually confessed that he blamed himself for not having moved away from Bethnal Green before war broke out, 'and if I had perhaps the Twins would then have turned out different'. But that was an old man's might-have-been and a very big 'perhaps'. Back in 1939, when he first went missing from the army, things were very different.

The truth was that Charlie wasn't stupid enough, or man enough, to have been a criminal himself. But as a deserter always on the run from the police he became *ex officio* a member of the underworld in order to survive. With the outbreak of war it was not surprising that in Bethnal Green there were some who felt no obligation to fight for a country which up to then had never shown any interest in them or in their families. In Vallance Road there were several more besides Charlie Kray who felt like him, so much so that the area around his house was known as Deserters' Corner.

When the Blitz was turning dockland into an inferno the Twins were evacuated to Tring in Hertfordshire and later they would recall nostalgically their earliest piece of villainy – stealing apples from Lord Rothschild's apple trees. But although they always said how much they loved the country – Ron actually once dreamed of ending up as a country gentleman – the Twins were city dwellers through and through and couldn't wait to return to Vallance Road.

They missed the togetherness of the family and back they came to their little house in Vallance Road. As a result, from the age of six and with a father who was on the run from the police, they became involved in a real-life game of cops and criminals which came to dominate their lives. Whenever their father was in London he generally holed up in Camberwell with an old villain he knew called Bob Rolfe. When he was there Violet kept in touch with him by sending him messages via the Twins, which helped to keep the family together; and the Twins began to idolise Bob Rolfe who told them gruesome tales of the bad old days and long-dead villains that he remembered.

During these exciting times the Twins' real heroes weren't only the old villains like Bob Rolfe that they met through their father. They were also the legendary characters of East End he loved to talk about. And throughout the war it was the police and not the Germans who were the real enemy, just as it was from their father that they first picked up his hatred of the Law together with his admiration for the villains and fighters he knew so well.

The Twins learned their hatred of the Law from the times when the police were searching for their father and turned the house over in the middle of the night. If a policeman asked them if they'd seen their father, Violet had taught them to reply, 'Our Dad an' Mum's divorced, an' we haven't seen our Dad for months,' although they knew that he was hiding in the coal hole in the yard or, as happened once, that he was underneath the kitchen table, hidden by the tablecloth while the police were searching for him everywhere.

It was a world that had its own mythology. At a time when, on the other side of London, small boys of their age dreamt of becoming fighter pilots or commandos, the shared ambitions of the Twins centred on characters like Dodger Mullins or Wassle Newman or Spud Murphy. Their roots were deeply sunk into the legends of these people and the code they learned was to be special through violence, never to grass, to understand that coppers were bent and not to care, and to fight the senseless fight until you dropped.

The most important thing the Twins were learning was the old East End's cult of criminal celebrity, which at the time existed nowhere else. Already they could see themselves as outlaws, modern Robin Hoods owing nothing to society and taking money from the rich to feed the poor.

What they had latched onto was the tail end of a long tradition of villains and so called Guv'nors of adjacent 'manors'. For true East Enders the real enemy had always been the Law, since the police, when they saw fit to intervene, were attempting to enforce the rules of the prosperous foreigners intruding from the world outside. It wasn't because they were frightened of the consequences that people didn't shop the Twins but because they had been taught that no self-respecting human being in Whitechapel or Bethnal Green or Hoxton shopped anybody to the Law. The first commandment of the old East End was still in force: 'Thou shalt not grass'. Had they tipped off the boys in blue, the consequences would have come less from the Twins or their henchmen than from their neighbours.

In spite of this the Twins were still isolated, still locked together in their claustrophobic world, and it was to overcome their sense of loneliness that they had already started to create a legend for themselves into which they could retreat and mentally act out whatever roles they fancied, based on a mix of legends from the time of Dickens and the American gangster movies that they would soon be seeing at the local cinemas.

6

Crime as Destiny: 1954–58

'WHAT YOU MUST understand about the Twins,' their old friend Dickie Morgan used to say, 'is that they were born to be criminals and there was nothing that they nor anybody else could do about it.'

Ron's favourite aunt, Aunt Rose, went further. 'Ronnie,' she'd say to him when he'd been particularly wicked. 'Your eyebrows meet in the middle, and you know what that means, Ronnie?'

'No, Aunt Rose, what does it mean?'

'It means you'll end up being hanged if you don't behave yourself.'

Most of those who knew the Twins as children were more or less convinced, like Aunt Rose, that they had been born wicked, and one can't avoid the feeling that by the time they reached their teens their lives had already been criminally mapped out for them.

To some extent this was obviously true. Since, as identical twins, they were born with the same genetic make-up, the views of the criminologist Lange, about what he termed 'crime as destiny' make a lot of sense when applied to them. Any genetic influence they inherited would have affected them identically, and if there really are certain genes that carry a propensity to violence and hence to crime, then there were a lot of very violent genes floating around in the gene pool of their immediate relations.

In their day both grandfathers of the Twins had been celebrated local fighters. Violet's family, the Lees, were gypsies who had settled here in the 1880s, originally to look after horses. But despite being such a strict teetotaller and something of a martinet within the family, the old grandfather, Cannonball 'the Eastern Southpaw' Lee, was a local character in Bethnal Green and one of the most unforgettable old men I have encountered. A skinny, gnarled old boy who was still living off his reputation as a fearsome fighter in his youth, he reminded me of a very ancient toothless crocodile who had ended up entertaining the visitors to the zoo.

In his day he'd been a famous East End boxer, and since he was left-handed his secret weapon was his irresistible left hook from which he derived his 'Southpaw' fighting name. If what he said was true, that old left hook of his had spelt the doom of many a brasher, bigger fighter during his long and varied fistic career, which hadn't prevented him acquiring an even greater reputation for battling outside the ring as well. One of his favourite stories, which he often told the Twins, was of how he broke the nose of the famous East End villain Mike Thomson, who had had the temerity to set about him with a brick one night in an alleyway in Wapping.

'Up came the old left hook, and down went Thomson. He never tried anything on me again.'

Cannonball also instilled into the Twins' childhood memories the stories of the famous local boxers he had known, including Jimmy Wilde of Stepney 'who had his strength in both his hands, where I had it only in my left' and the great Ted Kid Lewis, who grew up just around the corner and became world champion at three separate weights, 'a fine clean-living man he was, and one of the gamest fighters ever to enter a boxing ring.'

The Twins' formidable Aunt Rose was the only one of Cannonball's children who took after him. A powerful gypsy of a woman, she had inherited not only his dark hair but also his pugilistic prowess, including the family left hook which helped to make her one of the greatest female fighters in the old East End. In her prime she claimed to be a match in a straight fight with any one man or two women in Whitechapel and Bethnal Green combined.

The Kray connection was more mysterious. When I asked the Twins' father where the Kray name came from he simply answered, 'Buggered if I know.' But then he thought a while and scratched his head and added, 'My old man, Jimmy Kray, that was a costermonger, always said as the name was Austrian'.

'Why Austrian?' I asked. He shrugged and changed the subject. But I thought it worth consulting the 1967 Vienna telephone directory and found eight entries with the name of Kray as against two in the London phone book for the same year (Charlie himself and the Twins' elder brother, Charles Kray Jr). And when I got to know the Twins I understood what a valuable inheritance they had as criminals in the name of Kray. Depending on how it's spoken, it can sound both menacing and violent, with undertones of crab and craw and crow, making it a name that's not easily forgotten.

The other thing about the Twins' Kray grandfather is that they could have inherited their aggressive genes from him as easily as from old Cannonball Lee. For in his prime old Jimmy Kray – a.k.a. 'Mad' Jimmy Kray – also had a reputation as the sort of old-style bar fighter it was wisest to avoid.

If Lange's theories about criminal predestination were correct, as I suspect they could have been, this would mean that, as identical twins, whatever violent traits Ron and Reg had inherited from these battling grandparents would have had a similar effect on both of them. But although this could explain how they might have influenced each other on a life of crime, soon a more compelling force than this was prompting both of them to violence.

Once puberty began, the discordant nature of their identical-twin relationship increasingly affected them and made them utterly unlike any normal pair of adolescents.

We have already seen how the effects of Ronnie's childhood diphtheria had made his identical-twin relationship with Reg 'discordant', and how from early childhood Ron made Reg misbehave in order to maintain the identical-twin bond between them. The misbehaviour usually meant fighting, and with adolescence this dominating tendency increased dramatically.

The fighting between them had always been abnormally fierce for two young children. There is a famous tale of how, when they had just turned eight, they asked the man who ran the boxing booth in Victoria Park if they could compete, and since no other boys of their age would take either of them on they ended up fighting with each other. In the end the fight had to be stopped before one of them got seriously hurt.

In fact, this went on all the time. But this constant pattern, with Ron continually driven to involve Reg in this sort of mutual wickedness and brawling, was caused by something far more serious than a shared genetic tendency towards aggression. As we have seen, this compulsive fighting had started early on, but as the Twins grew stronger and Ron learned how to manipulate his brother he was actually discovering how to use violence as his means of survival.

Whatever the damage to his nervous system caused by that early battle with diphtheria, the result had left him at a crippling disadvantage to Reg and this was getting worse with age. As they developed it was clear that Ron was slower, lacking in dexterity, and appeared less mentally agile than his brother. He also clearly lacked Reg's charm and the social graces which are so important for a child's popularity.

This produced the sense of isolation and apartness from which

Ron suffered all his life, and which at times came close to destroying him as he retreated increasingly into himself. As he grew older and began to suffer from the schizophrenia that would finally attack his sanity he had to fight the demons that assailed him. Worst was the fear of loneliness, and the dread of being different from the normal world around him – and worst of all was the fear of being parted from the only people in his world who mattered – his twin brother Reg and his mother Violet.

Although Whitechapel and Bethnal Green were among the poorest districts in the old East End, they were also places where families stuck together in order to survive. The Lees had done exactly that, and had been there for so long that the locals called that part of Vallance Road 'Lee Street' (later on, 'Deserters' Corner'). Family solidarity was needed for survival and the twins took the spoiling and the loving from the women in the family for granted.

By the time they were in their teens it already seemed inevitable that they were heading for a life of crime. They had no skills or qualities that fitted them for anything, except violence and to follow in the footsteps of their heroes, the villains of the old East End. Just to encourage them in this, there was already an exciting range of lawless activity on their doorstep. As twins they'd inherited a double dose of toughness from their past, so they continued to assert their status as something special more than ever. They were strong, and the fact that they were not particularly big meant that they needed to assert themselves simply to survive. It was old Grandfather Lee who taught the boys to fight using the famous left hook that was part of the legend of Bethnal Green.

Theoretically at least, boxing also offered an escape route out of crime. As young professional boxers they were trained and learned exactly how to fight, but their greatest asset was the fact that they were twins. The extraordinary synergy they developed meant that when they fought they became the equivalent of a single person with four fists. And they loved the excitement and the reputation that it gave them of following in a great tradition.

So there were different influences working to ensure that the twins remained irrevocably together in the only life where they would stay united – by following the old East End traditions of the villains and street fighters they'd both been brought up to admire.

One was that deviant culture of the past which still held its magic for them. But most of all there was the sheer intoxication of asserting their supremacy in the street fights they soon began to organise.

It must have been particularly important for damaged Ron to have had this reassurance of supremacy in gangland culture, and these regular battles dispersed much of the aggression that was always building up between the Twins. It gave them a sense of power and adventure and esteem, all of which they needed. Surprisingly, it also gave them companionship, which Ron also needed.

It also bound the Twins themselves together. As long as they fought together, they stayed together, and the bond between the two of them endured.

In the tribal world of the old East End the local gangs were strictly territorial. The Bethnal Greeners' deadly enemies came from nearby Watney Street, a step down in poverty, where people still remembered the old women smoking clay pipes as they made brushes in the street. (George Cornell, the first man Ron would murder, came from Watney Street.)

The Twins weren't particularly big. According to their passports the measuring tape showed that they were 5ft. 10in. (Ron typically insisted that Reg was a half-inch shorter) but they were extremely strong through unremitting exercise and they had taught themselves to be extraordinarily vicious.

The point about this local gang warfare was that they did it because they were good at it, and it offered them an alternative society that they could dominate. And here at last the fact that they were twins became their greatest asset. It is scary to be up against an enemy in duplicate, and as fighters they were two in one. They were always eerily aware of the effect that their duality had on others. Word got round that because they fought in deadly silence they were telepathic. Neither of them denied this, and Ron certainly believed it.

With the Twins determined to improve their stamina and skill as teenage boxers, it's strange that it was boxing that finally became the greatest threat to their close relationship as twins. For as they trained and learned the rules of boxing, and trainers and managers began to notice them as possible 'young hopefuls' for the future, a difference between them which would for ever remain started to appear.

Throughout their teens they remained virtually identical both in facial looks and in physique, and only Violet could tell the two of them apart. But beneath the surface, differences between them were becoming evident, and nowhere more so than in the boxing ring.

According to one old trainer, 'Ronnie was a fighter. The hardest, toughest boy I've ever seen. To stop Ron you'd have had to kill him. But Reg was different. It was as if he had all the experience of an old boxer in his fists before he even started. Just once in a lifetime you find a boy with everything it takes to be a champion. Young Reggie was one of them.'

Reg was inevitably invited to turn professional. Ron wasn't, and something that Ron had always feared began to happen. The straight world of success began to beckon his brother, and Ronnie knew quite well that once his Reggie tasted real success he'd lose him for ever. On no account could Ronnie let this happen.

In the old days of the Twins' grandfathers, nobody objected

if a professional boxer had an occasional scrap with somebody as the result of an argument. But since then the rules had been tightened up, and it was now strictly forbidden for a professional fighter to engage in any sort of fight outside the boxing ring. So strictly was this enforced that for a professional boxer to become involved in a pub fight or a punch-up in the street spelled the instant end to his career.

On 11 December 1951, all three Kray brothers fought as professionals at the Albert Hall, on a programme headed by Tommy McGovern, the lightweight champion of Great Britain. This was the biggest chance that all three of them had ever had. Charlie Kray lost his bout on points, Ron was disqualified, and Reg won decisively in three perfectly fought rounds.

It was strange that Reg's Albert Hall success was followed, just a few weeks later, by a particularly fierce battle with another gang outside the Regency Club in Walthamstow. It was stranger still that the Twins were caught by the police and their names appeared in the local paper.

News of this inevitably reached the Boxing Board of Control, which was unfortunate for Reg who automatically lost his boxing licence and with it his hopes of becoming welterweight champion of Britain. It was a dreadful disappointment, but for Ron his brother's disappointment had a silver lining. He knew that Reg would never leave him now to become a boxing champion.

The other member of the family who was anxious to keep the Twins together was, of course, their mother Violet. Over the years she'd learned to play the part of the perfect cockney mother, and in many ways she was. But, as I finally discovered, she was not entirely the saintly figure she appeared. She was certainly utterly devoted to the Twins, who formed the purpose of her life and who for her could do no wrong. Luckily for her, the Twins were equally devoted in return, especially Ronnie who could never have survived without her. But this involved all three of them in varying degrees of deception, which at certain points in the Twins' career assumed considerable importance. Once I discovered this, I began to find Violet, the perfect mother, faintly sinister.

I got the first hint of something odd when I first met her late in 1967 in the kitchen of the Twins' house at 178 Vallance Road. Three china ducks which she proudly told me Ronnie had given her were frozen in perpetual flight across the kitchen wall, the kettle was boiling as it always did, and the large-screen television (another gift from Ron) was also on.

When she had made us both a cup of tea and we were sitting at the kitchen table where half the criminals in London must have sat before us, the first thing she showed me was an enormous album like a family Bible. In fact it was her own private bible, her large press-cuttings book dedicated to the most important people in her life – her Twins. I remember being puzzled at the time by the way she had pasted press cuttings of their successes in local boxing tournaments and pictures of them making contributions to some East End charity or other side by side with the sort of press reports which most mothers in the 'normal' world outside would have wanted to suppress – reports of violent fights in local pubs, gang wars, and woundings which were always featuring her boys. It was not until later that I realised how interchangeable the two activities of villainy and boxing were in Bethnal Green, – and also in the mind of Violet Kray.

As long as the Twins emerged unscathed and got themselves a mention in the press Violet was happy. She was still the centre of the trio, and still relied upon the Twins for her self-esteem.

Like many East End matriarchs, her role was sacrificial. But they had something else: they could fight, and in the old East End that also made you special.

After all, Violet had been brought up to respect her father who was equally respected in the local community as a famous fighter. But Ron and Reg could be more special still. They were the Twins and they still depended on her, and she on them. They were her boys and, whatever happened, she was always going to be proud of them. If her sister Rose was right, and Ronnie did end up on the gallows (as he would have done had he been born five years earlier, and Melford Stevenson had had anything to do with it) she would still have been proud of him. As she often said, 'What else are mothers for?'

Yet Violet would always be the nearest thing to a conscience that the Twins possessed. Thanks to her, a great deal was forgiven and a great deal more was overlooked; for the truth was that Violet was a faulty moral compass. Whatever the Twins chose to do she was always ready to condone; and if she felt she couldn't actively do so she would close her eyes to it.

'If you have to choose between the police and your own children, what choice is there?' she used to say.

At some point in their adolescence the Twins received one further all-important item in their package of predestination – the fact that both of them were homosexual. At the time this struck them both as so shameful that they attempted to conceal it, even from their mother, though given the set-up in the family, with its absent menfolk and its doting women, it can't have been completely unexpected.

On the one hand remembering the fitful presence of Charles Kray Sr, now promoted from rag-and-bone man to champion deserter, they had a father for whom they were rapidly losing whatever affection and respect they'd ever had. So much so that, having reached the age of fifteen, and returning home one night to find his father asserting his old East Ender's right to beat up his wife on a Friday night, Ronnie delivered his version of his grandfather's left hook and laid the paterfamilias out cold.

From then on, for a while at least, this became a fairly regular performance in the stuffy little house in Vallance Road; but the situation, far from discouraging Violet and convincing her that the time had come to end her marriage, made her more determined than ever to make the best of things. Boys would be boys and men were men, and with Mr Kray permanently on the run her Twins were, more than ever, all she had. Besides, though often absent, Charles Sr was still, and always would be, in close and jealous contact with her and maintained his role as family breadwinner.

He had his little ways, of course, but he needed her. Everybody needed her. Such was her chosen role in life. Which left stately Violet in the role of provider and protector whose first task was to hold the family together and who was always going to be there for those who needed her. For Violet, always ready with a blind eye or a consoling cup of tea, her Twins remained incapable of doing wrong. Mr Kray, unsurprisingly, felt differently but there was little he could do about it now. Certainly, if one imagined the Twins as the product of a bullying father and a rough, tough world of horny-fisted males, one couldn't have been more wrong. Once they were pubescent, if they weren't beating up their father the Twins were being spoiled by Violet, Grandma Lee, and their two aunties, May and Rose.

All of which conformed, of course, to a classic pattern; and with their warm, indulgent mother, their ineffectual father, and their surrounding cast of loving women, it was not surprising that, with adolescence, the Twins discovered that they were gay. Given their identical genetic make-up, it was virtually inevitable that if one twin was, the other would be too. What they didn't realise was that, particularly for Ron, the time would come when this was also going to be an important asset and a source of valuable connections. But for quite some time it would have to remain 'the sin that dared not speak its name'.

Within the macho world of 1950s East End villainy, to cast the faintest doubt upon another's masculinity was to invite fearsome retribution. So it was hardly surprising that, for the time being, both the Twins kept their sexual preferences to themselves. According to Ron, for quite a while they were so concerned to keep their secret hidden that the only sex they had was with each other.

7

God Bless the Royal Fusiliers: 1952–54

T HE GHOSTS OF the Twins have a way of suddenly appearing in surprising places but one of the most unlikely has to be the Tower of London. When the yeomen warders are conducting tourist parties round the ancient fortress and describing some of the famous characters who have been imprisoned here in the past, they always start off with the Princes in the Tower, followed by Anne Boleyn and Walter Raleigh, and these days they often end by mentioning 'those two murderers, the Kray Twins, who were imprisoned in the Wellington Tower for deserting from Her Majesty's armed forces in 1952.' Even this is fame of a sort, and serves as a reminder of an important episode in the history of the Twins that often gets forgotten.

Back in the 1950s it was always claimed that National Service was good for young tearaways like Ron and Reg and would end up making men of them; and undoubtedly the Twins' service with the Royal Fusiliers, did help to 'make' them what they were, but not exactly in the way the army wanted. Instead of learning how to fight *with* the Royal Fusiliers, the Twins put everything they'd got into fighting *against* them and emerged from the two-year battle even stronger and more determined to pursue a life of crime than ever.

The Tower of London had been the headquarters of the Royal Fusiliers from the time they were founded in the seventeenth century, and in the late summer of 1952 two identical official envelopes arrived at Vallance Road for Ron and Reg, containing orders to report to the Tower for their National Service with the regiment. Two years before, when their brother Charles was called up, he had loyally enlisted in the Royal Navy, became a model sailor, and ended up as light-heavyweight boxing champion of the Navy. Which goes to show that brother Charlie really wasn't like the Twins. Where they were crooked, he was fairly straight, and it was only the combined influence of the Twins upon a character as weak as his that would prove his downfall. As for the Kray Twins, back in 1952 weak was one thing that they weren't, and there was not the faintest chance of them following brother Charlie's good example.

They were just eighteen, and once they were in the army it's difficult to imagine them acting any differently. For by now so many antisocial influences − environmental, pugilistic, and genetic − had been at work on them that they were totally conditioned for a life of crime, and for none other. All that they lacked was practical experience of the use of violence. The Fusiliers provided it.

Not that the Twins joined battle with the British army unprepared. From earliest childhood they had watched their father's example as a champion deserter. Nearly twenty years later he was still on the run, but he had now been away so long that the local police had all but given up on him and he was more than ready to advise the Twins on how to follow his example. This was one occasion when the Twins were prepared to listen to him and he proved a good instructor in the art of humiliating the military. 'Whatever you do, you must start as you mean to go on,' he told them. 'Never weaken. Don't feel sorry for them and never obey an order. And just remember this: if things get really bad, pretend to be barmy!'

Not that Ron and Reg really needed much advice. And had the military authorities tried to organise a course in crime especially tailored for the Twins, they could hardly have improved upon their two years' service with the Fusiliers.

Although this was the first time they had been away from home so long, this never seemed to worry them. On the contrary, from start to finish the experience gave them added confidence. It showed them how to make a fool of authority, toughened them up and also taught them self-reliance. It gave them exercises in leadership and initiative, and ended up with a nine months' residential course in the country's most exclusive academy of crime, where they acquired further skills that would help them in the years ahead. In the process they enjoyed regular group discussions with other top young criminals, and made influential friends – and enemies – who stayed with them for life. But all of this came later.

Until now, all the Twins' street fights had been fought against 'their own', but this was different, and their two years' running battle with the army was their first real confrontation with organised authority. From the start they made it plain that they had no time for the army's notions of courage or nobility. Nor were they interested in official rules and regulations. Instead, they made up their own rules of engagement as they went along, following the precepts of non-caring villainy they had picked up from the old Guv'nors and villains of Bethnal Green. They fought as Dodger Mullins or Wassle Newman might have fought in a similar situation, and ended up by proving they could take whatever punishment the army could inflict – and in the process giving back more than they received.

On their first day at the Tower, remembering what their father had said about starting as they meant to continue, they stayed just long enough to receive their uniforms and equipment before being marched into a barrack room where a corporal told them how they should prepare their kit and explained the turnout that was expected from the Fusiliers. He was in the middle of telling them about the pride that they should feel at being made a Fusilier when the Twins began walking to the door.

'And where might the two of you be going?' the corporal shouted. When they didn't answer, he made the serious mistake of trying to stop them. The Twins still said nothing; nor did they stop walking, apart from pausing for a swift right hook from Ron which connected with the corporal's chin, leaving him sprawling on the floor. After this, no one tried to stop them and they walked back to Vallance Road in time for tea before going out to celebrate with friends.

Next morning, after breakfast, a police car collected them and returned them to the Tower, where they were put in the guardroom to await CO's orders. Striking an NCO was a court-martial offence, but it would have been ridiculous to court-martial two recruits after their first day in the army, particularly when they were so alike that nobody could say for sure which one of them was guilty. So after giving them a lecture on the need to settle down and be good soldiers, the Commanding Officer told them he'd be lenient and gave them seven days' confinement in the guardroom.

But from now on neither toughness nor kindness seemed to make the faintest difference to the Twins and no sooner were they out of the guardroom than they were on the run again, which was how their two-year war with the military started. And the truth was that there was nothing that the army could do to them that faintly troubled them. Neither the disgusting food nor the discomfort of the guardroom bothered them, and when the seven days were up they once again went missing. The Twins' one great advantage was that, unlike the army, they had nothing in the world to lose and were simply treating what was happening as one great adventure. Extreme discomfort didn't worry them. They were so tough that they treated the punishment cells, with bare boards to sleep on and a bread-and-water diet, simply as a challenge. Their powers of endurance were remarkable and, having once set out to call the bluff of the military establishment, they thoroughly enjoyed themselves.

Of course, their pugilistic skills were a great advantage. No ordinary recruit would have got away with the sort of liberties the Twins were taking with their NCOs. And anybody in authority who felt tough enough to teach the Twins a lesson invariably ended up wishing that he hadn't – like the big corporal who entered their cell 'to have a little word with them'. A few minutes later he was standing tied up by his braces to a pillar in the centre of the room, with the Twins doing an Indian war dance round him.

While they were obviously enjoying themselves, the Twins were learning other lessons. One of them was the art of surviving on nothing but a little thieving. Previously teetotal, they started drinking, and when they were bored there was usually somebody around who needed to be taught a lesson. For a time the pattern of recapture and escape continued, and just occasionally it looked as if the twins would settle down and soldier. Once they even got as far as the army rifle range at Purfleet where they proved to be appalling shots. Then after this Ron was in trouble for beating up another NCO who had tried to teach the Twins another lesson. And so it continued.

At one point the Twins refused to shave or wear a uniform, and the army retaliated with a month's sentence in the Colchester detention centre. After Colchester it was back to the Tower of London, and soon they were on the run again. This time they gave themselves an extended holiday in London's West End, living rather as their father had when he was on the run, helped by the members of the underworld they had befriended. Even now there was something about the Twins that always seemed to get them treated with the respect that they demanded, and all the time they were learning about other criminals and other forms of crime and how to live the life they wanted. It was now that they saw themselves as outlaws from society, for as Reg liked to say, 'What has society ever done for us?'

Whatever the answer, the fact was that society was becoming seriously concerned about them, particularly when they knocked down a policeman who was trying to arrest them and had to spend a month in Wormwood Scrubs together. After this they had their picture in the *East London Advertiser*, together with the headline 'Kray Brothers beat up PC'. The picture and the accompanying press cuttings were duly pasted into Violet's monster cuttings book, beside their boxing photographs and press reports of earlier misdemeanours.

Boxing or crime, crime or boxing, it scarcely seemed to matter any more. The Twins were on their way. Their name was getting known. From nobodies they were rapidly becoming somebodies. Their month in Wormwood Scrubs, far from being wasted, was seen as a further step up the criminal ladder.

After their time in the Scrubs they spent three months in the guardroom at Howe Barracks, Canterbury waiting to be court-martialled. According to Army regulations, before anyone could be dishonourably discharged he first had to be tried and punished. While this was going on, the Twins decided they would make the most of this boring period while the army got its act together. To pass the time they now decided to 'go the limit'.

One of them remembered their father's advice about acting barmy. For the Twins, particularly for Ronnie, nothing could have been easier. 'It was funny, but I felt that there was nothing that we couldn't do if we wanted to. So to start with I stopped shaving, then I shaved just half my face. Then we really did get going.' Both the Twins were natural actors, and Ron found no problem in appearing mentally unbalanced. It was as if he was rehearsing for the moment three years later when he would actually be certified insane, but at the time it was treated as a joke. In retrospect it all appeared distinctly creepy – particularly when the Twins began to stage a return to childhood with tantrums, screams and uncontrolled behaviour. Food was thrown against the walls and dishes smashed, followed by shouts and screams and hammering on the cell door. Both of them stripped off and cut their uniforms to pieces.

It now seems unbelievable that nobody could stop them, but when the sergeant of the guard decided to intervene and teach these hooligans a lesson the latrine bucket was promptly emptied over him. Next day when they burned their bedding and their uniforms the fire hose was turned on them but once again they didn't seem to worry. Finally they put the Twins in a cage. Reg asked a corporal for a glass of water. As he handed it to him through the bars, Reg produced a pair of handcuffs that he had kept hidden and handcuffed the NCO to the bars. As Reg put it, 'If you are weak and start worrying about others they've got you where they want you. If you can show you're tough and just don't care you become invulnerable.'

This was another lesson for the future, and the learning process went on unabated while the Twins awaited their court martial. Nobody in authority had had to deal with anyone like this before. The Twins could have escaped again whenever they wanted but they knew this would only delay their trial, and hence their ultimate release date from the army. So they waited. The truth was that by now the army was sick and tired of the Twins, the Twins were sick and tired of the army, and their court martial, when it came, was something of a farce. The list of their offences was so long that they could have been kept inside for twenty years. But as all the army really wanted now was to be rid of them – for good – they were given the smallest punishment that the court could reasonably accept – six months apiece in the military prison at Shepton Mallet in

Somerset, after which they would be ignominiously dismissed from the service.

For the Twins, those next six months seemed like the opposite of punishment. As for the dreaded military prison at Shepton Mallet, when they arrived there it was for them like two freshmen entering an Oxbridge College and finding themselves among a group of slightly older students of the higher criminality, selected by the army from all over Britain. The young Charlie Richardson was there, together with an equally young Freddy Foreman and one of the Adams brothers, together with other serious young offenders from all over Britain. This made those six months which the Twins spent at 'The Mallet' an invaluable experience. It broadened their minds, it started up a number of important friendships for the future, and it taught them something of the possibilities of organised crime, not just in Bethnal Green but throughout the country. As Reg often used to say, 'God bless the Royal Fusiliers.'

8

The Billiard Hall: 1954–59

IT'S UNLIKELY THAT the Twins' 'ignominious dismissal' from the Royal Fusiliers ever troubled them, and once they had shaken off the army and were safely back in Bethnal Green it was obvious where their latest ambitions would soon take them. Until they joined the army they were little more than youthful tearaways, engaging in their brawls and battles for the excitement and to keep a check on their discordant-twin relationship. Since then they had learned a lot from their battles with the Fusiliers, and two years in khaki had convinced them of the sort of life they wanted. Had they had any doubts before, they now knew for certain that they were going to be gangsters. But to be gangsters they first had to have a gang, and to have a proper gang they needed a place where it could meet. Someone remembered the old billiard hall in Eric Street, off the Mile End Road.

It had started life in the 1920s as the Regal Cinema, and in the depression of the 1930s, some optimistic property developer turned it into a billiard hall complete with fourteen snooker tables. Somehow it survived the war, but although there was now a demolition order on the place, no one had had the heart or the energy to demolish it. From the moment they saw it the Twins knew that it was what they needed. The only trouble was the rent, which they thought excessive, but that was something they could deal with.

What was strange was that no sooner had they set their hearts on having it than the billiard hall became the scene of unexpected aggravation. Fireworks were thrown inside, tables were mysteriously damaged, and senseless acts of petty vandalism occurred for which it would have been tactless but not inaccurate to blame the Twins. The police told the manager that there was nothing they could do about it and after several weeks of mayhem the owners were relieved when the Twins said they'd take it off their hands for a weekly fiver.

No sooner had they taken over than the trouble stopped as quickly as it had started – and one of the liveliest chapters in the story of the Twins began.

To start with, Reg was very much in charge. Unlike Ron, who could be described as ham-fisted, Reg could use his hands for many things besides punching people. Soon he had the hall cleaned up, the bar repainted, the snooker tables put in order, and within a few days it was as if the Twins had been in charge for ever. They kept it open night and day, and as word got round about the change of management it began to make a profit. But from the start the real attraction of the hall was not so much the snooker as the Twins, and since they rarely left the place, a lot of people caught the habit of dropping in to see them. These included former inmates from various detention centres in the army, old friends and friends of friends who had just got out of prison, hopeful villains with a sure-fire proposition, and a lot of bored teenagers who had heard about the Twins and were on the lookout for a good night's entertainment or adventure.

One of many unexpected things about the Twins was that they were naturally convivial. For obvious reasons, most criminals remain suspicious of the outside world and have a tendency to act as loners. But whilst I'm not convinced that the

Twins ever really liked their fellow human beings they none-theless loved to be the centre of activity and attention. They enjoyed having company around them and had little difficulty finding it.

One sees this clearly from the earliest days of the billiard hall. Whatever else they were, the Twins were rarely boring. They were what the locals used to call 'live wires' and had a knack of making something happen. It might be something funny. It was likely to be something dangerous and it would probably be unlawful, which ensured that evenings at the billiard hall were usually eventful. As one old regular put it, 'If you didn't turn up one night you'd find yourself worrying about what you were missing, and next morning someone would be sure to say, 'You should have been around last night. The things those Twins get up to. You should've seen 'em.'

Sometimes they would stage a full-scale battle, as on the night when members of a local Maltese gang arrived demanding money from the new management without previously having checked out who they were. The Twins were quick to disabuse them and a task force from the billiard hall pursued them down the road armed with cutlasses, after which no more was seen of the Maltese and no one else ever came demanding money. There were sometimes fights among the clientele to add to the excitement, but unless the Twins themselves joined in they disapproved of violence in the hall in case it undermined their authority.

One important feature of the lives of the Twins which started in the early days at the billiard hall was the emergence of a definite division of labour between them. Reg clearly was the worker. It was he who earned the money and he who paid – or, when he could get away with it, refused to pay – the bills and kept the whole place going. Reg had a straight side, which Ron lacked completely. Reg was sharper and more practical, with something of old Charlie's canniness and oily charm. Just as he'd been a classic boxer and Ron a bruiser, so Reg knew how to use his brain. He was keen on making money and on any wheezes that happened to be going.

Ron, on the other hand, remained the centre of attention and was increasingly the showman of the two. It was Ronnie whom people talked about, just as it was he who always needed people round him. I remember Dr Cline, a psychiatrist from the London Hospital who treated Ron for schizophrenia, saying he believed that 'a great deal of Ronnie's sociability and the need he seems to have for people who are dependent on him is almost certainly a compensation for the paranoiac's feelings of isolation and loneliness.'

If this was true, as I think it was, it goes some way to explain one of the enduring mysteries of the Twins and how they ended up as such iconic figures of the Sixties. But along with this there was another even more important feature of Ron's tortured personality, which was almost certainly related to his schizo-phrenia: his passionate involvement with a world of fantasy.

This seems to have begun with both the Twins during their childhood and early adolescence when they picked up all those stories of the criminals and villains of the old East End.

What was interesting was that although Ron had always been the damaged twin, and that emotionally he was increasingly at risk, it was he, not Reg who was always the centre of attention. He was the leader, he was the one who was really feared, and the billiard hall was the perfect stage for Ronnie to act out his favourite fantasies.

There were often evenings when for much of the time he'd sit there, sunk in silence. Then he could suddenly recover and when Ron was on a high he could usually be relied on to produce something crazy or outrageous. One night he brought along a donkey, placed a straw hat on its head and organised donkey rides around the hall. For some reason he had always loved dwarfs, and when he felt that things at the billiard hall needed livening up he would hire one from a theatrical agency for the evening to come and entertain them. Then one night for a change he hired a giant, and everyone had a great time trying to get him drunk. In the end he did become inebriated and when he fell asleep no one quite knew what to do with him. But beneath everything there always lurked an underlying threat of violence, and behind the fun and games the paranoid dreamworld of 'The Firm' was taking shape.

This could have been another of Ronnie's strategies to offset the earlier damage to his nervous system when it brought him terrible depressions. The criminologist Dick Hebdidge was the first to call the Twins 'actor gangsters' and during their time at the billiard hall one can see this tendency developing as Ron began escaping from acute depression into one or other of his favourite fantasies.

One can also understand how the billiard hall, having been originally built as a cinema, became a perfect stage for Ron's own criminal theatre. Every night it offered him a captive audience. Various members of what they were beginning to call 'The Firm', had walk-on parts, and lesser characters filled in as extras. Dickie Morgan played the part of resident comedian, and whatever happened Ron would always have to be the star, acting out whatever role the state of his emotions or the current situation called for.

His favourite role of all was to pretend to be his greatest hero, Al Capone. He had read a lot about him and began to copy the minutest details of his life. After reading how Capone, like the good Sicilian he was, used to have a barber come to shave him every morning, he got Violet to telephone the Italian barber from opposite Pellici's cafe to come and do the same for him at ten a.m. each day at Vallance Road. He also had a tailor measure him for a dark blue double-breasted suit, copied from an old photograph of his hero. But it was not until evening at the billiard hall that Ron came into his own, pretending to be Al Capone surrounded the members of his gang in some downtown pool room.

This would begin with Ronnie seated in the big armchair that was specially reserved for him, facing the door and watching as the regulars arrived. Then, as play began, the lights would flicker on above the tables, leaving the rest of the hall in shadow. 'Ron always wanted it to look like a den of thieves. He liked a lot of noise and lots of people and the air thick with cigarette smoke. He used to hand out cigarettes and shout, "Smoke up, you useless lot! There ain't enough smoke in 'ere." Then, when the hall was packed with people and play was going on at all the tables and the atmosphere was as thick as a Limehouse fog, Ronnie would be satisfied and would do something that you hardly ever saw. He would lean back in his chair and smile like an old tomcat.'

During nights like this, the drinks would always be on him and his favoured friends would play up to him, imitating characters in American gangster movies.

As well as Al Capone, Ron had other imaginary heroes, depending on his mood or whatever film he'd seen or what book he was reading. It was typical of him that, after all the trouble that he and Reg had endured to get thrown out of the army, he started calling himself 'The Colonel' and even dreamed about the sort of military hero he wished he'd been. Ever since reading *Seven Pillars of Wisdom* in Shepton Mallet he had been obsessed with Lawrence of Arabia. He also identified strongly with Gordon of Khartoum after reading Anthony Nutting's biography. When I asked him why, he said, 'Gordon was like me, 'omosexual, and he met his death like a man. When it's time for me to go, I hope I do the same.' For a time another hero was the daring leader of the SAS, Colonel Roy Farran. With Ron in full military mode, 178 Vallance Road became 'Fort Vallance,' just as he became 'The Colonel'. In a way the title rather suited him.

Reg, who would usually do anything to keep Ron happy,

would go along with this. He always liked to see himself as the practical member of the duo, as in fact he was – and as long as Ron was occupied, Reg got on with the practical side of running the Firm. It was he who generally 'did the business' which more or less financed Ron's fun and games. It was he, for instance, who tried to put some order into the protection rackets instead of relying, as Ron did, on the casual 'nipping' (the law called it 'demanding with menaces') of any sum you needed from anyone you thought you could frighten into giving it to you.

Ron's pathological love of violence could also cause unnecessary trouble between him and Reg, as it did when the minor incident of the Mile End Road second-hand car dealer nearly ended in disaster.

Ever since the Twins had taken on the billiard hall, Reg had begun to make arrangements for regular 'pensions' for protecting local businesses. This particularly applied to the many used-car dealers who had been appearing in the neighbourhood. He never had much trouble, persuading them to be sensible. Only in rare cases had force been necessary and even then a can of paint-stripper and a sledgehammer wielded against a car or two worked wonders.

Not that this kind of action was ever needed with this particular dealer Reg had been looking after down the Mile End Road. Reg always said that he was good as gold, never any trouble from his customers, and the money was always paid on time. As Reg put it, 'he made it a pleasure to do business with him. So when he told us he'd been having aggravation from this docker from the other side of the river over a car he'd bought and said he didn't like, we took it seriously. Then, when we heard that the docker was now threatening our friend if he didn't pay him all his money back, it was clearly up to us to do something about it.'

At this point Ron became interested in what was happening,

and when he heard the docker was coming mob-handed with a group of other dockers he decided he'd be there to meet them.

Reg was more practical. Instead of resorting to violence, he telephoned the docker, calmed him down, and then told the car dealer not to worry.

But when Ron 'ad the 'ump', as he often did these days, and all else failed to lift him from his black depressions, there was only one thing – sex apart – which never failed to restore his spirits: violence. Or failing that, the threat of violence. The most exciting moments at the billiard hall were when Ron would announce, 'Tonight I've decided that we're going to 'ave a little row with someone' and a fight with another gang would start for the fun of it.

Soon after this the Twins became conscious of their dress and adopted the sharp blue suits of another of their heroes, the film-star gangster George Raft. This formed the basis for what became the uniform of the Twins and the members of their so-called 'Firm' – dark blue suits, gleaming winkle-picker shoes, white shirts and tightly knotted slim dark silk ties. They wouldn't dream of fighting anyone, still less of killing him, unless they were wearing ties. In the same way, no matter how much blood there might be on their clothes when they staggered home to bed after a violent night out Violet would unfailingly ensure that next morning two fresh white shirts would be waiting for them on their beds, ironed with the love that only a devoted mother could give them.

It was during their time at the billiard hall that the Twins' homosexuality began to give its earliest indication of the part that it would play in the their criminal careers – especially Ron's. The days when the Twins were satisfied with sex with one another were over, and Ron had started paying local boys for it instead. Reg was warier, so unsurprisingly it was Ron who took the initiative, although Reg usually followed. Both twins were still anxious to keep their pleasures secret, and Ron used to claim that the teenage boys who had started hanging round the billiard hall were his 'little spies' and that he used them to pick up information – which, in fact, he did. But when he paid them it was rarely just for information. Although he only he really liked sex with young boys, he was technically not a paedophile but an ephebophile who confined his attractions, when he could, to youths between the ages of sixteen and eighteen.

Ron's ongoing relationship with his boys became tied up with several of his other fantasies. He once surprised me by saying that his favourite film was *Boys' Town*, starring Spencer Tracy as the priest who dedicates his life to saving boys from life on the streets.

Another of his favourite fantasies was what he liked to call 'politics', and he liked to see himself behind the scenes, using secret information from his boys to plot the downfall of his enemies. Before long this became an early symptom of his growing persecution complex.

During these carefree days at the billiard hall – at a time when the faintest hint of homosexuality would have shattered the Twins' credibility as up and coming gangsters – their pre-dilections tied them more than ever to a lasting life of crime.

Among the regulars who joined the Firm, it always seemed to be the same old story. When fresh recruits arrived they'd start off full of excitement and enthusiasm and for a while nobody would seem more devoted to the Twins and the thrilling life of violent action that they offered. Then gradually the new recruits would change, as local girls began to offer different pleasures which were harder to resist. Gradually the apprentice villain would begin to waver and all it needed was a pregnant girlfriend for the would-be gangster to be gone for ever. Cyril Connolly famously gave as the principal 'enemy of promise' for an aspiring writer what he called 'the threat of the pram in the hall'.

It was much the same for an aspiring villain in the East End of the 1950s, particularly now that there were beginning to be more well-paid jobs around than there had been even ten years earlier.

'Fuckin' women,' Ron would grumble. 'Make you end up like a fuckin' girl yourself.'

But there was no danger of that happening to Ron – nor to Reg either, if Ron had anything to do with it.

As for the billiard hall, its days were numbered. Before long the wreckers would arrive and the blocks of flats of the new East End would take its place. By then an equally dramatic change had hit the Twins as well, and but for an extraordinary stroke of luck their story would have ended there and then.

Thanks to the destruction of the traditional East End, its old gangland culture was in serious decline. This meant that the sort of home-grown violence that the Twins relied on for their fights was increasingly in short supply and on a wet March night in 1954 the Twins led half a dozen chosen followers on what would prove to be their last street battle. The Twins themselves were still unbeaten – and probably unbeatable – but in spite of this the battle turned out disastrously and came within a heartbeat of destroying both the Twins for good.

What both of them had been expecting was another bout of old-style gangland fighting, but this time it transpired that they were living in the past. The good old days had gone and the Watney Streeters weren't a proper gang. Some of them were drinking in a pub called The Britannia but they wisely disappeared when they heard the Twins were coming, leaving behind a local boy called Terry Martin who was simply finishing a game of poker with a friend.

Because Ron was expecting a full-scale battle and the red mist had descended, he wanted blood. Recognising Terry Martin – who had played no part in what was going on – he dragged him out of The Britannia, beat him up as only Ron could beat up someone and left him lying in the gutter. Those who found him thought that he was dead. He wasn't quite and the doctors at the London Hospital worked all night in an attempt to save him. But for the next few days it was a matter of touch and go whether he would survive.

During the days that followed, the lives of the Twins were hanging by the same slim thread as Terry Martin's. In 1954 capital punishment was still the mandatory sentence for murder and had Terry Martin died, as once or twice he very nearly did, the Twins would finally have proved Aunt Rose had been right as they took the dreaded nine o'clock walk together, Ron for murder and Reg as an accessory to the crime.

Instead, Terry Martin, by recovering, saved their lives as well as his own, but that was the only favour he would do them. When he recovered consciousness the police were by his bedside. And when they questioned him he talked – and went on talking when the case came up at the Old Bailey and he was the principal witness for the prosecution. By then the Twins had decided which of them should take the blame. Ron accepted that it was him and counted himself lucky to escape with only three years in prison. Reg was luckier still to be acquitted, and for the first time in their lives the Twins were parted.

9

Twins Apart

WHEN RON WENT off to prison, Violet was desperately
worried. How could her precious Ronnie cope without
his mother? Equally important, how could the Twins cope
without each other?

At first, to everyone's surprise, the answer to both questions
seemed to be extremely well. Overcrowded Wandsworth
Prison had a reputation as a 'tough nick' but after the baptismal
fire of that month in Wormwood Scrubs while serving in the
army, followed by the harsh regime of military detention
centres, Ron was prepared for whatever was in store for him
and seemed in the best of spirits. Priding himself on his
toughness, he actually enjoyed the challenge of what others saw
as unacceptably harsh conditions. If the prison authorities
believed that they could get him down with that, he'd show
them all what toughness really was and make them think again.

Besides, in Wandsworth he was in good company. Dickie
Morgan, old friend, ex-burglar and fellow deserter from the
army, was there already, having been caught attempting to
hijack a lorry-load of meat. Along with him there was the small
but influential jail fraternity of those who called themselves
'professionals'. They liked to see themselves as the elite of the
prison and regarded those beneath them as 'civilians'. Reg
understood this perfectly, of course. Most of the 'professionals'
actually came from the East End and through them he found it

easy to arrange things so that brother Ron's life in prison was a little easier.

He told him to obtain the family addresses of a number of his fellow prisoners, then arranged to send their wives regular small sums of money on the understanding that in return their husbands would make sure that Ronnie was all right. Soon Ron began finding fellow inmates offering to do his work for him. He started getting extra cigarettes, and since cigarettes were the unofficial currency in jail he could have anything he wanted, sex included.

What was the old lag's saying? 'If you can't do the time, don't do the crime.' Ron was perfectly prepared to do his time, no problem, and if this meant being parted from his all-important 'other half' for a period, so be it. Ron could cope – and so could Reg. For now that Reg was on his own, life without Ron was turning out to be much simpler than he had suspected. So were his ambitions as he started to enjoy his life in what would soon become the Swinging Sixties.

He had learned a lot from the experience of the billiard hall, and since the place was no more he started a new club of his own in a former fish shop up the Mile End Road. To set Ron's mind at rest and reassure him that the club was essentially a joint venture, he tactfully called it 'The Double R' – but unlike the long-lost billiard hall, the ethos of the Double R was far more social than criminal. As he put it, he was aiming at 'the young East Ender who wants somewhere he can take his girl for a safe but fun night out', which was very different from anything that Ronnie would have wanted.

In fact, The Double R brought something of a sea change into Reg's life. He would still have considered himself a criminal – and a number of his old rackets continued, together with a tidied-up version of the existing protection business – but no more violence for the hell of it, no more imitating Al Capone; and for that matter, no more gang fights without Ron to start them. On the other hand, Reg did not follow the advice of some old friends who urged him to reapply for his professional boxing licence. He bought himself a flash blue Pontiac instead.

Soon The Double R was making money and it was clear that with the club Reg had hit upon the formula for success – a clever combination of the authentic flavour of the old East End, the sentimental cockney ballads of Ron's favourite pianist, the hunchbacked Queenie Watts, and a handful of authentic underworld characters to convince the couples on a night out from the west of the city that they were experiencing a real-life adventure. As The Double R caught on, it was taken up by various showbiz celebrities like Jackie Collins, Sybil Burton and Barbara Windsor who liked the atmosphere and encouraged Reg to call them by their Christian names. For Reg's presence was crucial to The Double R's success. No longer overshadowed by Ron's dominating presence, he was in danger of becoming something of a celebrity himself. He started dressing well, and for the first time in his life began to take an interest in something else that had also been impossible when Ronnie was around – women.

Ronnie had always treated any show of interest in the opposite sex by Reggie as out and out betrayal, as in a way it was; for Ron knew that if ever Reg became seriously involved with a woman he would lose him. Not that Reg was ever likely to get sexually involved with a woman on a long-term basis. The ties that bind identical homosexual twins together are usually too strong for that. But with Ron no longer there, Reg could at least enjoy female company. He realised he was good-looking and when women started finding him attractive he felt flattered and made the most of it. He also started cashing in on the fact that the old East End was becoming fashionable and it only needed a few more show-business celebrities to arrive for The Double R to get a reputation as the 'in' place for an adventurous night out. Reg found it easy being independent.

True, life was no longer as exciting as it was with Ron around but there were other pleasures to enjoy. He still lived at home in Vallance Road and enjoyed having Violet to himself. He even got on better with his father. The next eighteen months were probably the happiest of his life.

As for Ron, he too continued to cope rather well in prison. Wandsworth was a tough nick but he could deal with that. He kept himself largely to himself, apart from his 'pensioners' and the company of a few close friends. Something about him made the warders treat him cautiously but the family kept in close touch with him and he had made a wonderful new friend – a good-looking giant of a man called Frank Mitchell who was so strong that he could lift Ron up with one hand. Frank Mitchell was in fact a gentle psychopath, childlike with those he trusted, dangerous with those he didn't.

Ron soon discovered they had certain things in common. As with Ron, the warders kept clear of Mitchell and having spent most of his life in institutions of one sort or another he was proud of being able to take any punishment the prison authorities could inflict on him. Ron admired him for that and did his best to cheer him up by promising that, after his release, he and his brothers would look after him.

As for Ron himself, he seemed in danger of becoming the last thing anyone would ever have predicted – a model prisoner – and ironically it was the prison governor's decision to reward Ron for his good behaviour that brought disaster. Having become eligible for an easier existence in a first offenders' prison Ron was sent to Camp Hill Prison on the Isle of Wight.

From the moment he stepped off the ferry from the mainland Ronnie hated everything that Camp Hill Prison represented. He was uneasy with the more relaxed regime, he detested games, which he couldn't play, and after the company of his hardened criminals at Wandsworth he despised the company of what he regarded as 'straight' prisoners. He also resented the staff trying to teach him a worthwhile trade to save him from becoming what they called 'a hardened criminal'. He had no intention of ever being anything else. In Wandsworth all the other old lags had respected him. Here there were no old lags, and nobody respected him or even bothered with him.

Had Reggie been with him none of this would have mattered. But Reggie wasn't with him, and without the presence of his 'other half' to help restore the all-important balance of the twin relationship, he had no way of controlling its 'discordant' element and really started going mad.

What was happening was that the mental sickness which had been lurking in Ron's damaged psyche since illness had struck him at the age of three was following the course that the doctors had predicted. He started to withdraw into himself; he refused to talk to anyone, and he lost the ability to read. All he could do was watch the world go by, and as he watched he realised the truth. Everyone had turned against him. He told himself that he was Ron Kray, and in the past Ron Kray had always been a match for anyone. But now Ron Kray was helpless and it was from his sense of helplessness that his fears began. When he and Reg had been together, they could make everybody fear them but now that he was on his own his enemies were out for their revenge. He couldn't sleep at night and lay awake for hours, brooding about what he'd seen and why everybody hated him. Obsessed by not knowing what he'd done, he began to fear that somebody had planned to kill him.

Suddenly he realised the truth. Everyone was thinking he had grassed. That explained everything – the silences, the way everybody turned against him, the sudden isolation. He had been brought up to believe that betraying anybody to the law was the most despicable act of all, so if those around him thought that that was what he'd done, they would feel justified in hating him.

He tried to tell himself that this was nonsense. He, Ronnie Kray, had never grassed to anybody in his life. It was ridiculous. He never could and never would. So all he had to do now was stay calm and tell himself that his time in jail would soon be over and he'd be back again with those who loved him and respected him. Take it a day at a time and after three hundred and sixty-five days his sentence would be over. All he had to do was to survive a year; but in the end a year proved far too too long.

By now he was clearly very sick. 'I was seeing secret agents everywhere, working on a plot to torture me. Somebody I didn't know was out to get me.'

Then came the final straw which broke him. Aunt Rose, his favourite aunt who could beat any two women in a stand-up fight, had lost her battle with leukaemia. When a warder gruffly told him that Aunt Rose had died it sent Ron off his head. From then on his condition worsened rapidly, and the prison authorities had to confine him in a straitjacket for his own protection. When his condition worsened two psychiatrists came and certified him insane. When they'd done this they sent him to a locked ward in the Long Grove lunatic asylum near Epsom.

Violet Kray never forgave the prison authorities for the way they broke the news to her about her Ronnie, so soon after Rose's death. The local policeman knocked on the door in the middle of the night with a telegram containing a single sentence: 'Your son Ronald Kray certified insane.'

Violet collapsed. When she recovered she was beside herself with fear that, if 'they' could treat *her* like that, what were they doing to her Ronnie? The family agreed, especially Reg, and there and then he swore a solemn oath to Violet that he would do everything he could to save him. As events would prove, he kept his word. But in doing so, Ron's madness, which at first had threatened to destroy the world that the Twins had shared together, became part of their legend and their destiny.

On 20 February 1958 Ron was admitted as a patient to a locked ward in the Long Grove lunatic asylum under twenty-four-hour supervision by trained nurses and there he stayed for several days in a state of abject terror.

'I wouldn't move, but sat all day huddled round the radiator. I wasn't sure of who I was, and because it was so warm I felt the radiator was the only friend I had. Apart from my friend the radiator I was on my own, and I remember daft things coming and going through my mind. There was a man in the bed opposite me and I thought he was a dog. I liked dogs, and I thought that if I could remember his name he'd come and jump into my lap, and then I'd have a friend. But I never got his name right. I couldn't recognise anybody else, not even Reggie or my mother when they came to see me. All I could think was that I'd better kill myself, before someone else did it first.'

According to Ron's medical reports, his delusions persisted for several weeks and he went on thinking that people were plotting against him and censoring his letters for sinister purposes. Then, slowly, the treatment seemed to work and by the end of April his doctor casually summed him up in his report. 'A simple man of low intelligence, poorly in touch with the outside world.'

For the Long Grove doctors that was that and the madness of Ronnie Kray was pigeon-holed as a run-of-the-mill mental breakdown of a simple man of low intelligence. It was a sad case, but the doctors saw such cases every day. He was never going to be completely cured but they could help him to recover from his breakdown, then stabilise him on regular doses of the tranquillisers that were beginning to revolutionise the treatment of the mentally sick. They prescribed Stematol, a powerful drug that damps down neurotic symptoms, hopefully without completely doping the patient in the process. And that, it seemed, was that – although, as things turned out, it wasn't.

The problem was that Long Grove was essentially a non-specialist National Health Service hospital for the mentally sick, and of its 1,800 patients when Ron was there only eight, including Ron, were criminals. Since the hospital authorities insisted on treating prisoners like Ron as patients, his criminal history was ignored and the doctors went on treating him as a case of fairly mild schizophrenia. Since the doctors had little or no experience of dealing with violent criminals like Ron they failed to recognise the telltale signs which should have warned them what he really was.

For Ronnie was no ordinary schizophrenic whose problems could be stabilised with Stematol. Schizophrenics form by far the largest single group of patients in Britain's mental hospitals but there are several different forms of the disease. The sickness usually develops over a long period and is sparked off by a final crisis in which sufferers find themselves unable to reconcile their delusions with the world outside. They are rarely violent, generally have a low sex drive and find it hard to deal with the world.

But among the various sufferers from schizophrenia there is one small group that is extremely dangerous and often difficult to spot – the paranoid schizophrenics. If a paranoid schizophrenic has a mental breakdown his delusions can persist unchanged for a long period afterwards, for he often has a frightening ability to use all his powers of intelligence to protect his distorted view of the world.

It is this that accounts for one of the scariest things about paranoid schizophrenics – the way that they can frequently appear quite rational and normal while inwardly their lives are being dominated by some all-powerful obsession. According to Kraeplin, who first described this condition in the 1890s, this condemns the paranoid schizophrenic to 'a vicious circle of ill-advised aggressiveness, self-protection, misinterpretation, the spread of delusional ideas and increasing watchfulness.' All of which very much applied to Ron.

Other symptoms of paranoid schizophrenia can include emotional coldness, absence of remorse and any feeling for others, coupled with delusions of grandeur alternating with periods of deep depression and an all-pervading sense of persecution. Some paranoid schizophrenics suffer from what is known as 'double orientation', living in the normal world while simultaneously identifying with Christ, Napoleon or some other great figure from the past. Sometimes they hear voices giving them directions, and this often accompanies a blunting of emotions, leading in extreme cases to 'callous and apparently motiveless crimes of violence' if their voices order them to commit them. Paranoid schizophrenics have been known to resort to the most violent crimes, which they see as their sole means of survival. Sometimes a trifling affair can throw them into a wild fury, just as something deeply moving or upsetting can fail to affect them.

Sometimes these qualities appear in history's greatest conquerors and religious leaders, and also in some of its most notorious criminals. Jack the Ripper, Al Capone, Charles Manson and the Boston Strangler are all textbook cases of violent paranoid schizophrenics. And, although none of the doctors had spotted it yet, so was Ronnie Kray.

By early May he seemed to be responding well to treatment and the doctors decided he was safely on the road to recovery. Soon they would recommend that he could return to prison and safely finish off his sentence.

While the Long Grove doctors were failing to appreciate the danger of Ron's condition, his family went still further and were claiming there was really nothing wrong with him at all. Violet was firmly, indeed passionately, of this opinion. After all, wasn't she his mother and wasn't she proved right that time when he'd had the diphtheria, and she'd saved his life by refusing to believe the doctors? She still knew her Ronnie better than any doctors. 'My Ronnie barmy? Don't be daft. He's just playing up, like he did when he was in the army.'

The rest of the family agreed with her, even Reg, although knowing Ron as closely as he did he must have had his doubts. But whatever doubts he might have had were quickly overruled when news arrived that one of the Long Grove doctors was advising that Ronnie should be kept in hospital a little longer to make sure that he was absolutely ready to return to prison to complete his sentence.

By now, really thanks to Violet, the whole family was in denial over Ronnie's madness and they seem to have persuaded Reg that it was his duty to do something to save his brother, 'otherwise they'll keep him in the loonie bin for ever.'

Reg was smart and had learned to pick the brains of people who were smarter still. After talking to a helpful lawyer he discovered something interesting. According to the law, provided someone who'd been certified insane could remain at liberty for six months or more the authorities would be compelled to accept this as evidence of a presumption of his sanity. If they still had doubts about it, the patient would have to be recertified.

This was all that Reg needed for the plan that followed. It was very simple. If Ron was to be rescued from spending the rest of his life in a lunatic asylum, there was one way Reg could help him to escape. After that, all they'd have to do was make sure he remained free for long enough to get an independent assessment of his sanity from their own doctors. After which he would give himself up to the police, serve out the remainder of his sentence, and emerge from prison freed from any stigma of insanity.

★

By now Ron was no longer restricted to the locked ward where he was placed on his arrival. He was allowed to see visitors on Saturday afternoons, when relatives could come and spend an hour or so having tea with the patients.

One must remember that in those days the Twins were still physically identical, and in the past they had often used their uncanny similarity to baffle the police over which of them was which. It was time to pull the same trick once again – and they both knew exactly what to do. On her last visit Violet had told Ron to be sure to wear his dark blue suit and red tie and when Reg arrived, accompanied by the Twins' old friend Georgie Osborne, he was wearing a raincoat but underneath was dressed the same as Ron. For the first half-hour of the visit the twins and Georgie Osborne sat talking and laughing over some holiday snapshots that Reg had brought along to show his brother. Then one of the nurses announced teatime. Tea was made in a scullery along the corridor, and since patients weren't allowed beyond the door to the visiting room one of the visitors usually went to fetch it.

The duty nurse noticed nothing strange when Ron's brother, who was still wearing his raincoat, went out to fetch the tea. He took his time but this didn't seem to worry the other two who were perfectly happy talking and laughing together over the photographs. So it was quite a while before the nurse became suspicious.

'Ron,' he said, 'where's your brother gone? He's taking an awful long time to get the tea.'

'I'm not Ron,' the twin replied. 'I'm Reg. You can look at my driving licence if you don't believe me.'

'Then where's your brother Ron?'

'How should I know? It's your job to look after him, not mine.'

At which point the nurse panicked and sounded the alarm. But by then Ron Kray had been picked up in a car being driven by his brother Charlie, who'd been waiting patiently outside, and was on his way to London.

The police arrived to question Reg and Georgie Osborne, but there was little they could do once Reg established his identity.

In fact, springing Ron from Long Grove was the easy part for Reg. After this he had to organise a complex operation to look after him.

First things first. Somehow Reg had to get reliable medical attention from a doctor they could trust not to turn Ron in to the police. There was one such doctor in the whole of London whom Reg was absolutely sure he could rely on: the villains' own medico emeritus, Doc Blasker, who operated from his second-floor surgery in a run-down semi on the edge of Dockland. Doc Blasker was as versatile as he was helpful. Over the years he had lost count of how many bullets, shotgun pellets and associated missiles he had extracted from the flesh of uncomplaining criminals without reporting them to the police – not to mention the damaged faces he had sewn up, and the discreet abortions he had carried out on the brown American-cloth-covered medical couch in his scruffy upstairs surgery.

In spite of which Doc Blasker was almost permanently broke. The more money that he made from ministering to criminals, the more he lost betting on horses. So when Reg brought his brother to his surgery late that February night, the good doctor was hardly likely to have turned the pair of them away.

There was something even more disturbing about the situation. Thanks to Doc Blasker and the misdiagnosis by the prison psychiatrists, in eleven months' time a potentially dangerous homicidal schizophrenic in the shape of Ronnie Kray was going to be released upon society when he had served out the rest of his original prison sentence.

In the meantime, Reg had to find somewhere Ron could live a secret life while keeping clear of the authorities long enough to prove his sanity. Easier said than done. Reg knew Ron well enough to understand that he would not be safe in a flat in town. People would talk about him and he would be suspicious. Once this happened he could well turn dangerous. It was altogether far too risky. Nor could one think of sending him abroad. There was one man and one alone that Reg could think of who would help them.

Geoff Allen was a man of many parts – con man, car dealer, professional card sharp, dedicated womaniser, property dealer, and Britain's most successful arsonist. When the need arose, as even for him it sometimes did, he employed the Twins as his enforcers. Ronnie, in return, used Geoff Allen as his private banker, knowing that he could always tap him for almost any sum, from a few hundred pounds to several thousand, if the need arose. Such was Geoff Allen's optimistic nature, that apparently they never had the faintest disagreement.

Geoff also owned a farm in Suffolk and when Reg told him of his problem with Ron and how he needed somewhere he could keep him securely hidden for several months, he offered him the use of an empty caravan on his land in Suffolk.

With Ron safely tucked away in Suffolk, Reg continued to make great gains at the helm of The Double R, revealing what he was really good at: living on the borderline of legality. He looked good in a tuxedo, and had a useful line of patter. Brother Charlie helped too. In this, as in so many things, the Krays were beginning to follow the pattern of New York gangsters, where showbiz and clubland overlapped with organised crime. Again, this was something new in London, as new money coming in from gambling started feeding through to clubland. As owner of The Double R, and its successor, the Kentucky, Reg even got to know a few visiting stars from America, including Judy Garland and her daughter Lisa Minelli. For the first time in his life, Reg was actually becoming famous on his own account. And for the first time in his life Reg was now free, which included being free from Ronnie: the conjoined life of twins who lived their life as one was in abeyance.

Everybody began to notice the signs of Reggie's newly found success, which were quite spectacular – the energy with which he started up his new club, the Kentucky, his new persona as its dinner-jacketed proprietor, the money he was making now that he didn't have to pay for Ron's crazier extravagances. Even his homosexuality seemed to be forgotten. Without Ron always there to turn him off the very thought of females and ensure that there would always be a boy to keep him happy, he started to enjoy the company of women, and the time was not far off when he would find his way to bed with them.

At the same time quite a number of fresh criminal activities were beckoning. In contrast there was poor, wretched Ronnie, on the edge of madness and terrified of anyone who passed his caravan.

He could not have seemed more hopeless, and more desperately in need of help, and as Reggie's heart went out to him, the contrast between the two of them could not have been more harrowing. Reg enjoying the new life that he had just discovered and Ron in the depths of abject wretchedness, terrified, unshaven, and dependent on his twin for his survival.

But it was still hard work for Reg, made all the harder by the way he always had to keep an eye on Ron. For Ron had become an even more pathetic figure, frightened of being on his own and terrified that Reg was going to abandon him. Reg was the only one who could reassure him that he hadn't been forgotten. When Ron forgot his pills he became hyperactive and was dangerous. When he took too many he would sink into a deep depression. Sex was an ever-present problem, and from time to time Reg would bring along a boy to keep Ron quiet. But this was dangerous. Boys could talk and sometimes did.

Besides, and understandably, few of them were over-anxious to oblige, however good the money.

Even with Reg, Ron wasn't easy. In a manic state he'd be immensely powerful and could turn dangerous, even to friends he'd known since boyhood, and sometimes even to Reg himself. 'You're not really my twin brother, you're just somebody who looks like him,' he told him once. For Ron the dominant emotion now was fear.

One of the very few people he never threatened was Geoff Allen, probably because Geoff made a point of visiting him in the caravan every day. In spite of this, Geoff realised how dangerous he was.

'But since he trusted me,' he said, 'I once took him up to London to a top Harley Street psychiatrist who told me afterwards that there was no question about it. He was definitely, incurably homicidal. But what was strange was the form it took with Ron. There were periods when he seemed absolutely normal and the only time there was any trouble was once when I was in the caravan with Ron and a chap I knew dropped in to see me. There was nothing in it and Ron seemed quite untroubled. But when I said, "I wish that wretched fellow wouldn't bother me like that," he started brooding.

'Then he said, "Geoff, you've been good to me and I'm going to do something for you in return. I'm going to kill that man who's been pestering you."

'From the way he said this I realised that he was deadly serious, and I had a dreadful job convincing him that I didn't want the poor sod killed'.

'And would he have killed him if you hadn't?'

'Oh, definitely', Geoff replied. 'It was only then that I realised that he was permanently suspicious and very dangerous.' When he saw a local farmer, he brooded over him for days and then told Reg his decision. He'd have to kill him too. It took all Reg's powers of persuasion to dissuade him and turn his mind to safer lines of thought. Soon the only way to cure his suspicions was to disguise him and drive him up on middle-of-the-night trips to London, to Vallance Road and even to The Double R. It was risky but leaving him in the caravan was riskier.

Torn both ways, it became an impossible situation for Reg. If he had wanted to survive, he should not have made that promise to Violet to look after Ron in the first place. It was Number One he should have been looking after now, not Ron. Others who were more experienced could have looked after him and he should have left them to it. For Reg would never get a chance like this again and the truth was that he could easily have taken it. He had so much going for him now – his club, his great new life, with his new friends and new celebrities to keep him happy. But it would have meant abandoning Ron, and Reg thought that God only knew what would have become of him. It would have also meant breaking from his mother who would never have forgiven him. Deciding to delegate the care of Ron would have been the most momentous decision of Reg's life and he must have known that he should take it. So why didn't he?

The answer now seems obvious, although it can't have been so obvious to Reg. The trouble was that he was still tightly locked in the same discordant-twin relationship with Ron that he had been in all his life and he could never break the pattern. And, at the same time, Violet was still acting as she always had. All she could think of was protecting her beloved Ronnie, although this meant that by doing so she was actually destroying Reggie.

Finally Reg took Ron to a tame psychologist in Harley Street and told him that Ron was planning to get married. Since his fiancée's parents had heard rumours of mental illness in his family he needed a doctor's letter to reassure them all that he was sane. After a brief and expensive consultation the doctor was happy to oblige, and with the backing of the letter Ron was also happy to return to prison, finish his original sentence, and emerge free from any suggestion of insanity.

The problem was getting Ron back to prison. It took Reg a long time to convince Violet that the time had come for Ron to surrender to the police, but he finally succeeded. Reg telephoned the local police station, and told an incredulous desk sergeant that his brother Ron Kray wanted to go back to prison. Having convinced him that it wasn't some sort of joke, Reg then arranged an appointment for a police car to come to Vallance Road after Ron had had his dinner. Since Reg had put sleeping pills in Ron's coffee, he went quietly.

This prisoner serving a three-year sentence for a violent crime that had nearly killed a man was someone they had declared sane, but he was not just mildly schizophrenic. He was a paranoid schizophrenic – and he was highly dangerous. Between them, the doctors and the prison authorities had released on the public a homicidal schizophrenic. In addition, there was a further source of danger for one person in particular – for Reg himself.

At the time it seemed inconceivable that the pathetic Ron could ever be a danger to anyone, least of all to his twin brother, especially as throughout Ron's illness the power relationship between the Twins appeared to have been dramatically reversed and Reg was clearly in command. It was he who was making the decisions, he who was making all the money and who was very much in control of life. Ron, by contrast, totally depended on his brother to survive.

Indeed, once Ron was back in prison the situation was tough on him, as the prison staff were not particularly understanding and Ron himself believed that he was cured. So did the family. He was weak, but with careful treatment he'd be fine. Doc Blasker would always be on hand to help if anything went wrong. And the family thanked God for Reg. Not only was he making money, the way he looked after Ron was wonderful. Reg had always been the strong one who could cope.

But in the long term, none of this was going to matter for once again it was Ronnie's weakness that would prove to be his greatest source of strength, and the more helpless and pathetic he became, the more Reg yielded to him; and somehow it was always Ron who ended up dictating what should happen, and Reg who ended up obeying. For Reg the real danger lay where it had lain since the Twins had emerged from their separate isolation hospitals at the age of three – in those unbreakable bonds that linked the two of them together. Had Reg been more self-aware, and more concerned about his own survival, he would have realised that, however mad he seemed, Ron would always find a way to reassert his domination and bring Reg under his control again. It might take time but, judging by what had happened in the past, it would be sure to happen once again.

The problem was that if Reg failed to understand what was happening to his brother so did everybody else, including those psychiatrists who should have seen the danger. The severity of Ron's mental state was always underestimated. He was regarded, if he was regarded at all, as a relatively mild schizophrenic who had suffered some sort of nervous breakdown from which he had more of less recovered, the breakdown mimicking the time when he had first pretended madness in the guardroom at Canterbury.

The family too were in denial, having convinced themselves that Ron was simply 'acting up' again. For Violet to have admitted that her own beloved Ronnie, whom she had saved when he had so nearly died of diphtheria, was actually a lethal madman would have totally destroyed her. So, following the pattern that she adhered to all her life when faced with something unacceptable about her twins, she closed her mind to it, and shifted any blame there was onto others, particularly, of course, the family's regular *bêtes noires* – the lawyers, the police and the prison authorities.

But that was not the point. Far more serious was the failure of the doctors at the Long Grove mental hospital to understand Ron's true mental condition. Even that was excusable: since Long Grove was an ordinary mental hospital, the doctors there had had little experience of criminals and diagnosed Ron as suffering from mild schizophrenia, which gave them little reason for alarm. According to a current psychiatric textbook, 'schizophrenics are usually the least dangerous of all the mentally sick and the least likely to go in for violent crime. They usually have a low sex drive, and a low energy quotient in general' – which, to judge by appearances, applied to Ron. The conclusion was brief and certainly not one to have given anyone concern. 'A patient of poor intelligence, and little contact with reality.'

What none of the doctors remembered, if they even knew about it at the time, was the existence of a small but separate group of schizophrenics known as paranoid schizophrenics, 'which in certain cases can produce the most dangerous criminals of all'. According to the textbooks, symptoms could include violent mood swings – from grandiose illusions to black depression – hearing voices, compulsive aggression, flattening of the emotions and, in adulthood, actual physical change which could include putting on weight, deadening of the voice and a pronounced coarsening of the facial features.

All of which was starting to apply with worrying precision to Ronnie. The truth was that his case had been misdiagnosed from the beginning. Far from being a harmlessly depressive schizophrenic with a low sex drive, he was in fact a paranoid schizophrenic and, potentially at least, a highly dangerous one. Certainly a disturbingly high proportion of the classic symptoms of schizophrenic paranoia applied with uncanny accuracy to him. He heard voices, he swung from highs of delusions of grandeur to lows of suicidal misery. He also swung rapidly between trust and irrational suspicion, and as his suspicions and fears of persecution mounted it would be only a matter of time before he became homicidal. With appropriate regular treatment his condition could have stabilised but this would have required expert and regular attention. With Ron there was not the faintest chance of this and, thanks to his erratic treatment by Doc Blasker, the family was able to convince themselves that Ron was cured when he wasn't.

With Reg so apparently successful, and Ron so pathetically in need of all the help that he could get, no one gave a thought to the dangers always lurking in their situation as discordant identical twins. But one of the reasons why a serious imbalance in a discordant-twin relationship so often brought disaster to them both, was because of their genetic similarities, which could not be changed and often made the weakness pass from one twin to the other.

What was particularly dangerous in the Twins' situation was that at this moment when the discordance in the relationship exploded due to Ronnie's madness, what everybody noticed were the differences which were all too clear in the separate situations of the Twins. At the very moment when Ron was in the depths of degradation and despair, it must have seemed that Reg had broken free from him at last, particularly when with the passing of the weeks the imbalance between the two of them increased dramatically and it seemed that Reg, finally released from Ron's irresistible twin demands, had started to enjoy his freedom for the first time in his life.

Although everyone, Reg included, now seemed to think that he was in command, nothing had really changed. With all the wayward cunning of the madman that he was, Ron had been playing games like these to keep Reg under his control since they were children. Alarming though it was, his recent breakdown only raised the stakes by making Ron more dependent now on Reg than ever.

This meant that, as long as the bond between the twins endured, the discordant-twin relationship could reassert itself and reunite them. If this happened there would be no stopping them, and since Reg was identical to Ron, anything could happen. I remember talking to Reg about Ron's first serious attack of madness in Camp Hill Prison, and him telling me how he experienced a sense of acute unease at precisely the same time, although nobody had told him that anything was wrong with Ron until much later.

This meant that in the short term Reg was in command and was free to enjoy his apparent independence. But in the long term the prognosis was alarming. As long as Ron remained alive and active it was a virtual certainty that he would reassert his domination over Reg and end up making him as mad as he was. The facts of their discordant-twin birthright were unassailable and would prove too powerful for either of them to resist.

10

Esmeralda's and After: 1960–64

THE 1960S STARTED well for the Twins. A few months earlier Reg had received an eighteenth-month prison sentence for demanding money with menaces. But there was such a strong suspicion that he had been framed by the police that in March 1960 he was released from Wandsworth pending his appeal. At the same time, Ron was beginning to cope with life and, thanks to his medication, was learning to live with his paranoia. But nonetheless the advance of his illness was beginning to change not only his appearance but his personality. The Twins' passport photos taken at the end of 1959 still show them as virtually identical, but since then the physical coarsening had set in. Ron had put on weight, his voice had become increasingly expressionless, and something was happening around his eyes.

Reg, in contrast with his brother, was in the best of spirits since leaving prison and was determined to exploit the opportunities of the new decade. For those with their wits about them, there had never been a better time to be a criminal – thanks largely to Parliament which was still debating what to do about the laws on gambling, some of which went back to the Middle Ages and most of which were unenforceable. So while the politicians went on arguing and the police gave up arresting people for illicit gambling, so many casinos and gaming clubs were springing up that London was getting known as the gambling capital of Europe.

During the late 1950s, the Twins had prospered from 'protecting' semi-legal gaming parties in Belgravia hosted by the gambling king of London at the time, John Aspinall. Reg was missing club life more than ever now and, remembering those parties, he was on the lookout for an upmarket gaming club of his own when someone mentioned Esmeralda's Barn.

Esmeralda's Barn has long since vanished from the ever-changing face of London, its premises demolished and its site in Knightsbridge now occupied by the unlovely bulk of the Berkeley Hotel. But the Barn used to be above a row of shops in fashionable Wilton Place and it was here that it began as a nightclub on London's debutante circuit in the 1950s, with soft lights, sweet music and a resident singer called Cy Grant.

Then, as the 1950s ended, a bright young man called Stefan de Faye took the club over and turned it into one of the West End's first legitimate casinos, with a bar, a dining room, roulette, and three full-sale tables for chemmy. Soon Alf Mancini, one of London's smartest gambling club managers, joined de Faye as co-director and it seemed that they could not go wrong. But in the hungry world of early 1960s London it was unwise to overreach yourself and, although he didn't know it yet, Stefan de Faye was in danger of becoming too successful.

It was always said that the Notting Hill property mogul Peter Rachman tipped the Twins off about the Barn in order to repay a favour. But more important was the fact that Billy Hill, who was rapidly becoming one of London's richest criminals, also encouraged them to go for it.

It would be unfair to Billy Hill to ascribe his attitude towards the Twins to fellow feeling for a pair of up-and-coming youngsters, still less to kindness or warm-heartedness. Mr Hill had given up on kindness and warm-heartedness many years before. As for encouraging young talent, after seventeen years in Her Majesty's prisons, forget it. The only motive Billy ever had was to do whatever suited Billy Hill. And it suited him to have the Kray Twins safely tucked away in Esmeralda's Barn to divert them from the richer pickings he was busily exploiting on the gambling scene of Mayfair and Belgravia.

Hill had changed a lot since the days of the billiard hall, when the Twins had first met him and refused to back him in his fight against Jack Spot. Sensing the new possibilities in London, he had reinvented himself as a big-time criminal tycoon. He had already masterminded the KLM gold job, eighteen months before, followed by a quarter-million-pound mailbag robbery, and apart from crime, he was now *en route* to becoming a multi-millionaire from the profits of gambling, property and a large-scale demolition company. He spent part of every year in Morocco, supervising his narcotics business from Tangier to London, and as a one-time burglar he enjoyed the luxury of his burglar-proof flat in Bayswater, opposite the Greek cathedral. From here he directed his criminal affairs like the chairman of a major multinational and it was this that made him keen to have the Twins on board. For Billy Hill was not naive, and he knew that the richer he became, the more vulnerable he'd be to violence. In London gang warfare was increasing but at the age of forty-nine Billy Hill had had enough of it to last a lifetime. Others could fight his battles for him now. Who better than the Krays?

Even with Billy Hill to back them it was unlikely that the Twins could have ever taken over Esmeralda's Barn. They would have started by threatening the owner, beaten up a croupier or two, then caused disturbances to interrupt the gambling. Ron was good at creating disturbances, and in the end it might have worked. On the other hand it might not. Stefan de Faye was no pushover and he would almost certainly have asked for police protection and toughed it out. All of which would have taken time and scared off the punters – and the Twins might well have found themselves back in prison, which was something that they seriously didn't want. To avoid this happening, they turned to one of the finest fraudsters in the country for assistance.

Leslie Payne was one of a new breed of high-powered con men who suddenly appeared in London in the 1960s. The son of an ex-solicitor, he was a big good-looking fair-haired man who would have had little difficulty making an honest living had he wished but who had long ago decided not to. His trademark was a casually tied polka-dot blue bow tie which, when combined with an equally casual lightweight suit, distinguished him from the other shady characters around him. Widely known as 'Payne the Brain' or 'the Man with the Briefcase', he was, as I wrote about him once, 'so plausible and so stylishly dishonest that I took him for an Old Etonian.'

He was also one of the few people round the Twins who had experienced violence on a scale that none of them had ever known – as an infantry sergeant in the war in Italy at the battle of Cassino. 'After that', he said, 'it was hard to take the hangers-on around the Twins too seriously.'

But Payne was never one to underestimate the Twins themselves, and he was interested in them for the same reason as Billy Hill was – he wanted the right to use the name of Kray to scare off any other hungry villains who felt like preying on his long-firm frauds.

The theory of the long-firm fraud was simple and probably started with the Ancient Greeks. It involved buying up large quantities of goods on credit, selling them off for cash as cheaply and as fast as possible, and then disappearing with the money. End of story. But there were endless variations on the way it worked, and with his ingenuity and the assistance of his partner, a mousy-looking ex-accountant called Freddy Gore, Leslie Payne had started raking in extraordinary amounts of money. But however smart you were – and Payne and Gore were very smart – there was always the chance of something going wrong. The fall guy you had paid to take the blame might go back on the agreement. Somebody might grass you to the police. Someone might even try to take your operation over.

Such things, alas, could happen, and when they did it was good to have someone on your side with a reputation that everybody feared. Which was why Les Payne had got to know the Twins. As he put it, 'when it came to organised, effective violence, they were quite simply the best in the business.'

In return the Twins asked Leslie Payne to help them hijack Esmeralda's Barn, which he did so skilfully that it was like having teeth extracted by a painless dentist. Stefan de Faye barely knew what had happened to his club until he lost it.

Payne began by renting an impressive office just behind the Albert Hall for a few days. Then he rang de Faye out of the blue, inviting him to call one evening at his office to discuss an interesting business proposition. Payne took a lot of trouble with his business propositions, which was why de Faye, who was not a stupid man, accepted. The address was reassuring and Leslie Payne sounded almost reassuring too. But all this ended when de Faye entered Payne's office and came face to face with the Twins.

It was not that they said or did anything, threatening or otherwise. They were dressed in their dark blue suits in honour of the occasion and all they did was sit silently for the next half-hour while Payne did all the talking. De Faye was not permitted to say much either, as Payne spelled out certain facts about the ownership of Esmeralda's Barn that he had recently discovered.

Unlike most con-men's patter, every statement in Leslie Payne's account was true.

He started with the Barn's monthly earnings. 'Correct me if I'm wrong, but during the last three months your total income from the gambling averaged £7,250 a month.'

Despite himself, de Faye could only nod.

'You are also one of four principal investors who are drawing money from the club but final control is vested in a holding company called Hotel Organisation Ltd. Again, correct me if I'm wrong, but I understand that Hotel Organisation Ltd is you, and you alone.'

Once again de Faye nodded.

'What exactly do you want?' he asked.

'My friends and I wish to purchase Hotel Organisation Ltd. And we are offering you a thousand pounds. My lawyer has already drawn up an agreement and I have it here for you to sign. You and your other three directors will keep your places on the board of Esmeralda's Barn. You will simply be relieved of all the worries you must have, running such a vulnerable club as this.'

'Worries? But I have no worries,' said de Faye.

Instead of answering, Payne turned his gaze upon the Twins who stared back at Stefan de Faye.

'I wouldn't be so sure,' said Leslie Payne. 'To be honest, were I in your position I would take the offer while you have the chance.'

De Faye still tried to argue but there was something about the presence of the Twins that made argument pointless and he finally did as Leslie Payne suggested. Stefan de Faye was never to set foot in Esmeralda's Barn again.

What was unusual about Esmeralda's Barn was its perfection. Thanks to de Faye and Alf Mancini it made money like a dream, and there was nothing for the Twins to do except enjoy it. With

Mancini in charge to supervise the gambling and Payne around to keep an eye on business, the Twins had no need to do anything at all.

Throughout the 1960s, London's gamblers were going chemmy mad. Unlike baccarat, that old favourite of the gambling classes in which the house retained the bank (and the profits), in chemmy the bank was passed around the players. (Hence its full name, *chemin de fer*, French for 'railway'.) Because of this it was generally believed that chemmy was the nearest one could get to a game of pure chance and – at least in theory – the odds were equalised between the players and the house.

But this overlooked the fact that in every game the players contributed what was known as the *cagnotte*. This was between seven and eight per cent of the money on the table and it was taken by the house. Since at Esmeralda's Barn the Twins and Leslie Payne were the house, every penny of the *cagnotte* went to them. So one can understand why Payne advised the Twins, whatever the temptation, never to interfere with such a fool-proof way of making money.

This suited Reg, who was increasingly busy now with his various protection rackets and the complicated long-firm frauds that he was running in partnership with Payne. In many ways Reg was not unlike his father, old Charlie Kray – a smart old-fashioned trickster who was keen to get his hands on any racket going. Given the chance, Reg could be extremely sharp, and he was particularly grateful to Billy Hill who had finally decided to 'educate' him about the various criminal possibilities emerging in the 1960s.

Many years later, in a deathbed interview, Reg paid Billy Hill the ultimate old lag's tribute by calling him 'my mentor'. But back then Reg was also learning fast from Leslie Payne, and compared with the money that the Twins were making from these other rackets Esmeralda's Barn was something of a side-show. During the first six months of 1960, their joint income with Leslie Payne from the long-firm frauds alone topped fifty thousand pounds, which in those days was a lot of money. The Twins took half of this, whereas at Esmeralda's Barn their weekly take was rarely more than £800 apiece. But then, it called for little effort.

Besides, for Reg, the fact that he and Ron were now owners of the club meant a lot to him. After so many setbacks in the past he was finally in the sort of West End club he'd dreamed of and, like many ambitious young East Enders in the 1960s, he felt that he had at last crossed the line between the old East End and the tempting pastures of the golden West.

Soon he was proudly inviting several of the celebrities he'd known at The Double R and the Kentucky to the Barn, and was in danger of becoming something of a celebrity himself. He'd already had dark blue dinner jackets made for himself and Ron, and he loved to play host to the Barn's rich clientele. On one gala evening Judy Garland came, while more frequent visitors included the singer Lita Rosa, a new young star called Barbara Windsor, and the blonde bombshell Diana Dors. Reg was in his element at last – but Ron was different.

During those early days at Esmeralda's Barn, Ron always seemed to be the odd man out. By completing his prison sentence in Wandsworth Prison he had done all that the law required of him to 'prove' his sanity. But although Doc Blasker was still trying to stabilise him with pills, this was not the same as being cured and whatever the law might say about his sanity there would never be a cure for his condition.

In contrast with the young and still handsome Reg, Ron in his dark blue dinner jacket looked increasingly like Dracula on a bad night out. Sometimes he even scared himself when he glanced in the mirror and saw the thickening features, the extra weight and something very odd about the eyes. The truth was that he was beginning to look like what he really was – a dangerous paranoid schizophrenic.

Throughout all this, one person in the Twins' small circle was totally oblivious to what was happening to Ron: his mother, Violet. During the early days at the club the Twins occasionally invited her for dinner, and after such occasions there was no prouder mother in the whole of Bethnal Green. Vi had always stood loyally by her Twins whatever happened and was thrilled to see them so successful. To please her, Reg always did his best to be patient with his brother, which wasn't easy.

To be fair to Violet, she was always grateful. But there was one thing that she wouldn't tolerate – any suggestion now that Ron was mad. Mad? Her Ronnie? How could anyone say such a thing, after all he'd suffered?

Because Violet felt so strongly on the subject the rest of the family had to follow her example; as did the members of the Firm, for whom Ron's mental health became a virtual test of loyalty. There was nothing wrong with Ron that time and kindness wouldn't cure, said Violet. Reg dutifully agreed and told himself that the more contact his brother had with ordinary people, the more he'd pull himself together and start to cure himself. Which to a point was true – but only to a point.

In fact the gap between the Twins was widening. Reg was more than ever now the live wire, the close friend of the stars, and the serious earner of the two. Reg was clearly going places. As for Ron, for most of the time he seemed to be living in a daze created by his sickness or his medication.

Then suddenly the situation changed, thanks to one of those twisted bits of luck which dominate the lives of criminals. Reg's appeal against his sentence was unexpectedly rejected, and back he went to Wandsworth Jail. In Reg's absence, Ron took over Esmeralda's Barn.

With hindsight one can see this as a crucial moment in the lives not only of the Twins but also of others in close contact with them. Indeed, it could be argued that the next six months with

Ron in charge of Esmeralda's Barn would see the start of something new and virtually unheard of in the world of crime in 1960s London.

To begin with, when he found himself in charge of Esmeralda's Barn Ron acted like a child who finds a magic money box and sets off on a spending spree. In the cashier's office there could be such large amounts of money that Ron found them irresistible and he started on a voyage of personal discovery round the rich West End of London.

He began in Savile Row by ordering several suits from one of the most expensive tailors in London. In Jermyn Street he discovered the shirt makers Turnbull and Asser, and ordered several dozen shirts from them as well. Then, finally, just around the corner from the Barn he found Harrods – not today's glorified shopping mall but the old Harrods, which still prided itself on getting anything its customers desired.

Remembering the success of his donkey at the billiard hall, Ron decided he would buy an elephant from the pet department[1] saying he wanted it to liven up the Barn. When someone told him that an elephant wouldn't go up the stairs, he bought a chimpanzee instead and ordered Turnbull and Asser to make the primate a dress shirt and a black bow tie. Then he brought his well-dressed chimpanzee to the Barn where he sat him down among what he saw as all the other monkeys trying their luck around the chemmy tables. When his monkey won he insisted that he was paid his winnings.

Say what you like about old Ron but there were times when he really was a joker.

With so much money coming in, Ron should have been free from all financial worries. But in fact it was now his attitude to money that landed him in trouble.

Since gambling clubs are legally obliged to pay winnings on the spot, in order to survive, most clubs insist that gamblers also

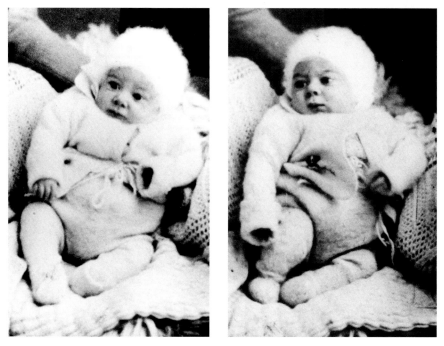

(*Above*) 'Twins is special' – Ron (left) and Reg (right) at eight weeks old.

(*Below*) The proud mother. Violet Kray between her two boys, Ron (left) and Reg (right), when they were still promising young boxers.

Indistinguishable from one another – the Twins' passport photographs
taken when they were twenty.

Not wanted in America – Ron's visa to
America which was cancelled on his arrival in
New York in the aftermath of the Boothby case.

Photograph of the Twins as young boxers, signed by Reg and given to the author and his wife.

(*Top left*) Ron and a friend enjoy a cigarette outside their hotel in Morocco in 1965.
(*Top right*) Reg was already dressing like his hero, the American movie gangster George Raft, in this photograph taken in 1964 at Steeple Bay in Essex. (*Above*) Gangster chic – a rare picture of all three brothers together taken outside 'Fort Vallance', their home in Bethnal Green.

Victory – Ron Kray (left) with his mother, Violet, and twin brother, Reg, looking on, being congratulated by his grandfather, 'Cannonball' Lee, outside the house in Vallance Road after their acquittal in the McCowan case.

(*Above*) The young reporter Michael Thornton at around the time that he was beaten up outside his home for 'not respecting' Ronald Kray. (*Above right*) The happy pair – Reg and Frances after their engagement. (*Right*) One of the family – a wedding day picture of Frances in her wedding dress, standing rather warily between her new brother-in-law Ron Kray (left) and her husband Reg Kray on the right.

In Loving Memory
of my dear wife
Frances
who passed away
7th June, 1967 aged 23 years

If I could write the beauty
of your eyes,
And in fresh numbers
Number all your graces,
The Age to come would say:
This poet lies,
Such heavenly touches
ne'er touched earthly faces'.

Reg's Wife

Doing the business –
Reg and Ron together on
the eve of their arrest in 1968.

(*Above*) Farewell to Frances –
the card which Reg Kray designed
for the funeral of his wife, Frances,
in 1965, complete with the poem
he wrote in her memory.
(*Right*) Still no escape – the last
resting place of Frances Kray in 'Kray
Corner' in Chingford cemetery,
next to her mother-in-law, Violet.

N° _____/9/DGR

six
soixante   dix-sept

Septembre

TEMSAMANI Mokhtar, Officier de Police Adjoint
Chef du Service Régional de la Documentation Générale
et de la Réglementation   Tanger

TANGER

l'arrêté provincial N°44 du 1er Joumada
Tani 1386 (17 Septembre 1966) ordonnant
le refoulement de M. ___ _____

K R A Y Ronald, de nationalité anglaise,

P.V. de notification
d'une mesure de re-
foulement du terri-
toire marocain.

_____ à Londres, fils de Charles et de Violet,
célibataire, directeur de Cie. demeuré 27, rue Grotius
à Tanger ; _____
Faisons comparaître à notre service l'intéressé à qui
nous notifions la mesure de refoulement du territoire
marocain prise à son encontre en vertu de l'arrêté provincial permanent précité émanant à M. le Gouverneur
de la Province de Tanger. _____
M. KRAY Ronald nous déclare : _____

La mesure dont vous venez de me donner connaissance
s'applique bien à ma personne. J'en prends bonne note
et quitterai le Maroc à la date qui me sera fixée par
vos soins.
_____, soit le jeudi 22 Septembre 1966.-
Lecture faite, signe et signons. _____

C/

KRAY Ronald, an-
glais.-

ROYAUME DU MAROC

PROVINCE DE TANGER

CONSEIL PROVINCIAL

ARRETE GUBERNATORIAL PERMANENT N° 44
---

du 1er. Djoumada Tania 1386 correspondant au 17 Septembre 1966,
ordonnant le refoulement du Territoire Marocain de M. KRAY Ronald,
de nationalité anglaise.-

LE GOUVERNEUR DE LA PROVINCE DE TANGER,

VU   l'article XII du Dahir du 15 Novembre 1934, modifié et complété
      par le Dahir du 26 Février 1951,

VU   la transmission N° 1349/D.G.R. du 15 Septembre 1966 de Monsieur
      le Chef de la Sûreté Régionale de cette ville,

A R R E T E :

ARTICLE 1er.- Monsieur KRAY Ronald, de nationalité anglaise, est
              refoulé du Territoire Marocain.-

ARTICLE 2.-   Le Chef de la Sûreté Régionale est chargé de l'exé-
              cution de cet Arrêté ./.

17 / 9 / 66

POUR LE GOUVERNEUR DE LA PROVINCE,
--- Le Secrétaire Général,

Signé: Abdeslam El Ouazzani.-

Farewell Morocco –
the banning order from
the Governor of Tangier
excluding Ron Kray
from his country as
an 'undesirable' in
September 1966.

(Above) The man from the Mafia who was Ron's most faithful visitor in Broadmoor.

Lord Boothby and Ron Kray with another gay friend – 'Mad' Teddy Smith.

Ron Kray (third from right) having dinner at the old 'Society' restaurant with Christine Keeler as his guest.

pay their losses straight away; for once dud cheques start piling up it's usually a sign of a gaming club that's on the road to ruin. One of the reasons for Alf Mancini's continuing success was that he never offered credit to even the most favoured punters.

But here, as usual, Ron was different. Apart from treating Esmeralda's as his private money box, he also started offering friends and fellow criminals endless credit, encouraged them to over-spend, and then enjoyed putting the squeeze on anyone with money. During his first month on his own Ron landed the club with debts of £1,500; by the second month they had reached £3,500; and by the end of the third month Mancini had offered Ron £1,000 a week to stay away. When Ron told him to get lost, Mancini understood that the time had come to follow Ron's advice himself. Within a few weeks he was running another gaming club in Curzon Street; within a year he owned the place.

Mancini's departure brought an instant dip in the profits at the Barn. Most of Mancini's regulars were in the restaurant business and had been coming to Esmeralda's since the club began. They gambled heavily, drank sparingly, and always paid their debts; but when Alf Mancini left most of them went with him.

Ron barely seemed to notice. If the club was getting into debt, so what? He liked to think that people were grateful to him for his generosity, although what he really liked was to put the fear of God into those who couldn't pay. He rarely used violence on them but he loved tormenting them and sometimes sent members of 'the Firm' to call on them at home. In spite of which the club began to grow and the membership began to change. So did Ron, who was about to experience something of a personal revelation.

In the basement under Esmeralda's a girl called Ginette had recently opened a lesbian disco called the Cellar Club, which became a free and easy meeting place for gays of every sexual inclination. As a serious male chauvinist, Ron had always said that he hated lesbians. But Ginette was an exception and when he started visiting her club he discovered something that surprised him. None of its members seemed to feel the slightest sense of shame at being homosexual.

Soon in the the Cellar Club he started meeting other gays who, far from disguising their sexuality, obviously enjoyed it. When Ron saw some who even dared to flaunt their nature, he realised that being gay could actually be fun and he started to enjoy it too. Then, finally, he plucked up courage and decided it was time to emerge from the closet.

Ron was far too square ever to be considered camp and he hated effeminacy in men as much as he hated it in women. He also made it clear exactly what he was. In gay parlance Ron was a 'giver', not a 'taker'. 'I'm not queer,' he used to say. 'I'm 'omosexual'. And from then on, as far as he was concerned, in matters sexual that was that.

But for Ron this change of attitude had one all–important side effect. With the awareness that his sexuality was no longer any cause for personal embarrassment came a rapid increase in self-confidence, and along with gay liberation much of the sense of class inferiority that had always bothered him began to disappear as well.

Interestingly, it was the opening of the Cellar Club in the basement under Esmeralda's Barn that helped to bring about a change in the Barn's membership as more 'playboy gamblers' took the place of the restaurateurs and head waiters who had left the club along with Alf Mancini. Some of the newcomers were gay, some weren't, and some were not particularly concerned about what they were. But since since this was the Swinging Sixties none of this seemed to matter very much at Esmeralda's Barn.

Certainly Ron felt more at ease among them than he had with Alf Mancini's friends and for the first time he began to feel at ease in the club that, partially at least, belonged to him. It was now, with Reg away, that he started to use it rather as he used the old billiard hall in Eric Street. Not only did he make the Barn his headquarters but at times he used it as his personal theatre to perform in front of the members who became a sort of captive audience. It was now, as Aunt Rose used to say, that 'Ronnie started acting up.'

By its nature big-time crime is silent crime, and the criminal tycoons of the 1960s, like Billy Hill, the Adams brothers and the Richardsons trod softly and had no desire to advertise their business or themselves. Even the elusive Freddy Foreman, whose criminal empire was beginning to rival Billy Hill's, never courted personal publicity.

Characters like these were as much a part of the enterprise culture of the 1960s as any takeover tycoon or merchant banker. Like them, they were primarily concerned with money, and like them they conducted their activities with considerable discretion. Ronnie could not have been more different.

The Twins patterned themselves on the old-style villains of the past whose legends they had grown up with. This specially applied to Ronnie, and the more publicity he got, the better.

With Ron it was partly due to the necessity of feeling 'special' – and partly to the dominating influence of his paranoid nature. Driven by its overwhelming mood swings, and depending on his mood, Ron could play many parts. His appearance helped. It was the criminologist Dick Hebdidge who first called him an 'actor criminal'.

This did not mean that they weren't also real criminals, and didn't do appalling things. Of course, as we have seen already, Reg, like his mentor Billy Hill, was seriously into making money and was already a successful organising criminal. He was also in close contact with the American Mafia.

But in the early 1960s, as organised crime increased, there was a vacancy for somebody to be the public face of villainy. This showed in the way most fascinating creations of thriller writers like Ian Fleming were their villains. Monsters were suddenly in vogue, but they had no real-life equivalent, and it wasn't what you were but what people thought you were that mattered.

How much was gossip, how much was grim reality didn't really matter very much. What *did* matter was the growing impression created in the minds of those who came in contact with them that the Twins were the most powerful and ruthless criminals in London. It was at Esmeralda's Barn that London found the monster it was seeking.

First, of course, came Ron's appearance. He really could look very frightening. Indeed one of his most bankable assets as a real-life villain was that he looked like a murderer several years before he actually murdered anyone.

It also helped that he had episodes of real madness and that his moods depended largely on whether Doc Blasker's pills were working. This made him irrational and unpredictable and potentially extremely dangerous, which all added to his legend.

With Reggie still 'away' Ron was at liberty to turn the Barn into what he'd always wanted – a richer, more accommodating version of the old billiard hall. Here chemmy could take the place of snooker to provide the necessary background, and for Ron and any friends he invited food and drink were on the house.

When in the right mood Ron would put on an unforgettable performance with a sudden demonstration of his lethal virtuosity. All the stories being told about the Twins concerned violence and the fear of violence. One vicim who had 'taken the liberty' of beating up the son of an old friend of the Twins (and should obviously have known better) needed to be taught a lesson, which Ron did by taking him into the kitchen when Esmeralda's Barn was closed, heating up a steel knife-sharpener on the gas and branding him with it on the cheek.

It was also true that Ron had 'disciplined' another villain who had unwisely told him that he had put on weight by taking him into the washroom at the club and slashing off half his face.

At a club as respectable as Esmeralda's Barn a little violence went a long way.

There were also incidents of mayhem and skulduggery at the club that lost nothing in the telling, and other stories that originated in the minds of some of Esmeralda's clientele. I don't believe, for instance, that as legend had it, Ron imprisoned somebody all night with a hungry Dobermann – 'to teach him a lesson'. Still less do I believe the story that he anally assaulted an accountant with a red-hot poker.

But the best stories were the ones that only Ron himself could have invented, and by the time that Reg returned from prison late that summer, he could see that Ron had changed.

Reg made light of Mancini's departure, nor did he mention the pile of dishonoured cheques in the secretary's office. That was Ron all over, and as long as he was happy and Violet was pleased that was all that mattered. But one thing troubled Reg. After his absence, not only did the club feel different, with its changing clientele, but no one took much notice of him any more. It was Ron they wanted, Ron that people talked about, and Ron who seemed to rule the roost.

Although this rankled, Reg had other things to think about while Ron was still enjoying the company of his gay friends in the Cellar Club downstairs. Cannier and warier, Reg kept his sexuality to himself and had openly started courting pretty Frances Shea, the teenage sister of a boy that Ron had once fancied. And while he was in prison Reg had started dreaming of life with her in the distant future with marriage, children and a settled home life. This would mean, of course, that he would have to break from Ronnie, which he longed for all the more because he knew it was impossible.

With his telepathic way of knowing what Reg was thinking, Ron knew exactly what was going through his mind but didn't worry. He knew that Reg could never get away from him. He was Reg and Reg was him – and that was all that mattered.

One gets a clear idea of how Ron's power was growing from the painter Francis Bacon who met the Twins together in Morocco early in 1962 when they were in Tangier as guests of Billy Hill. Hill had business interests that he wanted to discuss with them, principally protecting his highly profitable trade in hashish and heroin against the threat of the American Mafia in Europe, as well as from the criminal element in Tangier itself. Reg was interested and promised Hill that he would help, but whenever Ron was in Morocco he was interested in one thing and one thing alone – the local boys. When he had visited Tangier back in 1959 – he'd said that he found them 'unbelievable'.

Francis Bacon felt the same, which was why he spent several months in Tangier every year, and while he was there in 1962 his friend, the wild young actor Stanley Baker who was there on holiday introduced him to the Twins. Baker had got to know Reg by visiting The Double R and all four of them went out to dinner at a local restaurant.

Once they were sitting down comfortably, Ron noticed a boy he knew at a nearby table and called him over. Then, instead of introducing him, he ordered the boy to kneel down and kiss his shoes. Clearly frightened, the boy obeyed. Ron said nothing, took no notice, and the boy scurried off, looking terrified.

Ron's behaviour made a great impression on Bacon who was deeply shocked and later told his biographer, Michael Peppiat, that he 'felt this was a horrible thing to do to anyone.' But while Ron's behaviour repelled him it also fascinated him.

According to Peppiat, Bacon believed, like many in the 1960s, that East End criminals 'possessed some ruthlessly virile sense of amorality', and what particularly turned him on was the thought of 'succumbing to a man like Ron who was beyond good and evil, totally immoral, and would stop at nothing', even murder.

Clearly a masochistic homosexual like Francis Bacon offered an extreme example of the psychic force that Ron projected, which makes the reaction of a strictly heterosexual tough-guy actor like Stanley Baker to the Twins particularly interesting. Even for him violence came into it, for Baker apparently told Francis Bacon afterwards that he 'thought it was terribly smart to get to know the Twins, because of their reputation as the most violent and feared operators in the London underworld with a number of grisly murders to their credit.'

What is fascinating about this is that although by 1962 the Twins, and Ron in particular, had inflicted every known form of grievous bodily harm on somebody or other, the one crime that he and Reg would both avoid for nearly four more years was murder. In 1962, there was still capital punishment for murder and like most of their predecessors, the old East End villains, the Twins actually had no intention of taking the 'nine o'clock walk' to the gallows. In spite of this, now that they were fast becoming the legendary twin monsters of the 1960s the rumours grew that they were killers.

Until the end of 1962, most of the tales about the Twins came from members of, or visitors to, Esmeralda's Barn. Then suddenly all this changed with the arrival on the scene of a keen admirer and self-appointed publicist of the Krays who began the process of turning them into the monsters who would haunt the imagination of the 1960s.

David Litvinoff was one of a family of Russian Jewish immigrants who settled in the poorest part of Whitchapel in the 1890s. One of his brothers, Emmanuel Litvinoff, was a poet, and another, Barnet Litvinoff, was the friend and biographer of

Ben Gurion. As a child, great things were predicted for the third son, David, who was very bright and had a gift for words. But he also had a wicked streak and became the black sheep of the family. He was homosexual, loved low life, and tried to be a villain. The 1960s found him living with a pretty ex-stable boy called Bobby Buckley in a flat in Ashburn Gardens, off the Gloucester Road in Kensington.

By now, rather than do anything as dull as working for his living, Litvinoff was involved in the only true career he ever had – as a talker, joker and teller of elaborate tall stories to some of the most interesting people in Chelsea. Before long he was at the centre of one of the most colourful and influential cliques in Swinging London.

As well as talking, Litvinoff also loved to gamble, but when he tried his luck at Esmeralda's he was less successful, and he finally confessed to Ron that he owed the club over £3,000. Keen as ever to take advantage of this sort of situation, Ron suggested an agreement that would suit them both.

In lieu of payment Ron accepted the short lease that Litvinoff owned on the flat in Kensington, provided that his boyfriend Bobby Buckley was included in the deal. Litvinoff could go on living there together with Ron and his former lover, to which Litvinoff agreed. So it was that for the next eighteen months Ron came to be living at a smart address in fashionable Kensington with Litvinoff and Bobby Buckley, and all three of them getting up to God knew what together.

It was largely thanks to Litvinoff that Esmeralda's Barn began to form a bridge between two separate and dynamic worlds in 1960s London which had already begun to intermingle – the nostalgically resurgent world of East End villainy of which the Twins were becoming the most famous representatives and the celebrity-conscious showbiz world of Swinging Chelsea.

Time and place are crucial for most things in life, and one of the many fascinating things about the Twins is how they now invaded the imagination of a small but influential group of celebrities, headed by Mick Jagger and the Rolling Stones who lived near to one another in the most desirable parts of Chelsea. These were glamourous people, artistic, rich and highy influential. They were trendsetters who stood emphatically for certain things – youth and freedom from the old taboos of sex and class. At heart most of them were self-indulgent anarchists. And as pioneers and eager practitioners of the new drug culture, which brought them into unwelcome contact with the law, culminating in the notorious 'Redlands bust', which ended up with Jagger and several of his friends in prison, they had little sympathy with the law or the police. They were easygoing over sex, on the basis of the more of it the better, and they loved Morocco for the climate and the easy availability of drugs. Those who were jealous of them called them the Chelsea mafia, but George Melly got nearer to the truth when he called them the Chelsea Popocracy. By the time that Ronnie got to know him, Litvinoff had become their 'unoffical court jester'.

The group's king across the water was young Paul Getty who was still clinging on to his position as the favourite son of the reputedly richest and meanest man in the world, the oil billionaire J. Paul Getty. Young Paul had recently bought beautiful Queen's House on Cheyne Walk and commuted between there and his house in Tangier. He and his glamorous wife Talitha were often high on drugs themselves. Other Rolling Stones were near neighbours, including Jagger, Brian Jones and Keith Richards, together with their girlfriends such as Marianne Faithfull and Anita Pallenberg.

There was also a rich young bisexual painter called Donald Cammell who wanted to be a film director and rented a room above the Pheasantry Club in King's Road Chelsea to be near his teacher Annigoni. According to his brother David, Donald Cammell was 'utterly fascinated' by the Krays and couldn't hear enough about them. So was another all important member of the Popocracy, the influential young art dealer gay 'Groovy Bob' Fraser. Soon, in one way or another, most of the Popocracy was becoming obsessed with Litvinoff's stories of the Twins, and the day would come when Mick Jagger and his Chelsea friends would play an all-important role in adding to their legend.

This was the point at which the cult of criminal celebrity from the old East End began to meet the new pop culture of the Swinging Sixties in earnest. As much as with any of the other iconic figures of the time, the Twins were truly children of the Sixties. Without gay liberation, changes in the gaming laws, and the abolition of capital punishment, their phenomenal career would not have been a possibility. In addition there was one other largely unsuspected social change which now proved crucial in their rise to fame and notoriety. This was the breaking down of centuries old barriers in London between the West and the old East End, where the Twins had grown up. This was a process which the historian of the East End, Iain Sinclair, has compared with the coming down of the Berlin Wall, as two-way traffic expended between the east and west, and London began to reunite itself.

In his own strange way, David Litvinoff played a part in this, through his after-dinner magic and the stories he told about the Twins and the world they came from. But there was also a more sinister side to Litvinoff's activities.

Ever since the days of the billiard hall, Ron had encouraged a following of teenage boys for sex. As a cover for their activities, he used to call them his 'information service', which they also were, since he paid them for any scraps of information they could find about his enemies. Once he was settled in Esmeralda's Barn he revived the information service, and ran it from the flat in Ashburn Gardens for himself and for a few gay friends. Typically it was Litvinoff's idea to extend the information service to a number of rich and influential homosexual members of his widespread West End social network, supplying them with rent boys and way-out sex shows. Besides broadening the acquaintanceship with 'important' people, both Ron and Litvinoff were very much aware from the start of the possibilities for blackmail which their little scheme could offer.

11

Enter Boothby: 1964

THIS IS THE point at which the Kray Twins enter the secret history of the 1960s through a scandal brought about by Ron which thrust them into politics at the highest level. Because it was hushed up by the political establishment the Twins, predominantly Ron himself, became the untouchables of London Crime. For the next three years the fallout from this scandal would leave parliament, press and the police impotent to deal with them, and as the Twins' reputation as untouchables grew this proved to be the basis for everything that followed. To make sense of how this happened we must turn briefly to the old scoundrel who by the early 1960s was probably the most popular political celebrity in the country, and trace the political and criminal events which brought him and Ronald Kray together with such fateful consequences for politics and crime in Britain.

At the beginning of 1964, Robert John Graham – Baron Boothby of Buchan and Ratray Head as he had styled himself since receiving a peerage six years earlier – had been leading a dangerous double life. During the thirty-eight years he'd been in parliament he'd had his share of ups and downs, but his emergence as a TV celebrity had given a much-needed late-life boost to his ego and his erratic career.

But there had always been a hidden side to Robert Boothby.

Behind the famous public figure was a drunk, a liar, a reckless gambler and a bisexual with a taste for rough-trade sex and teenage boys. With fame and age his recklessness had been increasing and since it was his hidden life that brought him into contact with the Krays, it is to this that we must turn.

Back in 1924, Boothby's election at the age of twenty-four as Conservative MP for East Aberdeenshire had made him the youngest member of the House of Commons. The spoiled only son of a Scots insurance magnate who sent him to Eton and Oxford to acquire the accent and the manners of the English upper classes, he was ambitious and good-looking, and could talk the hind leg off a haggis. Churchill took a shine to him, and on becoming chancellor of the exchequer in 1926 the great man appointed him his parliamentary private secretary. For a while Boothby was being tipped as a future prime minister himself. But his prospects were not quite as rosy as they seemed.

At Oxford a homosexual scandal had briefly threatened his university career. It was sorted out, as these things tend to be at Oxford. But the truth was that, until the early 1960s when homosexual acts between consenting adults began to be decriminalised, anyone hoping to combine an openly gay existence with a serious career in British politics had problems. And that included Robert Boothby.

'I thought men shot themselves for that sort of thing' was King George V's reaction to the news that Lord Beauchamp had been caught in bed with a man; and as recently as 1954 Lord Montagu of Beaulieu had spent six months in Wormwood Scrubs for an indiscretion with an aircraftman. Boothby was very much aware of the danger. If the trouble at Oxford had taught him anything, it was the need to be discreet – and so his double life began. Since he was technically bisexual, this wasn't difficult, particularly as his behaviour wasn't camp. This meant that while he was primarily attracted to men he was also attractive to women and was perfectly prepared to go to bed with them if necessary. He even got himself engaged to an American heiress until she grew bored when nothing happened and sailed back to America.

Then, at the age of twenty-eight, he very nearly came unstuck. He was a considerable snob and particularly enjoyed the company of the English aristocracy, as did an older Scots MP from a similar background, his friend and colleague Harold Macmillan. Some years before, Macmillan had married a daughter of the Duke of Devonshire, Lady Dorothy Cavendish. They were already the parents of three children when, to complicate the lives of all concerned, the Macmillans invited Boothby to join them on a shooting party. Lady Dorothy's hand touched his, the lightning struck, and she discovered that she was passionately in love with him.

As the daughter of a duke, Lady Dorothy was used to getting what she wanted and, feeling painfully frustrated, she pursued her husband's friend with all the eagerness of her passionate nature. A foreign holiday together convinced her that they were made for one another, but when she broke the news to her husband he was so upset that, according to one account, he threatened suicide. On recovering his self-control he made it clear that whatever happened he would never divorce her. This must have come as a considerable relief to Boothby and his affair with Lady Dorothy continued.

At times he seemed unable to resist her. At other times he was so anxious to escape that he married Dorothy's young cousin Diana Cavendish, hoping this would put Dorothy off. (It didn't, and the marriage ended two years later.) Which was more or less how things remained until war broke out in 1939, with Boothby stringing Dorothy along and the infatuated Dorothy always coming back for more. Oswald Mosley, who knew them both, recalled several occasions when an excited Dorothy was on the point of bolting, but at the last minute Boothby always let her down.

Poor Lady Dorothy. Her husband wouldn't divorce her, her lover wouldn't elope with her, and the truth was that the situation rather suited both the men involved. For Macmillan, who was more interested in politics than in sex, a divorce on any terms would have been disastrous to his all-important political career; while for Boothby, who had even less intention of exchanging his political career for a life with passionate, garden-loving Lady Dorothy, his 'affair' provided invaluable cover for the double life that he was leading. In the gay parlance of the time, Dorothy had become his 'beard' and he her 'walker'.

On one occasion, Lord Lambton, who was in parliament with Boothby before inheriting his title, asked him, as one bounder to another, what Boothby saw in her.

'To tell the truth,' Boothby said, 'she reminds me of a caddie I once seduced on the golf course at St Andrews.'

Boothby may have been more honest in the reply he gave his cousin, Ludovic Kennedy, who asked him the same question. 'Dorothy has thighs like hams and hands like a stevedore, but I adore her,' he replied. Possibly he did; but, whatever the truth behind this curious relationship, as the years rolled by the lies and the deceptions needed for his double life, combined with worries over his mounting gambling debts, can't have helped whatever judgement he might have possessed. As his debts rose, so did his reputation for accepting money in return for political favours. When war broke out and Churchill rewarded him with a place in his wartime government, Boothby was either stupid enough or desperate enough to make a deal with a rich Czech refugee, to use his influence to free his assets, impounded under wartime regulations. More stupid still, he lied about this to a parliamentary committee. When Churchill heard about the matter and sacked him, Boothby asked him what to do. 'Get yourself a job with a bomb-disposal unit,' the old warhorse growled, thus ending a long friendship – and Boothby's political ambitions – until the arrival of TV brought his salvation.

Suddenly he was like an old pirate fallen on good times. He called himself a maverick, and like many an old rogue was an accomplished raconteur with a fund of stories, many of them untrue. When the students of St Andrew's University voted him their Rector he claimed that he was the most popular politician in the country. Quite possibly he was. At one stage the *Any Questions?* TV programme, in which he was a star performer, claimed an audience of seventeen million. But he was also dangerously conceited and attributed his success to his memorable 'deep brown' voice. 'Tony,' he once boasted to Lambton, 'it's as if I've got my cock in my throat.'

'Are you sure it's not someone else's, Bob?' Lord Lambton answered.

Like Lambton, Boothby loved to be outrageous and it seemed that he could get away with anything. Few men, on hearing that an old friend whom he'd been cuckolding (at least in theory) for nearly thirty years had just become prime minister would have instantly asked him for a peerage. Still fewer men in Macmillan's situation would have said, 'Of course Bob must have a peerage if he wants it', and promptly raised him to the House of Lords.

Since Boothby finally destroyed all Dorothy's letters – and Macmillan burned all Boothby's – we'll never know for certain why the prime minister acted as he did. I once did have a chance to ask him. 'Because I thought it would please Dorothy,' he replied, and changed the subject. My own feeling is that Macmillan, who liked to play the aristocrat that he was not, wished to demonstrate that sexual jealousy was too tediously middle-class to have seriously bothered him – which was almost certainly untrue.

As for the new Lord Boothby, by now he really should have been content. Verging on sixty, he was the Houdini of British politics and had got away with so much in his lifetime, that he probably felt that he could get away with anything. The demanding double life that he'd been leading now for nigh on forty years was flourishing. He had a fine flat in Belgravia and a perfect butler with the similarly perfect (and actually quite genuine) name of Goodfellow who shared his tastes and tended him like the wife he almost was. Now, to gild his lily, came his title, which as a man of inordinate vanity he loved, together with the deference, the robes, the embossed coronet on his writing paper, the right to sign his name with effortless simplicity 'Boothby' which went with it.

He also cultivated influential friends in the highest places including press lords like Beaverbrook and Camrose, important journalists like William Haley, editor of *The Times*, and Colin Coote, who edited the *Daily Telegraph*. This meant that, despite his rakish reputation, Boothby was beginning to enjoy an enviable position at the very heart of the British Establishment.

There was, however, just one danger. Transgression can become addictive. Having got away with so much for so many years the new Lord Boothby started taking bigger and yet bigger risks. It was a dangerous game, even though imminent changes in the law on gay behaviour meant that almost anything was now more or less acceptable. In Boothby's case a great deal clearly was, particularly since he had recently acquired an experienced enabler. This was another rogue politician notorious for his own erratic sexuality, the journalist, future peer and Chairman of the Labour Party, Tom Driberg.

It was, in many ways, a most unlikely friendship. Driberg was on the extreme left of the Labour Party while Boothby was embedded in the Tory establishment. One of the best informed journalists in London, Driberg had started the William Hickey column in the *Daily Express* and, according to its defence correspondent Chapman Pincher, not only had he been a close friend of both the spies Burgess and Maclean but he himself spied regularly for Russia and held the rank of colonel in the Soviet KGB. This sounds unlikely but was not impossible. With

Tom Driberg almost anything was possible. Certainly he was one of the highest-paid journalists on the *Express* and Lord Beaverbrook treated him accordingly. Driberg and Boothby were both 'good company' and the two of them would often meet at Beaverbrook's famous dinner parties at Cherkley, his country house near Leatherhead in Surrey.

Driberg's friend, the theatrical producer Joan Littlewood, had already introduced him to Reg Kray at The Double R Club, and the meeting was apparently a great success. Driberg got on well with criminals and Reg was quick to see the value of a friendly politician. This was as far as things had gone until the late summer of 1963, when Driberg discovered Esmeralda's Barn.

He must have thought he was in paradise. Downstairs boys and criminals. Upstairs gambling and yet more criminals, among whom was one of Ronnie's latest hangers-on, 'Mad' Teddy Smith, aspiring villain, would-be playwright and seriously rough-trade homosexual. Neither he nor Driberg could resist each other and a close relationship began. Rumour had it that, along with other favours, Driberg used to tell 'Mad' Teddy about rich friends' houses he could burgle; and he couldn't wait to introduce his friend Bob Boothby to Esmeralda's Barn, where he had already spotted the perfect boy for him, a good-looking late teenager called Leslie Holt.

The son of a cockney dustman, Holt was already one of Ron Kray's ever-growing band of lovers. Ron had appointed him a trainee croupier at the club and when he wasn't working there he doubled as a cat burglar and male prostitute. He was small, blond, blue-eyed and apparently immensely charming. As Driberg had predicted, from the moment he clapped eyes on him Boothby was besotted.

Although Ron Kray was not remotely interested in gambling, he always insisted that when anyone 'interesting' turned up at Esmeralda's Barn he was to be informed instantly. That evening, when Holt reported back that he had just hooked Boothby, Ron ordered him to get to know him better. One never knew. He might be useful.

By now, having helped the Twins acquire Esmeralda's Barn and earned them large amounts of money through his long-firm frauds, Leslie 'The Brain' Payne, was very much in favour with them both, and was wondering how he could exploit the situation. Protection rackets and long-firm frauds were fine, but they could get boring, and like the lively Sixties con man that he was, Les Payne, was thinking big. He had been hearing of a fascinating scheme, backed with foreign capital, to build a great new town near Enugu in Nigeria. To set his own ball rolling and with the help of his astute but equally crooked accountant Freddy Gore, Payne had already set up his own company, the impressively named Imperial Development Corporation. The Corporation soon attracted interest from the Nigerian government and also from the reputable British construction company Turriff International. Payne even claimed to have the blessing of the British Colonial Office. Things were moving. Detailed plans were drawn up for Les Payne's new Enugu, and the Nigerians became excited by the news that a high-powered delegation from his Imperial Development Corporation would visit Enugu if their government invited them. What Payne didn't tell them was that the delegation would consist of Freddy Gore, the Kray Twins and himself.

When Payne informed the Twins about the invitation Ron was particularly excited. He had always dreamed of visiting black Africa. The Nigerians paid their air fares and he and Reg enjoyed the novelty of being flown first-class to Enugu where they were feted by welcoming Nigerians. Ron brought back a four-foot ebony model of an elephant to take the place of the live one he had tried to buy from Harrods. He was more interested still in tales he heard about the local leopard men, ritual assassins who supposedly ate their victims. But, most of all, what Ronnie really loved was being treated as a VIP.

For a while it seemed that Les Payne's biggest scam was working. It had all the elements of a genuine proposal which he hoped might get financial backing from the British government and soon he was talking to the Twins of making more than two million pounds in profits if the plan succeeded. All it needed was some famous and respected public figure as his company's chairman. What about Lord Boothby? Billy Hill had recently put Reggie Maudling, the chancellor of the exchequer, on his payroll and Boothby, with that famous voice of his, could have sold ketchup to a cannibal.

Leslie Holt appears to have arranged the meeting and Boothby duly invited Ron to his flat in Eaton Place, which also served him as an office, to discuss his proposition. Holt was already there when Ron arrived, together with Teddy Smith and a photographer called Bernard Black. When he was introduced to Boothby, Ron explained that he liked to have his photograph taken with famous people. Presumably flattered, Boothby agreed and Black took several photographs, one of Ron and Boothby sitting together on the office sofa and another of Ron and Boothby sitting with Leslie Holt between them. After this there were two more meetings at the flat to discuss the proposal before Boothby, sensible for once, decided to withdraw from the project – but not from his relationship with Ron Kray, and still less from the one with Leslie Holt. It was shortly after this that Lord Boothby invited Ronald Kray to dinner at the House of Lords.

In its way it's hard to imagine anything more socially unthinkable – and hence to Boothby irresistible – than entering the dining room at the House of Lords with a psychotic gangster like Ron Kray as your guest. But if there had been something even more unthinkable, it would have been to have taken him on afterwards for a nightcap at that embatttled stronghold of clubland, White's Club in St James's. Still, Boothby was the man who could get away with anything and for him the unthinkable had a way of becoming overpoweringly attractive. (When he asked Ron what he was drinking Ron supposedly replied 'I've always wanted to try one of those prawn cocktails.' This suggests that Ron was onto his lordship even then.)

When Ron told me all about this some years later he said that while he was in White's Club, Boothby introduced him to another member of the club, the distinguished judge Lord Cohen, 'and we 'ad a very interesting conversation about life in prison.'

But bringing violent criminals into social contact with distinguished law lords wasn't Boothby's primary concern when mixing socially with Ronnie Kray. Transgressing socially was only a beginning. Transgressing sexually was his ultimate obsession.

As a compulsive gambler himself, Boothby must have known the addictive fascination of disaster, but when he started to frequent a second-floor flat in Cedra Court, Cazenove Road in Walthamstow he was indulging in a far more hazardous gamble than chemmy or losing on the greyhounds at White City Stadium. For when it came to sex Ron was all too ready to oblige, though not in person. Neither he nor Bob were into sex with grown men.

In the old East End there was a long tradition of catering for the more exotic sexual tastes of Victorian and Edwardian gay gentry in the male bordellos of Limehouse and Wapping, where the police had always known better than to intrude. Apparently this old tradition lingered. If one's taste was rough-trade sex it can't come much rougher than with Ronald Kray.

When Ron took on the lease on David Litvinoff's flat in Ashburn Gardens and moved in with him he also took on Litvinoff's boyfriend, the young Irish ex-stable boy called

Bobby Buckley. Soon Buckley had a new job as a croupier at the Barn and it was from there that he brought in Leslie Holt to console his former lover David Litvinoff.

Ron had always been promiscuous. Back in the early days at the billiard hall he would take his pick from the boys who formed his so-called 'information service'. He did the same at Esmeralda's Barn and since he was able to ensure that many of the croupiers and waiters were handsome, young and homosexual, the Barn inevitably became the centre of Ron's own private vice ring. Ron was always too chaotic to have organised everything that followed but he had someone close at hand who was all too willing to oblige.

It was around this time that one of the regulars at Esmeralda's Barn was the painter Lucien Freud, who used to gamble there along with his friend and fellow painter Francis Bacon. Unlike Bacon, Freud was not interested in boys, but like many others he enjoyed Litvinoff's way-out company and conversation, and ended up by painting his portrait. Sometime later, something happened which brought their friendship to an abrupt conclusion. Freud has never disclosed what this was but he made it fairly clear what he thought of Litvinoff in the title he now added to his portrait. He called it *The Procurer*. Freud wasn't wrong in this, for among the many services which Litvinoff performed for his gay friends in Chelsea was, as Freud suggested, procuring, or pimping, providing boys for sexual purposes.

Since Ron already had his own informal vice ring there had been no shortage of boys at Esmeralda's Barn anxious to supplement their earnings, and between them he and Litvinoff were soon organising sex shows for their friends at Ashburn Gardens and later on at Cedra Court, Ron's flat in Walthamstow. As well as the inevitable blue movies, there were performances specially tailored to the tastes of those whom Ron wanted to impress. According to one witness, one of Boothby's particular pleasures was to watch boys excrete above him as he lay beneath a glass-topped table. On one occasion he brought along his friend and fellow TV celebrity, A. J. P. Taylor. What that great historian made of these proceedings is not recorded.

As for Ron, one would be underestimating him to imagine that he was doing this for fun or simply to amuse his friends. It was more serious than that. Obsessed with the idea that the upper classes always save their own he was enjoying the sense of power he got from indulging their perversions, particularly those of powerful politicians like Driberg and Lord Boothby who would otherwise not have come within a mile of him. One never knew when help from such a quarter might be useful.

Boothby's motives were also interesting. This sort of thing was fine for Francis Bacon, who liked the company of criminals and had no reputation to lose. But Boothby must have been aware that he was mixing risk with pleasure, when Ron repaid him for his dinner at the House of Lords by taking him to his favourite West End restaurant, the old Society in Jermyn Street (better known today as the nightclub Tramp). Ron was accompanied by a cat burglar called Charlie Clark and a ganster called Billy Exley, together with their wives. Boothby brought along the goodwife Goodfellow.

Once again Ron was careful to arrange for a photographer to record the happy scene. But far from letting this worry him, from the smile his lordship presented to the camera Boothby was remarkably pleased with himself and quite unconcerned by any risk he might have been running.

The various photographs that Ronnie made a point of getting are more interesting than they seem. Had he wished to blackmail anyone he could have easily obtained obscene pictures. But that was not what Ronnie had in mind. Mad he might have been, but stupid he was not. What he wanted was evidence to prove his friendship with important public figures whose help he felt he could rely on in an emergency.

In contrast with Ron Kray, Boothby strikes one as a touch pathetic. He clearly loved the fact that as a TV celebrity everybody knew him, and he must have known that his blatant presence in the company of criminals would sooner or later be brought to the attention of the law. But presumably he was also so conceited that he thought that no one in authority would dare to do anything about it. This went with the true insider's confidence that if anything *did* go hideously wrong somebody somewhere would always be around to sort things out for him. The first assumption was correct. And so, at enormous cost to all and sundry, was the second.

Thoroughly infatuated by now with Leslie Holt, Boothby began to push his luck and for several weeks became a regular visitor at Cedra Court. I remember Violet Kray mentioning to me that Ron brought him several times to Vallance Road. 'He was very nice and very fond of Ronnie. A real gentleman,' was her reaction. Members of the Firm thought differently. For them, Boothby was an old fool who should have known better. Behind his back they started calling him 'the Queen Mother'.

It was around this time that Lord Beaverbrook's old journalistic instincts got the better of him and, thinking that it might make an interesting story for the *Express*, sent Michael Thornton, one of his young reporters, round to Eaton Place to interview his old friend Boothby. 'The Beaver' should have known better, particularly as Michael Thornton was both young and good-looking. When Thornton telephoned the flat in Eaton Square, Lord Boothby answered. When Thornton mentioned Beaverbrook's name he was invited round straight away and arrived to find Boothby considerably the worse for drink. With him was Leslie Holt who made it clear that he had just moved in with Boothby.

Thanks presumably to the whisky, Boothby was absurdly indiscreet and when Holt had left the room, and Thornton inquired if Holt was an actor, Boothby answered, 'No, dear boy, he's a burglar and I'm in love with him.' He went on to say that, following the example of his friend Tom Driberg and another gay burglar Teddy Smith, he sometimes encouraged Holt to burgle rich people he disliked while they were away on holiday.

While Thornton was listening, fascinated by all this, a third person arrived who was also introduced. 'Michael, this is an old friend of mine: meet Ronnie Kray.'

For Thornton this was the beginning of what proved to be a nightmare evening. To start with Ron insisted on taking everybody out to dinner, and afterwards they all moved on to Esmeralda's Barn. Thornton had done his best to leave by now, but Ron wouldn't hear of it, and Boothby whispered to Thornton, 'just play along with him,' adding, 'he's not a man to offend'.

Then, when Ron abruptly made it clear that he fancied Thornton, and Thornton made it just as clear that he wasn't gay, an angry scene broke out. Boothby did his best to calm things down, but Ron was furious to be spurned and, but for Reg's tactful intervention, Michael Thornton would have been seriously hurt. But, thereafter, Ron felt that he had been insulted and wanted his revenge, although it took more than a year for him to get it.

Thornton had returned late one night to his small mews house in Marylebone and was just unlocking his front door when somebody he never saw attacked him from behind and beat him up so savagely that he later needed several stitches in his head. All he could remember afterwards was that, just before passing out, he heard someone saying, 'that'll teach you to show respect to Ronnie Kray in future'.

This sort of close relationship between a famous and instantly recognisable public figure like Boothby and a criminal as notorious as Ron could hardly go unnoticed, and reports began to circulate between the local police and Scotland Yard about an inadvisable connection between the gangster and the peer. With blackmail and scandal – even physical harm – a possibility in this sort of situation, this was something the police could not ignore. Accordingly Detective Superintendent John Cummings, head of Scotland Yard's fledgling Intelligence Section, C11, was ordered to keep Boothby and the Krays under constant observation by plain-clothes officers. As a result, by the spring of 1964 a considerable dossier was building up at C11, not only concerning the sexual shenanigans at Cedra Court and who attended them but also about the more serious criminal activities of the Twins, including detailed information on their protection rackets, extortion, organised crime and major fraud.

While this was going on his lordship was still blithely unconcerned by the interest he was arousing. He might also have been getting dangerous advice from his friend Tom Driberg. According to Superintendent Cummings, whenever Driberg was arrested – as he was with ridiculous regularity for soliciting, or 'cottaging' as it was called, in public lavatories – he always made a point of complaining directly to the Home Secretary in person of 'harassment' by the police. This would usually result in proceedings being dropped. If they weren't, Driberg was not above begging his friend and employer Lord Beaverbrook to use his influence. At first Beaverbrook had been prepared to tolerate Tom's escapades, but he was starting to become impatient. 'Tom, how many times do I have to save you from arrest? It can't go on' he used to say.

Lord Beaverbrook was about to be proved right. The time had come when even he would be unable to save his star columnist from trouble, now that he was going on the prowl with a TV celebrity as notorious and recognisable as Boothby. By early summer 1964, C11's work was almost done and Scotland Yard was on the point of launching a major offensive against the Krays. Had this occurred at this stage in their career it would have been the end of them and their threat for ever, together with the reputations and careers of Lord Boothby and Tom Driberg. This would certainly have happened but for Norman Lucas.

Norman Lucas was one of the last of the old-school crime reporters and he was something of a Fleet Street institution. Like many of his kind he was a former policeman. But Norman had a sentimental streak: over many years a considerable part of his generous expense account had gone on keeping in contact with his old friends at New Scotland Yard. All he asked for in return was to be kept informed if anything interesting cropped up in their line of duty. Over the years these contacts proved to be a useful source of information, but everything depended on trust between them. Norman's Scotland Yard friends trusted him to be totally discreet, and Norman trusted them to be absolutely accurate. A slip-up either way could have been embarrassing. But Norman's friends didn't make mistakes; nor did Norman, and it was thanks to this that he was regarded as one of the best-informed crime writers in London. By 1964 he had become chief crime reporter of the *Sunday Mirror*, a newspaper with a weekly circulation of five million.

During that first week of July 1964, one of Norman's contacts at the Yard informed him that the major investigation of the Krays and their followers was complete and arrests would shortly follow. Apart from details of the Twins' involvement in organised crime throughout London, including their contacts with the American Mafia, C11 had turned up sensitive information about a number of public figures and politicians involved with one of the Twins in a homosexual vice ring. The most sensational of these characters was a member of the House of Lords 'who is a household name'. When Lucas asked his informant to be more specific, Boothby's name was mentioned, together with those of several other politicians and celebrities.

★

As it happened, C11 and Norman Lucas weren't the only people suddenly aware of what Boothby and Tom Driberg had been doing. What Lucas couldn't know – because it would be thirty years before the papers of Sir Timothy Bligh, private secretary to the then prime minister Sir Alec Douglas-Home would be placed in the Public Records Office – was that serious concern about the antics of these two important politicians was coming from another quarter, quite independently from C11. And because of this a still more high-powered investigation was just about to start. On the orders of the prime minister, Sir Alec Douglas-Home himself, two of his top ministers were making urgent inquiries into the behaviour of Lord Boothby and Tom Driberg.

What had happened was that just before Norman Lucas got his tip-off from his friend at Scotland Yard, Martin Redmayne, Conservative Chief Whip in the House of Commons, had been approached by a pair of worried Conservative backbenchers, Brigadier Terence Clarke, and Barnaby Drayson. Some of their constituents had been complaining about the behaviour of two politicians, accompanied by obvious criminals, whom they'd witnessed soliciting rent boys at White City dog track. The two MPs had duly visited White City to check out the story for themselves and had actually seen Boothby and Driberg behaving as their constituents described.

In fact the behaviour of Boothby and Driberg wasn't quite as far-fetched as it sounds. Gambling, particularly on greyhound racing, was fairly common practice by criminals needing to account for their illicit earnings. One of those who did so was Driberg's current lover, the burglar Teddy Smith, who not only was a keen greyhound fancier but might well have needed an explanation for the proceeds from the burglaries that Driberg had put him up to.

When the two MPs reported back to Martin Redmayne with the news he was so disturbed that he instantly informed the prime minister, who was even more alarmed. Since Driberg was a Labour MP his behaviour was strictly not Sir Alec's business but the possibility of a criminal and homosexual scandal involving a Conservative politician as famous as Lord Boothby emphatically was. It was less than a year since one of Lord Home's own parliamentary colleagues, John Profumo, the then Minister for Defence, had been forced to resign from the government after lying in parliament over an affair with the call girl Christine Keeler. The ensuing uproar ended with the resignation of Harold Macmillan, the then prime minister, who was succeeded by Alec Douglas-Home.

Sir Alec didn't panic easily but the scars from the Profumo business had still to heal and he was so alarmed at the prospect of a rerun of that terrible disaster that he actually called in his home secretary Henry Brooke to question Boothby personally. It is an indication of how seriously the prime minister treated it that he also summoned the secretary to the Cabinet, Sir Timothy Bligh, to record his actions, along with the home secretary's reply. He'd spoken to Boothby who totally denied any suggestion of involvement with the Krays. More reassuring still, the home secretary said that he'd had a word with the Commissioner for Police, Sir Joseph Simpson. A great careerist who was every inch a politician's policeman, bland Sir Joseph had a knack of saying what senior politicians wished to hear. He did so now, assuring worried Henry Brooke that not only was there 'no ongoing investigation of any organised criminals' by Scotland Yard but that 'organised crime is actually decreasing now in London'.

When the home secretary reported these glad tidings back to the prime minister and the members of his committee the members appear to have been reassured, with the exception of the down-to-earth Solicitor General, Peter Rawlinson, who remarked that it all sounded, 'pretty unconvincing'.

As for Norman Lucas's story, which by now had reached the newsroom of the *Sunday Mirror*, it would normally have gone straight to the Mirror Group's editorial director Hugh Cudlipp, widely known as one of the great crusading journalists of the day. But ebullient Hugh was off on holiday and at that very moment all his energies were going on repainting his yacht in Honfleur harbour. Had Cudlipp been a little less concerned about his boat and been in London to deal with Norman's story, things would have turned out differently.

For quite some time Hugh Cudlipp had been cultivating close personal relations with Harold Wilson and the Labour Party's high command, and he would certainly have checked with them before running such a dangerous story in the paper, just as Harold Wilson and his advisers would certainly have urged caution before running such a story with a general election looming that autumn. But during Cudlipp's absence editorial control of the Mirror newspapers was left in the nervous hands of the chairman of the Mirror's proprietors, the International Press Corporation, Cecil Harmsworth King, who was a very different character from that crusading journalist Hugh Cudlipp.

That July, Cecil Harmsworth King had two particularly busy bees buzzing in his bonnet. The first, as befitted the great-nephew of Lord Northcliffe, the intolerable father of modern popular journalism, was that he absolutely must assert himself against the dangerously ambitious Cudlipp and make himself the undisputed boss of IPC. The second, which was closely linked with this, was to use his position of chairman of Mirror Newspapers to take his place among London's movers and shakers. Cecil King was longing to assert himself and make things happen.

Sensing, correctly, that Sir Alec Douglas-Home had almost had his day, Cecil King had recently decided to offer Harold Wilson and the Labour Party the support of Mirror newspapers in the forthcoming election and was driving round London in his big Rolls-Royce with a red flag flying from its radiator. And now Norman Lucas had given him just the story he needed to show his loyalty to Labour and to demonstrate the power of the Mirror newspapers. The Profumo case had brought down one prime minister already and had sold an awful lot of papers in the process. Imagine the effect of the revelation that the most popular right-wing politician of the day had been involved in a homosexual scandal with the most dangerous gangster in London.

According to Norman Lucas 'Cecil King was cock-a-hoop' when he read his story. Understandably. Single-handed, he and he alone was about to shaft the rickety Conservative government, and help to send Harold Wilson to Downing Street as prime minister in the forthcoming general election. In the process he could also show crusading journalist Hugh Cudlipp how to edit a newspaper. At one smart stroke Cecil King would have made himself master in his own house and put himself in line for that longed for peerage that would place him on a par with his fearsome great-uncle, the legendary Lord Northcliffe.

The year before, at the start of the Profumo scandal, Cecil King had actually asked Prime Minister Macmillan if there was any truth in rumours he was hearing of a 'relationship' between Jack Profumo and the call girl Christine Keeler. 'Not a shred. You have my word upon it,' said Macmillan. Two days later, when the *Sunday Mirror's* deadly rival, the *News of the World* openly accused Profumo of lying to the House of Commons, Profumo admitted it and resigned immediately. Shortly afterwards, Macmillan followed. Once fooled, Cecil King had no intention of being caught out like this again over Robert Boothby.

There was, however, just one tiny problem. King hadn't checked with Transport House as to whether Labour's high command actually wanted his story. Not that this made any difference once the presses had begun to roll, and five million copies of the *Sunday Mirror* fell on five million doormats that Sunday morning.

'PEER AND A GANGSTER. YARD INQUIRY' proclaimed their headlines, and according to the accompanying article 'the Police Commissioner, Sir Joseph Simpson, has ordered a top-level investigation into the alleged homosexual relationship between a peer who is a household name and a leading thug in the London underworld, involved in West End protection rackets.'[1]

12

Cover-up:
August–September 1964

AFTER THOSE UNEXPLAINED reports from the two Conservative MPs concerning the behaviour of Lord Boothby and Tom Driberg at the dog track, one place in Britain where the *Sunday Mirror* story must have caused some consternation was at Chequers, the official country residence of the prime minister, where on that memorable Sunday morning, Sir Alec Douglas-Home was enjoying his breakfast with the Sunday papers – except that he can't have enjoyed anything very much when he saw the front page of the *Sunday Mirror*. This was what Sir Alec had been fearing all along. How typical of bloody Bob. Disaster loomed.

Faced with this suddenly appalling crisis, Douglas-Home was powerless. There was nothing he could do except send once more for the home secretary, who couldn't do a great deal either. But politics can be an odd old business, and few things were odder than what happened next and how help and consolation were to reach Sir Alec in his hour of need by courtesy of his arch-enemy Harold Wilson, the leader of the opposition. To understand how this happened we must return to the central character in this imminent disaster, Lord Boothby.

★

France was a popular destination for top people that July, and while Hugh Cudlipp was putting that final coat of varnish to his yacht in Honfleur harbour, Boothby, oblivious to what Cecil King was up to, not to mention the discoveries of his own party's parliamentary chief whip, had spent a more relaxed few days taking the waters at the spa town of Vittel with his old friend, Colin Coote, editor of the London *Daily Telegraph*. That Sunday morning as they returned to London one of them picked up a copy of the *Sunday Mirror* at the airport.

'We were both completely baffled by its front-page story and spent the flight back to London trying to work out who on earth the famous peer could be,' Lord Boothby told me later. (Interestingly, another member of the House of Lords who felt genuine alarm was Lord Montgomery of Alamein who thought that since he was one of the few members of the Lords who could claim to be 'a household name' the press had discovered some fearful indiscretion from *his* past.)

Boothby, on the other hand, insisted that in contrast with the Field Marshal his conscience was crystal-clear, and that he had never imagined for a moment that the as yet unnamed peer in the *Sunday Mirror* might just conceivably be him. He also claimed that after he was safely back in Eaton Place he rang his old friend Driberg out of simple curiosity to find out who it was. 'As one of the best-informed journalists in London, Tom was sure to know the peer's identity.'

All this, of course, like most of what Lord Boothby uttered in the days ahead, was sheerest nonsense. What in fact had happened was that no sooner had he read the front page of the *Sunday Mirror* than he panicked, and his hurried call to Driberg was not to inquire who the fuss was all about but to beg him to do anything he could to help him. Here he was clutching at the flimsiest of straws but he had no one else to turn to. Besides, Driberg, as we now know, was not uninvolved himself and having wriggled out of so many sexual scrapes in his own distinctly lurid past there was just a chance that he might help them both to wriggle out of this one.

But, clearly, clever Tom didn't sound too hopeful. And when, shortly afterwards, the doorbell rang and the home secretary and the Conservative chief whip were standing on the doorstep with orders from the prime minister to ask what Lord Boothby now intended doing about the *Mirror*'s accusations there was not a great deal he could say, apart from using that deep brown TV voice of his to deny everything and send them on their way. His visitors had made it fairly clear, to say the least, that they were not impressed. Once they'd gone, despair and desperation descended on Number One Eaton Place.

Several years later, when I was trying to make sense of what had happened, I was put in touch with one of the minor characters involved, a rich Lithuanian timber merchant called Harold Kissin, who was said to have helped Boothby at the time. When I met him he struck me as an extremely amiable rich middle-aged businessman; apparently by chance he too had arrived at Eaton Place soon after the two top Tory politicians had left.

But did he really come by chance? It was only later that I discovered that Kissin was a close and trusted friend of Harold Wilson and a member of his so-called 'Hampstead Circle'. In the past Wilson had even done unofficial business for him during trips to Russia. Now was the time for Wilson to request a favour in return. For Kissin apparently knew Boothby quite well and was just the sort of tactful understanding character one would turn to in an awkward situation. At the time he told me that he found Boothby 'in a dreadful state, poor fellow. He'd been drinking heavily, and was threatening to kill himself.'

Kissin also told me how he did his best to calm Boothby down and told him not to panic. He had good friends who would help him and he was sure that everything could be arranged. Before he left he gave him what would prove to be extremely sound advice. Get in touch at once with Arnold Goodman.

I was always puzzled over why the Labour Party's most influential lawyer, Arnold Goodman, came to represent a Conservative peer as notorious as Robert Boothby. What made it particularly strange was that not only was Goodman very much a Labour lawyer but he was also one of Harold Wilson's most trusted and dedicated advisers. So why should he, of all men, have helped to get the Tory Lord Boothby off the hook in his hour of greatest need?

I actually interviewed Boothby at the end of 1969 and in all innocence asked him the same question. Who was responsible for Goodman's intervention in his defence, which on the face of it seemed most unlikely? Had it really been down to the influence of kindly Harold Kissin? Boothby shook his head. 'Certainly not', he said. 'It was the little man.'

'Little man. What little man?' I asked.

'Who d'you think I mean? The little man. Harold Wilson.'

The mystery deepened. But when I tried to probe, Lord Boothby clearly felt he'd said enough and changed the subject.

Even so, I found it hard to believe that Harold Wilson would have acted so decisively to save an old scoundrel like Boothby – and a Conservative scoundrel at that – out of the sheer kindness of his heart. There had to be some other reason. Not until 1995, when the Cabinet papers were finally released under the thirty-year rule, did I find out what it was. What I couldn't know in 1964, because the evidence would be suppressed for another thirty years, was that when the Boothby scandal burst that summer Harold Wilson had a desperate need to destroy all traces of what was actually a far more dangerous scandal than I realised. For it was not until 1995 that I learned that Tom Driberg, who was one of Wilson's oldest and most trusted friends in politics, the man he would finally ennoble and make

Chairman of the Labour Party, had also been so perilously involved with Boothby.

This was plainly crucial to any understanding of this whole extraordinary affair. For it meant that both government and opposition shared a common interest – to make absolutely sure that Cecil King's story went no further. It also explained why bulky Arnold Goodman was so hurriedly wheeled in to succour Boothby in his hour of need. With a general election in the offing, all that really mattered now to Harold Wilson was not to bail out the unfortunate Boothby but to save the skin of one of his most influential political advisers. Should this scandal ever have spread to Driberg, the Little Man might soon have been saying sad farewells to any hopes he had of becoming prime minister in the election set for eight weeks' time.[1]

So this, and not the milk of human kindness, was why Arnold Goodman was so hurriedly brought in to save the skin of Robert Boothby.

Not for nothing was the man whose appetite and girth had earned him the nickname of 'Two Dinners Goodman' also known as Harold Wilson's 'Mr Fixit'. After the *Sunday Mirror* revelations he was probably the only man alive who could have put the lid back firmly on this highly toxic can of worms – and made absolutely sure it stayed there.

Whatever one may think of the late Arnold Goodman's lawyerly integrity, one must admire his cool in such a very awkward situation. The problem was that, then as now, the village of Westminster kept afloat on gossip and everyone in politics who was not born yesterday knew at least something of Bob Boothby's reputation – and probably even more about Tom Driberg's. Frankly, it would have been hard to find a dodgier duo in public life to have landed in a mess like this. And the longer it was permitted to drag on, the more the rumour and the gossip would increase and the more difficult it would be to save the pair.

Normally Goodman would have launched a strongly worded writ for libel against the International Press Corporation, its chairman Cecil Harmsworth King, its editorial director Hugh Kinsman Cudlipp, and the *Sunday Mirror* editor Reg Payne – then left the law to take its course. But Goodman knew quite well that this would be disastrous. There had recently been too many barely veiled press reports and suspicious incidents involving Boothby which made it clear that if things ever reached the point where he was forced to defend his reputation in a court of law against any but a brain-dead barrister he would be shot to pieces in the process. Also, as someone with a considerable appetite not just for food but also for political gossip, Arnold Goodman would certainly have known that not only were the *Sunday Mirror*'s accusations broadly true but that the longer the paper had to put its case together the more the truth was likely to emerge, including as the final clincher Boothby's close involvement with Tom Driberg.

In such situations Goodman had a favourite saying – 'The greater the truth, the greater the libel.' And the more the truth about this case emerged, as it certainly would do if it ever went to court, the bloodier would be the carnage that would follow. To avoid this happening, speed was of the essence and Goodman was quick to pick on three potential advantages – and, like the clever lawyer that he was, proceed to make hay with them.

The first was a widespread feeling among politicians of all parties that the sleaze and scandal of the Profumo case the year before had done politics no favours, and that the last thing any politician wanted now was another catastrophic scandal, especially one involving a notorious old rake like Robert Boothby. Taken on their own, of course, such feelings would not have been enough to save him. But they would undoubtedly reinforce the second point, which could be vital. Since the scandal involved a prominent Conservative *and* a prominent member of the Labour Party both main parties had a strong interest in suppressing it. The prime minister, Sir Alec Douglas-Home and the leader of the opposition, Harold Wilson, both wanted it to disappear and neither was going to object, still less play party politics over the *Sunday Mirror* story, if the scandal could be painlessly persuaded to vanish quietly.

Thirdly, and most importantly of all, smart Arnold unerringly homed in on one last crucial fact for the plan he was devising to succeed, and which in turn permitted him to deliver his master-stroke. This was the dominant position of Hugh Cudlipp at the centre of the whole affair. If Harold Wilson and Sir Alec Douglas-Home both fervently desired to have this story killed, the one man who could wield the knife was Hugh Kinsman Cudlipp.

Goodman might well have earned his nickname 'Mr Fixit', by being the greatest fixer of his day but had he not been sure of Cudlipp's absolute support not even he would ever have dared to pursue the course that he did.

The point was that no top investigative journalist as sharp and as well informed as Cudlipp would have had the faintest difficulty digging out the mass of evidence, much of it in the public domain already, which lay around to add credence to the *Sunday Mirror*'s allegations. It was not as if Boothby, still less Tom Driberg, had ever been particularly discreet about the company they kept or about what they did. There had already been press reports of suspicious incidents involving Boothby's relationships with boys and it would not have taken a journalist as smart as Cudlipp long to ferret out yet further morsels such as Ron Kray's dinner with Lord Boothby at the House of Lords or the return dinner party that Ron had arranged in Boothby's honour at the Society restaurant. Had Cudlipp also felt inclined he could have fairly easily found out, through Norman Lucas, what had been going on at Ronnie's flat. But did Hugh Cudlipp really wish to waste his precious time assembling evidence to support a scoop on which his greatest rival at the *Sunday Mirror*, Cecil King, had firmly staked his reputation?

This question, or something very like it, must have swiftly passed through Goodman's agile brain as he pondered on how to act in the most important case of his career. Or, to put it more directly, how could he organise the perfect cover-up of what would otherwise become the most damaging political scandal of the 1960s.

One thing to remember about Arnold Goodman was his impressiveness. This was partly down to his size. Not only was he very fat but he was also very large. He had what politicians once called 'bottom'. His pronouncements carried weight. Because of this people trusted him, and he had made himself the unofficial spokesman for what was known as 'the Great and the Good' throughout the country. In *Private Eye*, he was habitually referred to as 'the Blessed Arnold' and his admiring biographer Brian Brivati actually calls him Britain's 'most distinguished citizen outside government'. In other words, if the English Establishment had a physical presence in the 1960s, it was Arnold Goodman. Only this explains what happened next and how this most impressive but extremely devious old lawyer got Lord Boothby, Tom Driberg and a lot of other very worried politicians off the hook – and saved the Kray Twins in the process.

We'll never know exactly how he did it. But since everything depended now on Hugh Cudlipp for his plan to work, Goodman must have had a very serious discussion with him very early on. One says this for the simple reason that without a watertight guarantee from Cudlipp nothing of what followed would have been remotely possible. But from what we know of both the characters involved it can't have been too difficult for them to have reached an understanding, particularly when someone as persuasive as Arnold Goodman set out to remind someone as ambitious as Hugh Cudlipp of the simple benefits of seeing sense.

We'll never know precisely what was said to whom but Hugh Cudlipp can't have needed much persuading. And, once he had been persuaded, the time had come for big fat Arnold to batten down the hatches and proceed full steam ahead.

Since it was far too dangerous to risk a full-scale libel action in a court of law Goodman was left with only one alternative. He must somehow make Cecil King retract his story in the *Sunday Mirror*, publicly apologise to Boothby and sign up to appropriate – i.e. extremely large – damages for libel.

As a young journalist on the *Sunday Mirror*, Derek Jameson witnessed what ensued from the vantage point of the paper's newsroom during the first two crucial weeks following the breaking of the story in the paper. He is quite specific over what occurred.

'To begin with we were all excited by what was going on. None of us doubted for a moment the truth of the story, nor did we question our ability to prove it. We already knew a lot about Boothby. So did Norman Lucas, and we were just about to start gathering together the proof we needed to back the story up when everything ground to a halt. There was no explanation but suddenly the story died. I remember feeling baffled and frustrated at the time. So were quite a lot of others but there was nothing we could do about it as the orders had come down to us from the editorial director, Hugh Cudlipp.'

And that was that. Without the necessary proof to back the story up the paper was powerless, and the moment had arrived when Arnold Goodman gave the final touch to the biggest gamble of his career.

Bearing in mind how much was now involved, it was a scheme of remarkable audacity. It was nothing less than to persuade

Boothby to make a public declaration of his total innocence of all the *Mirror*'s accusations and get it published in the letter column of *The Times*. In those days, when that newspaper still used to claim that 'Top People Read *The Times*' it was still the tribal noticeboard of the Establishment and as Goodman knew quite well a letter at the head of its famous correspondence columns would carry far more weight among 'those who mattered' than it would do anywhere else.

Bereft of any other way of escaping from his nightmare situation, Boothby had to go along with this, and at Goodman's personal dictation he sat down to write what his biographer, Robert Rhodes James rightly called 'the letter of his life'.

In essence it was perfectly straightforward: a simple five-hundred-word denial of all the *Sunday Mirror* allegations, and it went in part as follows: 'I have never been to all-male parties in Mayfair. I have met the man alleged to be King of the Underworld (Ron Kray) only three times, on business matters, and then by appointment at my flat, at his request, and in the presence of other people. The police deny having made any report to Scotland Yard or the Home Secretary in connection with any matters that affect me. Lastly, I am not, and never have been, homosexual. In short, the *Sunday Mirror* allegations are a tissue of atrocious lies.'

The letter ended with a challenge. 'If Mirror Newspapers possess any documentary or photographic evidence to the contrary, let them print it and take the consequences.'

To ensure that there was no misunderstanding Boothby personally delivered the letter to the editor of *The Times*, Sir William Haley, to whom he gave his absolute assurance that every word he wrote was gospel truth. Goodman also took the further precaution of involving the distinguished barrister Sir Gerald Gardiner QC in his plan to seek an instant settlement from the *Sunday Mirror*, by persuading Boothby to engage him as his counsel.

At first Sir Gerald seems to have been reluctant to take on this role and he finally accepted only after getting Boothby's absolute assurance that there was not the faintest truth in any of the *Mirror*'s allegations.

'You have my word of honour on it as a gentleman,' said Lord Boothby.

So much for honour as far as Lord Boothby was concerned, and so much for his assurances to the Labour Party's future Lord Chancellor. For, as we now know, every one of the letter's positive denials was false. Boothby *had* been meeting Ron Kray on numerous occasions since the end of 1963. He had been to all-male parties (admittedly not in Mayfair but elsewhere in London). He *had* been the subject of an ongoing investigation by Scotland Yard's intelligence section, and he unquestionably had been and still was homosexual. In short it was his letter, not the *Sunday Mirror*'s article, that was the 'tissue of atrocious lies'.

Once the letter had been published in *The Times* on the second of August it was time for action. 'He who hesitates is lost.' But Arnold Goodman didn't hesitate and it was Cecil Harmsworth King who lost. For the time had come for the Blessed Arnold to make that all-important telephone call to Cecil Harmsworth King that would leave him no alternative but to repudiate his story.

Against the voice of the Establishment the wretched Cecil didn't really stand a chance.

As Derek Jameson recalls, 'everybody in the press was terrified of Goodie' – especially when he habitually introduced bad news on the telephone with the remark, "I think that you should know."'

When Goodman rang up Cecil King and started off with 'Mr King, there is something that I think you should know . . .' Jehovah could have been announcing Judgement Day to him.

And when Cecil King attempted to reply, it must have been like arguing with God Almighty – in spite of which he did his best.

'Where is your evidence for these damaging allegations, Mr King?' the Almighty asked him.

Reply came there none, and the voice of the Establishment continued: 'I can't imagine that your shareholders would appreciate the costs. For if you leave my client no alternative but to pursue this matter through the courts the cost to your shareholders will be fearsome. The course that I'm suggesting would mean letting your shareholders off cheaply by comparison with the sort of figures they'll be facing if, heaven forfend, this sorry business ever comes to court.'

By the time the conversation ended it must have felt as if the Blessed Arnold was offering Cecil King salvation on the cheap.

'How much would you suggest?' asked Cecil King.

'Fifty thousand pounds,' said the voice of the Establishment.

'I was thinking more in terms of thirty thousand,' ventured Cecil King.

'Mr King, we mustn't be ridiculous. Bear in mind the suffering these outrageous falsehoods must have caused Lord Boothby and all you come up with is thirty thousand pounds. I must urge you, think again. In the meantime I'm prepared to compromise. Forty thousand plus a full apology on the front page of the next edition of the *Sunday Mirror*. And that's my final offer.'

'Done!' said Cecil Harmsworth King, or words to that effect.

And done he truly was.

At this point there is one thing that one must understand – the sheer power behind the blow that Goodman had struck in defence of Boothby. It wasn't only Cecil King who had to suffer. This was the mail-clad fist of the Establishment at its most formidable, and the blow was intended to intimidate anyone who dared to challenge it. Goodman knew exactly what he was up to and how much was at stake, and he took no chances. Back in 1964, £40,000 – nearly a million pounds in today's inflated currency – were unprecedented damages in a libel case, as Goodman intended them to be – less to compensate Lord Boothby than to stand there as a fearsome warning against anyone ever reopening the case.

There was one final grace note that, lawyer-like, Goodman insisted on, revealing the perfectionism which made him such a master of his trade. Partly in order to cover his own tracks, along with those of many others, he insisted that none of those involved in the agreement was ever to discuss or comment on it afterwards. The Establishment had spoken. The greatest coup of Cecil King's career was rubbished, and Arnold Goodman's stitch-up was complete, leaving Harold Wilson free to go ahead and win the general election. Thanks in no small part to Arnold Goodman, Labour was elected that October. And Arnold Goodman soon received a peerage from a grateful Labour government. As his fellow lawyers put it, he could rest his case.

Or as the *Mirror*'s lawyer Philip Levy (lover of its top columnist, Marjorie Proops) told me: 'once the deal was signed, the shutters came down on the case and no one was ever going to raise them in a hurry.'

Goodman – not to mention Boothby and Tom Driberg – were all extremely lucky with the timing when the scandal broke and the way the settlement coincided with the official dissolution of parliament in preparation for that autumn's general election. It meant that every active politician in the land now had that one single thought in his or her mind, in comparison with which the lies and antics of Lord Boothby could be conveniently forgotten.

What nobody appeared to notice was that Arnold Goodman's actions had not only given the law's protection to this elderly ennobled catamite, but also to a psychotic and potentially homicidal gangster: Ronnie Kray. The possibilities for blackmail were enormous and, as we shall see, would soon be made the most of by the Twins. At the same time, during the next four years the megalomania and madness of the Twins would grow apace until fear of them spread far beyond Scotland Yard and started to infect the nation.

In 1969, when the Krays and their followers were finally brought to trial, there was much talk about what was called 'the conspiracy of silence' around them. What nobody remembered was the behaviour of friends and politicians round the undeserving form of Robert Boothby, who for reasons of their own had stayed silent as an increasingly dangerous and out-rageous actual conspiracy of silence rolled smoothly into operation.

The point was that by the standards of the day a libel settle-ment which would approach one million pounds in today's inflated currency was enormous – and a truly fearsome demon-stration of the power of the Establishment when threatened, as Arnold Goodman had intended it should be. Not only had the Establishment spoken – it had put its victim's money where its mouth was by demanding these formidable damages, along with grovelling apologies from the offending newspaper. Rarely was closure bought at such cost. With retribution such as this, the argument was over. The Establishment, in the bulky form of Arnold Goodman, had given notice to the media that no further mention of the Boothby scandal would be tolerated.

But in spite of this impressive legal edifice which Arnold Goodman had created to protect Lord Boothby's reputation at such a vast expenditure of other people's money there remained one simple fact which left at risk the whole performance. Henceforth, everyone involved in it would be haunted by a secret that could not be spoken. Lord Boothby was actually a liar and it was his case not the *Sunday Mirror*'s, which had been a tissue of atrocious falsehoods.

I am still amazed that at the time nobody, but nobody, spoke out against this. Instead, a mood of smug congratulation followed from a group of Boothby's friends and admirers. Michael Foot, for instance, wrote to him, 'adding my congratulations to the multitudes you must have received and richly deserved. You showed great nerve and courage. But who would have expected otherwise.'

In an editorial, the left-wing *New Statesman* congratulated him still more fulsomely. 'Boothby has demonstrated, for all the world to see, that the right way to tackle a newspaper smear is to hit back hard and openly. Not all have his courage. Perhaps more will do so in future as a result of his actions.'

For those who like dwelling on the hollowness of power, the absurdity of the great, and the inflated claptrap of earthly honours, let us end by listing the winners and the losers in this whole affair.

First in the list of winners come the politicians, who were left free to fight that autumn's general election undistracted by a sordid scandal at the heart of the body politic. Since he became prime minister as a result, Harold Wilson proved to be the greatest beneficiary of all – which in the circumstances was fair since it was he who had ordered the cover-up in the first place.

The former prime minister Sir Alec Douglas-Home also benefited since the cover-up allowed him to forget the cares of his unwanted premiership along with the dirt and debris of a scandal which would certainly have upset his reputation and his last few weeks in office.

But it was Arnold Goodman who outdid everyone in the honours following this case, including, of course, the almost instant peerage, the chairmanship of the the Arts Council and the Observer Trust, and – perhaps the most enviable gift of all – the Mastership of University College, Oxford.

Goodman was closely followed in the honours stakes by Hugh Cudlipp. Some months later when the unfortunate Cecil King lost the chairmanship of IPC in the fallout from the Boothby business Cudlipp inevitably replaced him. His peerage followed two years later, along with the emoluments that make life in the Establishment so profitable and so enjoyable. In 1976 someone with, one hopes, a sense of humour made him a member of the Royal Commission on Standards of Conduct in Public Life. For Cudlipp was not entirely devoid of humour about himself. Not long before he died he published a sequel to his early biography which was called *Publish and be Damned*. He called his final book, *The Prerogative of the Harlot*.

And what about Lord Robert Graham Boothby who, after all, had been the man that all the fuss had been about?

One can't disguise the fact that he did very well indeed. Nearly a million pounds in today's money was not a bad reward for mendacity and rough-trade sex – although, as we shall see, there wasn't all that much of the money left by the time the Krays had got their hands on it.

And what about the losers? First, of course, comes Cecil Harmsworth King who bore the disaster bravely as he signed the £40,000 cheque for Robert Boothby, 'thereby proving', as Randolph Churchill pointed out, 'that he was not the master in his own house'. A point made more cruelly eighteen months later when Cudlipp displaced him from his chairmanship of IPC and got that precious peerage that had been the cause of so much trouble.

There were some other losers too, but not among Top People, still less among the Great and the Good. Reg Payne, nominally the editor of the *Sunday Mirror* at the time of the affair, had played little part in the disaster, but since he was unimportant and someone had to take the blame he was sacrificed. No longer the editor of the *Sunday Mirror* he was made editor of IPC's downmarket magazine *Tit-Bits*. And, inevitably, there were some East End criminals who would lose their lives – once Ron got going. George Cornell, Jack 'The Hat' McVitie, the 'Mad Axeman' Frank Mitchell and, although few know about it, Driberg's boyfriend Teddy Smith would all get their comeuppance in the fallout from the scandal.

Because of all this the Boothby case must count as the cause célèbre of the Sixties, an all but unbelievable and still largely unacknowledged secret scandal that dwarfs the other scandals of the time for the number of top people who were involved, for the extent of the involvement of politicians with known criminals, and for the cynicism with which it was so neatly brushed beneath the carpets of both Houses of Parliament – not to mention, of course, the people who were subsequently murdered, and the cost in time and money spent on bringing their murderers to so-called justice.

But the most extraordinary thing about the scandal was, as we shall see, the way in which, over the next three years, the cover-up would make the Twins 'the untouchables' of the underworld and in the process turned them into the mythical monsters who still haunt us.

13

Blackmail: 1964–65

I T WASN'T LONG before the Twins were enjoying the first fruits of the hushed-up scandal. By getting Boothby forty thousand pounds for perjuring himself in public Lord Goodman had made him vulnerable to anybody who could prove that he was lying – which, life being what it was, meant Ronnie Kray. Had there been any argument there were the contents of the small brown suitcase that Ron had deposited with his mother, comprising various photographs including those taken in his flat and at the Society Restaurant, a personally inscribed copy of Lord Boothby's memoirs and, most damaging of all, a number of handwritten letters to Ron from Boothby on his crested paper, some of them dating back to long before Ron's first visit to his flat and all of which proved conclusively that Boothby, in the famous phrase of a former Secretary to the Cabinet, had been 'somewhat economical with the truth' and his friendship with the King of the Underworld was far more extensive than those three brief business meetings on which he had staked his reputation in his letter to *The Times*.

The little brown suitcase was Ron's weapon of last resort but at the moment he had no need to use it. The truth was, of course, that Boothby was scared to death of Ronnie Kray. For those unacquainted with the sadder facts of life, this is what so-called rough-trade sex is all about – fear as a sexual switch-on, violence as an aphrodisiac, brutality and domination at the service of the addict's sexual pleasure. In the words of Leopold von Sacher-Masoch, the Austrian novelist who gave his name to this condition: 'Show me a sadist and I'll show you a masochist.' Ron had been the sadist while Boothby and the members of their circle had been the masochists.

Make no mistake, Ronnie could be seriously scary, particularly when he hadn't had his Stematol and what it was like for idiots like Boothby playing masochistic sex games with a potential murderer like Ronnie Kray, I still don't care to think.

As far as the situation between him and Boothby was concerned, by early that autumn one thing was crystal-clear. All Ronnie had to do was say the word and Boothby would jump. At present there was no need for Ron to do this but should the need have arisen, all he would have had to do would be to be to put the squeeze on him for what he rightly saw as his fair share of the money from the *Sunday Mirror*.

At least Boothby had the decency to say that he regarded those forty thousand pounds as 'tainted money'. But he was always curiously vague about what he actually did with a sum which, in today's debased currency, would have fallen not far short of a million pounds.

Apart from telling Driberg that he'd bought himself a house in France (which Driberg apparently could never find) the old fabulist mentioned a number of other possible recipients – including Sister Agnes Hospital, 'in gratitude for having saved my life', the British Heart Foundation, and trusts that he supposedly set up for various unnamed godchildren. Perhaps some of them did receive something but that didn't stop most of the 'tainted money' ending up with the Krays. Their attitude to tainted money was like that of the Roman Emperor Vespasian who, on picking out a coin from the imperial privy, said, '*Non odet pecunia*' – money doesn't stink. When it came to money, Ronnie felt the same.

As far as I could discover, no sooner had the bank cleared the *Sunday Mirror* cheque than Boothby sent Ron £5,000 – which in the circumstances was sensible, if only to keep him sweet and pay the costs of the libel case which he was just about to launch against the *Sunday Mirror*. It would seem to follow that since Cecil King had now apologised to Ron for calling him 'a homosexual thug' he had *ipso facto*, libelled him as well, but the judge felt otherwise and dismissed the case on the grounds of fair comment. This would always be a sore point with Ron. 'Proves what I always said. One law for the fucking rich, and another for the poor,' an observation so obvious that it hardly needed Ronald Kray to make it.

This was, however, only the beginning of the Kray Twins' squeeze on the highly squeezable Lord Boothby. For, as it happened, by that autumn they were going through a cash-flow problem. Thanks to Ron's habit of using Esmeralda's Barn as his personal money box the club that should have been a small gold mine for the Twins was going broke. To save the day Reg installed the Twins' uncle, old Charlie's brother Alf, as manager. But Uncle Alf was not John Aspinall, bills continued to pile up unpaid, and soon the bailiffs were fixing padlocks on the doors.

Realistically, the Twins should not have let this bother them unduly. They had wisely continued to keep clear of banks, insisting that whatever they were owed from protection rackets, rents and profits from their long-firm frauds and associated scams, was handed over weekly and in cash. Ron kept the details in his spidery writing in a small black book, and he and Reggie shared the proceeds. The only trouble was that Ron had been in the habit of treating the money from the Barn as his and when it stopped he began to feel the pinch. He was always more extravagant than Reg (who, truth be told, was rather mean) and large sums now began to disappear on clothes and jewellery and boys – especially boys – who knew that they could always earn themselves a gold bracelet or even a diamond-studded watch if they were suitably inventive.

Now that the gold mine of the Barn had disappeared the Twins' largest source of income was the Mafia-owned Colony Sporting Club in Mayfair which, according to Les Payne, was still paying them £500 a week in protection money alone. It wasn't extortionate, but it was regular, and there were many other gambling and illicit drinking clubs across London making regular contributions to the Twins. These were mainly Reg's concern. Unlike Ron he was methodical, and it was thanks to Reg that the business side of the Firm went on ticking over so profitably. But this didn't suit Ron who was attracted by the bigger picture. Now that the Barn had gone he wanted something that would take its place and bring in real money. That autumn he set out to find it.

Ever since those early evenings in the billiard hall when he had played the part of the boss among his underlings Ron had continued his obsession with the American Mafia. In the early 1960s, when Castro kicked the Mob out of Cuba and they started seriously investing in gambling in London, the Twins had met several major figures in the Mafia, such as Dino Cellini and Angelo Bruno, and above all the hyper-rich boss of bosses Meyer Lansky. For many years Lansky controlled most of the gambling in Las Vegas, and was currently in London. He regarded London, unlike Vegas now, as a source of endless possibilities for organised crime, gambling and large-scale trafficking in drugs.

When he was setting up the plush Colony Sporting Club in Mayfair as his London showplace Lansky installed the actor George Raft, star of many forgettable gangster B-movies, to front this extremely lucrative operation and the Twins soon got to meet him. In a way they felt that they already knew him – from all his early movies, especially *Scarface*, the 1932 film that made his name. It was *Scarface* that had brought him to the attention of big-time mafiosi such as Lansky, who employed Raft in the part he played so often in his films – as the public face of the Mafia in their top casinos.

After 1966, when the Home Office would make him a scapegoat for the Mob in London and sling him out of Britain, Raft would recall his years in London as the happiest of his life. 'I had a chauffeured Rolls-Royce, I had a penthouse apartment in Mayfair, and I had beautiful women with me every night.' He also had the Krays to guarantee the Colony Sporting Club 'protection' and make sure that nothing untoward upset his plans for highly profitable gambling 'junkets' when groups of rich punters were specially flown in to London from America.

But by that autumn Ron was getting bored with this arrangement and, knowing that the Mafia was planning to extend its activities in London to a range of crimes including trafficking in stolen securities, drug dealing and money laundering, he felt the time had come to assert what he felt should be the Twins' rightful share of the action. Reg said he'd talk this over with George Raft. Ron angrily (and truthfully) insisted that Raft had no authority and that this was the moment to be tough and up the ante. Reg passed the gist of this to Raft, knowing that he in turn would pass it on to Lansky who was now in America – which he did.

Lansky was surprisingly accommodating. 'Invite the boys over. Let's discuss this face to face,' was his reaction. Reg made it clear that he wasn't going to America, saying he didn't want trouble with the FBI, which made Ron decide immediately that *he* was going.

I was always puzzled over how Ron got his US visa. Perhaps he just got lucky, and the US Consul in London, Ray E. White Jr, hadn't been paying enough attention to the British press. Otherwise he was hardly likely to have granted the recently proclaimed King of the London Underworld unlimited access to America. At all events, on 16 October 1964 Ronald Kray –

occupation: 'General Dealer' – got his tourist visa for as many visits to the USA as he cared to make, up to and including 16 October 1968. Since Ronnie wasn't one for wasting time he took advantage of his luck and booked a New York flight for early that November.

Boothby meanwhile was not as happy as he might have been, considering the scandal and the depths of unplumbed misery that he had so narrowly avoided. And that autumn, when Boothby's 'Little Man', the Labour leader, Harold Wilson, duly became prime minister, this should have led to what would probably have been the proudest moment of his lordship's life.

Long before the trouble started with the *Sunday Mirror* one of Boothby's oldest friends, Labour's shadow foreign secretary Patrick Gordon Walker, had suggested him to Harold Wilson as an ideal choice for Labour's next ambassador to France and Wilson had seen the point. As a popular celebrity politician, with cross-party appeal and a reputation for independence, Boothby would have been the sort of maverick appointment that Wilson wanted for his new regime, signalling the end of the stuffy image of the previous government. This was how things stood when Labour was returned to power and the London *Evening Standard* broke the news a few days later that Boothby was about to be Britain's next ambassador in Paris.

What followed then was fascinating. Had everything been as it should have been if Boothby really had been innocent of any involvement with the Krays nothing would have changed. He had been vindicated thanks to Arnold Goodman, the *Sunday Mirror* accusations had been exposed as a 'tissue of atrocious lies' and there was no earthly reason why the new prime minister should not have happily confirmed Lord Boothby's long-awaited elevation as Britain's man in Paris.

But this didn't happen and the fact that it didn't rather gives the game away. Now that we know the truth, and since many members of the Establishment, including Harold Wilson and his close advisers, unquestionably knew it too, it is obvious that there was actually no way that popular Lord Boothby could ever have been appointed to anything. However brilliantly Arnold Goodman had seen off the *Sunday Mirror*, no politician or senior civil servant with the remotest contact with reality would have dreamt of risking his career by backing Boothby for a five-pound loan, let alone to an ambassadorship as sensitive as that of Paris. The thought of the Kray Twins at some later date blackmailing Her Majesty's Ambassador in Paris has a certain wild appeal but is also quite disturbing.

However, just as the Establishment had saved Boothby for reasons of its own, so it was now dropping him as fast as possible – because it had to. Lady Luck had done enough for Robert Boothby and as a lifelong gambler he knew better than to push her any further. As a gambler he also knew the meaning of the phrase 'a busted flush'. His usefulness to anyone except the Krays was over.

In the Public Record Office there is a letter that he wrote to Harold Wilson, which in the circumstances is so rich in irony and reveals so much about the man who wrote it that it's worth quoting.

'My Dear Prime Minister,
I am down with bronchitis for the fifth year running and my doctor says it is no longer funny. He added yesterday that although there is no immediate reason for alarm, if it continues it can be a killer. He has therefore ordered me to the Caribbean for a minimum period of two months, and I am leaving for Barbados next week. In many ways it is a great relief.

One final word, if I may. If it is not an impertinence for me to say so, after forty years of unbroken public service in parliament I have not got what I ought to have. This, I know, means little or nothing to the public. But if, at any

time, you could see your way to put it right, it would give
very great satisfaction to,
Yours very sincerely,
Bob Boothby

As with his letter to Macmillan asking for his peerage, one can
only marvel at Boothby's extraordinary effrontery and wonder
just what further honours he may have thought he 'ought to
have'. Having already picked up a peerage and a KBE, it left
only the Companionship of Honour, the Order of Merit and
the Order of the Garter, any one of which in the circumstances
might have seemed a touch excessive. Certainly, Harold Wilson
and his government had clearly had enough of him by now, and
whatever honour Boothby might have thought that he deserved
was not forthcoming.

As for the talk about bronchitis, like so many of his utterances
this was only partly true. For him the real relief and the reason
he was leaving London for Barbados was not in obedience to his
doctor but to take a break from Ronald Kray, whose demands
were now becoming increasingly insistent.

While Boothby and the faithful Goodfellow were preparing to
exchange the fog of London for the warm sands of Barbados,
Ron was heading for New York and was looking forward to his
meeting with the 'aristocracy' of the American Mafia, including
Meyer Lansky, Angelo Bruno, and the Gallo Brothers.

In the meantime, someone in the security section of the US
Embassy in London, must have been hearing things about the
'general dealer' to whom Ray E. White Jr had granted a tourist
visa. For Ronnie never got that friendly welcome he had been
expecting on his first trip to America. Indeed, his only human
contact in New York was with a grim-faced member of the US
immigration service who examined his passport, asked him if his
name was Ronald Kray and, being told that it was, stamped his

visa, with a single word in large black letters: INVALIDATED. Having done this, he dispatched Ron back to Britain on the next plane to Heathrow.

After sitting for twenty hours high above the ocean getting nowhere, it must have been hard for Ronnie to control himself. But once back in London he saved his anger for his call to Eaton Square where Lord Boothby and his faithful butler were in the throes of imminent departure. One can but imagine how the conversation went. What did the so-and-so Americans think they were up to, giving him a visa and then cancelling it without an explanation? And what the so-and-so was Boothby going to do about it? And while he was on the subject, he and Reg had been getting too much aggravation in the last few weeks from a copper by the name of Gerrard and a younger one called Read who had both been poking their noses into their affairs. If his lordship knew what was good for him he'd better sort this out for them and be quick about it. Etc., etc.

Whatever form the actual conversation took Ron clearly put the fear of God into Robert Boothby. Not only did his lordship promise faithfully that before he left he would raise the question of his visa with the American ambassador, he also promised that he would have a word with the Police Commissioner, Sir Joseph Simpson, about the police harassment. As usual when receiving orders from Ron Kray his lordship did as he was told.

We can be sure of this because, no sooner were Boothby and his faithful butler Gordon Goodfellow safely ensconced in Barbados's luxury Miramar Beach Hotel than one of their first priorities was to write a letter back to Ron, a missive that was mysteriously preserved and found its way into the National Archive at the Public Record Office where it is today. Judging from the tone of the letter Ron had already helped to blight the couple's holiday by sending them a threatening message through a friend called John, complaining of the lack of action. Boothby was clearly so upset by this that he ordered

Goodfellow to pen an immediate reply for him on hotel stationery; and like nothing else, this letter demonstrates the vicelike grip that Ron Kray exercised on Boothby and the extraordinary lengths to which the peer would go in order to placate him.

After saying how distressed he and LB (short for 'Lord Boothby') had been by Ronnie's message, Goodfellow continued: 'I have spoken to LB and he says that no living man could have done more for you than he has done. As regards the American visa, he has made personal representations to the American ambassador, who undertook to look into the matter himself.'

As for Ron's complaints that he and Reg were being victimised by the police, Goodfellow wrote that 'LB has spoken on your behalf to the Chief Commissioner of the Metropolitan Police, Sir Joseph Simpson, and also to Chief Inspector Gerrard, who took down the statement that he made. In the course of this LB said that he had found you perfectly straightforward in any dealings he had had with you, and that he firmly believed you were now engaged in business which was absolutely legitimate. LB also said that he had reason to believe that the police were "hounding" you, and Chief Inspector Gerrard included this in the statement which he took down.'

After tactfully expressing LB's 'great regard' for Ronnie Kray, Goodfellow ended by saying that 'although LB of course has no control over the behaviour of either Scotland Yard or the American embassy, he is nevertheless a great friend of the editor of *The Times*, and if there is any further trouble from that quarter he will be glad to do what he can when he gets back.'

By this stage it's hard to imagine either Twin being terribly impressed by Boothby's 'great regard', still less by his promise of support from the editor of *The Times*. (Sir William Haley). After Ronnie's failed trip to America, what the Twins really needed now was money. Which was why they had recently been taking so much interest in the appropriately named Hideaway Club in Gerrard Street, Soho, over which Chief Inspector Gerrard (no connection) had been making such a nuisance of himself.

Thanks to Ron's gay information service the Twins had been among the first to hear that a 'rich socialite' called Hew McCowan had bought the club and was planning to turn it into a fashionable night spot for an upmarket clientele. They had been trying to use the same tactics on McCowan as they had when they took over Esmeralda's Barn and since the Twins regarded Soho as their territory they were expecting a substantial slice of the action. The only question was how substantial. There had already been tentative discussions on the subject between Reg and Hew McCowan during which Reg had suggested they adopt their going rate and that out of estimated earnings from the club of £2,000 a week the Twins should start with thirty per cent of the profits, rising by monthly increments to fifty per cent. For this payment McCowan would be provided with a doorman, a 'dedicated' minder and an inclusive security service guaranteeing full immunity from any bother or aggravation from other criminals or random hooligans. Through his friendship with the film star George Raft, Reg also promised personal appearances at the club by Frank Sinatra and Nat King Cole.

Reg was all for patience and had everything been left to him he almost certainly would have worked things out with McCowan as he usually did. But since his return from New York Ron had been impossible. Frustration, sexual or otherwise, was bad for him, and no sooner had Reg mentioned Hew McCowan than Ron started breathing fire and fury. Reg was getting soft with all this women's talk of negotiation. What McCowan needed was a fucking lesson that he would not forget.

While this was going on Teddy Smith, who was with them,

was listening and getting very drunk. He decided it was time to do the Twins a favour.

Mad Teddy was in many ways an unusual character to have found in the company of the Twins. At barely five foot seven, he was really too small to be a villain, and had begun his life of crime as a burglar before gravitating to the Firm. Apart from the Twins he was one of the Firm's few other homosexuals. He was also something of a fantasist and after winning a BBC writing competition with *Top Bunk*, a play he wrote in prison, he always claimed to be a writer.

He was also something of a mystery. As well as being one of the very few West Londoners in the Firm he had no known dependants and, after starting off as one of Ron's many boyfriends, had made him his hero and tried to model himself on him. Like Ron, he was probably psychotic and had earned his nickname 'Mad' from the way he spiralled out of all control when he was drunk. When drunk he could be dangerous and he loved mentioning the name of Kray to scare his enemies. He did so now and, thinking he was bigger and smarter than he was, went round to the Hideaway Club to teach Hew McCowan a lesson by smashing the place up.

As the full extent of the damage he inflicted on the club was subsequently valued at just twenty pounds, it would seem that the violence was mainly verbal. But since it was strongly spiced with threats and insults from the Krays it was enough to make McCowan summon the police, who soon arrived and promptly cautioned Edward Smith, writer, on suspicion of demanding money with menaces on behalf of Reginald and Ronald Kray.

For Chief Inspector Gerrard and Inspector 'Nipper' Read, the two Scotland Yard detectives who had been unsuccessfully targeting the Krays for several months, Mad Teddy's antics at the Hideaway seemed something of a godsend. Unlike the

Police Commissioner they were seriously concerned about the menace of the Twins and felt that this could be their chance to catch them before something worse occurred.

Of course, as we now know, they were absolutely right, but as an appropriate response by Scotland Yard to the threat of those who had only recently been called 'the most dangerous organised criminals in London' this case against the Twins for demanding money with menaces was somewhat flimsy, especially after all the information C11 had been gathering about the Twins' involvement in blackmail, extortion, protection, large-scale fraud and connections with the US Mafia. Still, in the circumstances, anything was better than nothing, and there was a fighting chance that it might work. After all, after evading the FBI for years, even Al Capone was finally caught for tax evasion, and the fact was that Ron's paranoia and Mad Teddy's drunken idiocy had landed the Kray Twins in a potentially dangerous situation – just when they didn't need it.

Even now it took a lot of effort from the two detectives before they received permission to pursue the case and there seemed little enthusiasm for it from their masters at the Yard. Remembering that the Commissioner, Sir Joseph Simpson, had only recently been telling the Home Secretary that C11's investigation had not taken place and that organised crime in the capital was decreasing, Simpson was not over-anxious to be forced to eat his words. Also sensing, quite correctly, that no one in the new government wished to hear another word about the Kray Twins or Lord Boothby, his instinct was to let sleeping gangsters go on sleeping – so long as they didn't cause him or his friendly politicians any trouble.

Gerrard and Read felt very differently. They were starting to believe that this time round they really had a chance and where there was a chance, they'd take it. They had several reasons to be optimistic. This was the first time for several years that the

Twins had permitted such a breach in their defences, and Mad Teddy's outburst had occurred in front of witnesses, including McCowan's agent Sydney Vaughan and Peter Byrne, a small-time villain who professed to hate the Krays. In addition both detectives had been favourably impressed by the club's new owner, Hew Cargill McCowan. I suspect that this was largely down to their sense of class. The police rarely found a man in McCowan's position willing to stand up in court against the Krays but McCowan was unusual. The son and heir of Sir David McCowan, the putative second baronet and laird of Menzie Castle, Perthshire, Hew McCowan displayed all the self-assurance of his class and the detectives were particularly struck by the way that he refused the offer of police protection. Clearly he was wealthy, brave and a thorough gentleman, which might have made them underplay one further fact about him. As Inspector Read put it, 'McCowan was an active homosexual but he did not dress flamboyantly, nor had he exaggerated effeminate gestures.' In other words, he wasn't camp but he was a gentleman.

What the detectives failed to realise was that there could be more complexities to Hew McCowan's sexual history than flamboyant dress and effeminate gestures, and that by failing to discover them they were in danger of overvaluing him as a witness. This was to prove a serious mistake once they had the go-ahead for their investigation, particularly as the case continued with a health warning from the powers above that this time they were on their own and if they failed there'd be no second chance. This was a risk they had to take, and on 18 December the Kray Twins were arrested at the Glenrae, a residential hotel in Seven Sisters Road, Islington where they often stayed in order to escape police surveillance or the cramped surroundings back at Vallance Road.

Together with Edward Smith, 'writer', they were charged with demanding money with menaces. When they appeared before the stipendiary magistrate he refused them bail and sent them up for trial at the Old Bailey at the end of January.

Gerrard and Read would have been encouraged had they known of the anxiety this caused the Twins. Reg was particularly incensed and said that he had no intention of having his private life destroyed by a further spell in prison, thanks to the behaviour of Ron's drunken so-called 'writer' friend 'Mad' Teddy Smith. Ron stuck up for him and after several fairly bitter arguments on the subject they agreed on one thing. They would move heaven and earth to avoid the hefty prison sentence that was almost certainly awaiting them if they didn't take things very seriously indeed.

Their first requirement was to get out of prison on bail fast and start sorting out the hostile witnesses, but even this was proving difficult. After the magistrate's refusal of their bail application they applied to the high court, followed by the Lord Chief Justice, without success. Once more the time had come to apply a little pressure on their old friend Bob Boothby, and see if he could fix it.

As luck would have it, Boothby and his butler had just returned from Barbados and Ron ordered his brother Charles to pay what proved to be the first of several visits to the flat in Eaton Square. From his prison cell Ron briefed his brother on what to say. This time he must really scare the daylights out of Boothby. He must emphasise that he and Reg meant business and that, after screwing up with the American ambassador and the Police Commissioner, it was up to him to get them bail through the House of Lords.

Boothby was many things, but he was not entirely a fool and he knew quite well that the Twins' request was theoretically impossible, and that as a member of the House of Lords he had absolutely no right to speak in parliament on a case that was still *sub judice*. To do so, and particularly on the Twins' behalf, could land him in serious trouble.

But thanks to the contents of Violet Kray's small brown suitcase he had to do something, and faced with the alternative of total ruin he assured Charlie he would do his best. Two days later he tabled a question in the House of Lords asking the Lord Chancellor if it was the Government's intention to keep the Kray Twins and Edward Smith in prison on remand indefinitely.

After forty years in parliament Boothby knew, if anyone did, that since it was parliament's job to make the laws, and the judges' to enforce them, members of parliament had no right to question a judge's decision, particularly in a case like this where there was really nothing to object to in the courts' behaviour. Since the Twins and Teddy Smith were down for trial in three weeks' time, it was hard to claim that they were suffering undue hardship and to speak as if the judges were keeping them on remand 'indefinitely' was ridiculous.

So Boothby was not just breaking the rules of parliament when he lumbered to his feet and in that famous voice of his put his question to the Lord Chancellor. He was also being fairly fatuous. Even as he started speaking he was met with cries of 'Order, order' from his fellow lords and a swift rebuke from Lord Dillhorne, the former Lord Chancellor, for asking a question on a matter which was still *sub judice*. Lord Rea, the Liberal spokesman, observed that the noble lord's question was not in accordance with the traditions of the House. And saintly Lord Longford, who could forgive almost anyone anything, including the moors murderer Myra Hindley, warned that 'his noble friend was going to regret this intervention when he reads it afterwards in cold blood.' The Lord Chancellor, Lord Gardiner, in his role of Speaker of the House, did not deign to pronounce.

And that it seemed, was that. Lord Boothby had once more acted under orders from the Krays, finally in parliament itself.

He had been expecting an uncomfortable ride but it could have been far worse, and as the owner of one of the thickest skins in politics he made a show of saying that he had nothing to regret, and left the chamber.

One wonders if he realised how fortunate he had been to have got away with it so lightly. For while they were shouting 'Order, order' none of his fellow lords could have possibly been ignorant of his recent case against the *Sunday Mirror*. To hear him pleading now for the very criminals concerning whom he had recently been awarded £40,000 for maintaining that he had met them on only two occasions meant that something very strange indeed was going on. And unless the noble lord was off his head – which in the circumstances just might have been possible – Lord Boothby had committed something so outrageous that it struck at the very heart of parliament itself.

There were no ifs and buts about it. By asking his question in the House of Lords over the bail application of the Krays and Teddy Smith, Boothby had not been raising any question of principle about the rights of prisoners on remand. He had been acting as a parliamentary spokesman for the Krays and as such had been in serious contempt of parliament. The strong likelihood that he had been doing this because he was being blackmailed only made the situation worse.

This should have been a matter of profound concern to Gerald Gardiner, the Lord High Chancellor, who was not only Speaker of the House of Lords and as such responsible for the integrity of the House but was also head of the judiciary with a similar responsibility for the judges. So one must wonder why the Lord High Chancellor stayed silent, why Lord Boothby was permitted to depart, and why nothing was ever done about it.

Since the answer goes to the very heart of the story of the Krays and explains much about the nature of their future crimes, their mythic status in the years ahead and the invulnerability that would soon surround them it is important that we understand it.

Let us begin with the behaviour of Lord Gardiner. The son of a rich Midlands businessman, educated at Harrow and Magdalen College, Oxford he had served in the Coldstream Guards at the end of the first world war; he was also an honourable, heterosexual, upper-class Englishman. Far from being a stuffy old reactionary he was slightly to the left of centre and a paid-up member of the Labour Party. As a lawyer he had successfully led the campaign against capital punishment. It was this combination of legal eminence and left-wing credentials that explains why Arnold Goodman had been anxious to involve him in Boothby's case against the *Sunday Mirror*, and why, after Labour won that autumn's general election, Harold Wilson had appointed him Lord Chancellor.

Unlike Boothby he was not a rogue, and unlike Goodman he was not a hypocritical old fixer. But remembering that, as Lord Chancellor, he was also an important member of Harold Wilson's cabinet, one begins to see the dilemma he was in. It was in many ways a similar dilemma to that faced by his Conservative predecessor as Lord Chancellor, Lord Dillhorne.

One should not insult the memory of either of these politicians by suggesting that they sat through Boothby's intervention unaware of what was going on. But they also knew quite well that as soon as either of them questioned the relationship between Boothby and the Krays the whole elaborate stitch-up that had been so deftly woven by Arnold Goodman round the Boothby scandal would have started to unravel. They also knew that, once this happened, the political mayhem that had followed John Profumo's admission that he had lied to parliament about sleeping with a call girl would have been a minor storm in a relatively small teacup compared with the hurricane that would have struck the Wilson government – and also the opposition – once the whole truth of the Boothby scandal was revealed.

Cover-ups frequently occur in politics and are usually forgotten. What was so unusual about Goodman's cover-up of the Boothby scandal was that so many people knew about it from the start and that the stakes were so enormous, especially now that, with Ronnie Kray actively blackmailing Lord Boothby, there was a very real danger of the whole thing cracking open.

This could well have happened after Boothby's intervention in the House of Lords had the consequences not been so alarming and posed such a a profound threat to the Establishment itself. All political establishments, the world over, are ultimately concerned with power and share a tendency to close ranks in an emergency. The British Establishment was no exception. Faced with a direct threat to important members of the government and opposition, it now retreated into what amounted to collective denial over this whole extremely dangerous affair.

One sees this happening even as the two lord chancellors backed off from initiating an investigation of the intrusion of the Krays into the business of the House of Lords. One also sees it with the press, where a sudden blanket of discretion stopped any comment in the media on Boothby's highly suspect behaviour. Once again the contrast with the Profumo scandal is revealing. In the Profumo scandal it was the press, and not the politicians, who performed what should always be the duty of the media, namely to expose serious corruption even in the highest ranks of society and government. But at this point in the Boothby scandal the opposite was taking place.

For political reasons a distinguished but over-influential lawyer had been able to suppress the truth about the intrusion of organised crime into British politics; and in so doing not only did he kill the truth but he also helped to gag the British press from any meaningful discussion of the scandal for years to come. For out of craven fear of Arnold Goodman – and because of the iniquities of the English law of libel – the press had effectively gagged itself over anything to do with either Boothby or the Krays.

This happened largely through the operation of the Establishment's traditional secondary line of defence, the so-called 'old boy network'. This was an area in which Boothby himself had always been a wily operator and he still had powerful allies whom he could trust.

Foremost, of course, was his old friend, and fellow holiday-maker, Sir Colin Coote who edited the *Daily Telegraph*. His frequent host Lord Beaverbrook, proprietor of Express Newspapers, had always been another close admirer and, as Boothby had recently been telling Ronnie Kray, the editor of *The Times*, Sir William Haley, was yet another influential ally. Since Goodman had already tightly gagged the Mirror papers and the *Sun* through the terms of his agreement with Cecil King, this left few papers willing or able to risk breaking ranks on the subject. What was soon to prove of such importance to the Krays was not that the Establishment, and virtually the entire media with it, had now closed ranks so tightly round Boothby and Tom Driberg. Frankly, the Krays themselves didn't care remotely for either of these deeply dodgy politicians. What *did* concern them was ensuring that, with the Establishment and the media now in denial over the whole Boothby scandal, the cover-up covered them as well. They were very much aware of this when, with barely four weeks left before their trial began, they started making active preparations for a masterclass in the not so gentle art of fixing a trial at the Old Bailey.

Until now the Twins had been acting on their own, but although they were still on remand in Brixton Jail, there remained one person they could turn to for advice – their legal adviser Manny Fryde (pronounced Freedy). He was a character who would have fascinated Dickens. Officially he was no more than the Twins' legal adviser because he was not a qualified solicitor, but whether this was because he'd been struck off as a lawyer in his native South Africa or because he'd never qualified was one of many mysteries that surrounded him. Another mystery was how, although he was no more than the managing clerk of the law firm of Sampson and Co. which employed him, old Manny ran every aspect of the business from his office in the company's decrepit premises in the shadow of the Old Bailey, which he haunted like a hungry undertaker.

As a total outsider to the cliquey world of lawyers, whatever human sympathies Manny might have had were saved for the criminals he represented. He spoke like them, felt like them, and looked wickeder than any of them. Since he was probably more cunning and unscrupulous than any other lawyer in the business, he and the Twins were made for one another.

When they said that all they wanted was to avoid going back to prison, he told them that that was simple. As with most things in life there was a simple answer – money, and a lot of it.

If the Twins were happy to rely on legal aid and take whatever barristers the system offered to defend them, they might as well forget the next few years and go to prison straight away. But provided they had money and knew how to use it, they could have the finest legal brains in Britain to defend them.

Reg saw the point at once. He always blamed his spell in prison on Paul Wrightson, the formidable prosecuting counsel, and said that this time round he wanted Wrightson on his side. Ron agreed, and asked Manny who would be the best barrister to defend him. He suggested the influential barrister politician Sir Peter Crowder MP, QC, with young Ivan Lawrence as his junior.

Apart from advising them to get the top barristers in London to represent them Manny made another shrewd suggestion. It was always claimed that he remembered something suspicious in McCowan's past which might make him vulnerable in cross-examination, and because of this he advised hiring George Devlin who was known as the smartest private eye in London. He would cost as much as a top barrister but Manny guessed correctly that in a case like this he could be worth every penny.

Finally, of course, there were the members of the Firm. There was now a lot of work for them to do and they too would need paying.

This was a problem. Thanks to the Twins' expenses and loss of earning power during their current troubles that sort of money was the one thing that they lacked. Living very much from day to day and relying on people they could tap for contributions, their finances were, as usual, quite chaotic.

When I asked Ron how much he and Reg spent on their defence he said around £10,000. But this was probably an underestimate: Manny's services did not come cheap, and as the Twins always lived beyond their means, I have estimated that they spent between twenty and thirty thousand pounds on their defence, most of it up front. By now they were running short of money. They could raise something from friends and victims but nothing like enough. There remained one obvious source who they knew could not refuse them – Boothby; and there was one thing they wanted from him – the rest of the 'tainted money' from the *Sunday Mirror*. A few days later brother Charlie made another trip to Eaton Square to put the final squeeze on Boothby.

Charlie was kept busy as he had to see two equally important characters who had been at the Hideaway Club when Mad Teddy had made his fateful visit – Sydney Vaughan and Peter Byrne. At the remand hearings they had appeared for the prosecution but how could either of them now argue when Charlie paid them both a visit accompanied by the Twins' old friend, the eighteen-stone ex-wrestler Tommy 'The Bear' Brown and made it plain where their best interests lay. Charlie had no problem getting Byrne to change his story. Vaughan took longer, but finally he too agreed that he had appeared for the prosecution only under extreme duress. Later Charlie took them both back to his flat where they met Father Foster, the young priest from the local church of St James the Less, who duly witnessed their sworn statements to that effect.

On 7 March, when the trial opened, everything had been so carefully set up by Manny Fryde and the Twins that, thanks to Devlin and the work of several members of the Firm, the prosecution really didn't stand a chance. The first shock came when the prosecution learned that their two key witnesses, Vaughan and Byrne, had inexplicably gone over to the defence. But there was worse to come. It had not been hard for Manny Fryde to discover the names and the addresses of the jurors and pick one or two of them who, for a slight consideration, might be prepared to do the Twins a favour. As Manny knew quite well, a vulnerable point in the legal system was the rule that a jury's verdict had to be unanimous. And as the trial proceeded, trouble started with the jurors. One was suddenly hit with a mysterious illness and, to avoid arousing the interest of the press photographers, had to be driven from the court lying on the floor of his taxi. Manny had been hoping this would lead to a retrial but instead the judge ordered the trial to continue with eleven jurors. But even then, all was far from lost. By a strange coincidence, when the jury retired to consider their verdict one of them was unable to agree with the others – and went on disagreeing for the next four hours, until the judge had no alternative but to discharge the jury, and order a retrial eight days later. Those eight days allowed Devlin to follow the advice of Manny Fryde and spend some time in Edinburgh, working through recent Scottish court records. He returned with his notebook full of information on the private life of Hew McCowan.

With the two witnesses Byrne and Vaughan now on the side of the defence, the prosecution at this point depended more than ever on McCowan. But as soon as Reg's counsel Paul Wrightson rose to cross-examine him it was clear that what remained of Boothby's 'tainted money' had not been spent in vain.

Wrightson was at his most effective. Was it true, he asked Mr McCowan, that on such-and-such dates you appeared as a prosecution witness in no less than three homosexual-blackmail cases, two of them in Scotland.

Then, with gentle sarcasm, he continued: 'Mr McCowan, I am wondering how it is that you have been in this unfortunate position three times already. Did you think that you would be getting public acclaim for giving this evidence today, or did you have some other reason?'

By the time that Wrightson had finished with him, McCowan's credibility had gone and for all intents and purposes the trial was over apart from one remaining possibility – a guilty verdict from the jury. But, of course, it would have to be unanimous. Was there any chance of this, Judge Arvold asked the foreman of the jury.

'None at all, my lord,' replied the foreman of the jury, leaving Judge Arvold no alternative but to dismiss the case, for the second time. After this there could be no question of another retrial. Mad Teddy and the Twins walked out of the Old Bailey to freedom.

The Twins' victory was, in fact, even greater than it seemed. Not only had they avoided imprisonment, but they had finally scared off Scotland Yard, who now retreated ignominiously.

It had been entirely against the wishes and advice of the Police Commissioner to tangle with the Kray Twins in the first place, and the whole operation had subsequently been absurdly feeble and half-hearted. To have allowed the Krays to win by scaring prosecution witnesses and suborning jurors, and then to rely on a chief prosecution witness as vulnerable as Hew McCowan – what sort of top Scotland Yard investigation was that?

Gerrard said nothing, but later Nipper Read would admit that it had been the worst defeat of his career.

But then, what did anyone expect following the Boothby cover-up? When top criminals are protected by distinguished lawyers on behalf of the Establishment, and famous members of the House of Lords decided to intervene on their behalf in parliament, it would have taken a courageous Commissioner of Police to have still gone all out to convict them.

But, as we know, Sir Joseph Simpson was not courageous in the face of the political establishment, any more than were those members of the Establishment itself who had colluded in the cover-up in the first place.

So what one witnessed now in the wake of the McCowan disaster was an ignominious retreat. If Goodman's perjured victory over Mirror Newspapers halted any meaningful attack on the Krays by the media, the craven defeat of the prosecution in the McCowan case did much the same at Scotland Yard. For Scotland Yard, of course, had shared in the defeat and now they shared in the results of Arnold Goodman's cover-up. By any standards of policing or of law enforcement the whole affair was shameful.

Gerrard, who would soon retire, was moved to other duties, and Nipper Read, who was the one detective with the awareness and the knowledge of the Twins to have still been capable of tackling them, was instantly transferred as far away from London and the Twins as possible. Having stated that no blame attached to him for what had happened, he was exiled to a murder case in Ireland and spent the next three years free from all concern about the Twins as far as ordinary policing was concerned.

As for Sir Joseph Simpson, he seemed to have gone into what is known as 'denial' over anything relating to the Krays. Like the three wise monkeys he could see no evil, think no evil, and certainly do no evil to the Twins for the remainder of his life. What made this so extraordinary was that after the McCowan case, although there was no outcry in the muted media, there was one thing that they had done by exploiting the jury system that was so serious that it couldn't be ignored.

Since members of the press were so anxious to say nothing that could be construed as criticising either of them, the Kray Twins never got the credit they deserved for having brought about a fundamental change in one of the most important laws of England, a law that had been in existence for at least six hundred years. Rarely had one of the protective pillars of the English legal system been changed for ever with so little discussion or publicity. Thanks to the McCowan case English jury law was abruptly changed – and, thanks largely to the Twins, it was announced that a jury's verdict no longer had to be unanimous but could be settled by a majority. And so, whatever else they'd done, the Twins had made their mark on the country's legal history.

14

Sing, Fuck You, Sing!

WHEN IT FINALLY arrived, the Twins' acquittal from the McCowan case was not entirely unexpected and they made the most of it. Someone had tipped off the press, and as the Twins came down the steps of the Old Bailey the family was out in force to greet them, including Violet and Auntie May and their old grandfather, Cannonball Lee, who was soon boring the reporters with tales of how he had taught the Twins to box. But the star of the occasion was Reg's new fiancée, Frances Shea. While he'd been in prison Reg had proposed and Frances had finally accepted. Now she was there to greet him.

The April sun was shining and for this one brief moment in their lives the pair of them looked truly happy. Unlike Ron, Reg had kept his looks and there was something childlike about Frances with her shy girl's smile and auburn hair. She was not quite the girl next door but she lived with her parents in Ormsby Street, which from Vallance Road is just around the corner. Reg had known her since she was a child and had written to her every day while he'd been on remand. Whatever else it was, his love for her was deeply sentimental. She was his little goddess, his treasured Frankie, and he had courted her and written poems for her and showered her with gifts. Now, having proved his innocence in court, he was free to marry her.

Given the circumstances, the engagement was a natural for the press and the reporters and the press photographers made the most of it. At that moment even the most cynical of them might just have thought that the fates could still be cheated and that the twisted story of the Twins would have its happy ending. But by now there was little chance of that for, as always with the Krays, the subplot was somewhat different from the story in the press.

The Sheas were Irish. The Krays had known them for years and Frances Shea's father, Frank Shea Sr, had worked at the Regency Club as a croupier. The family were all good-looking and at one stage Ron had fancied Frances's brother Frank Shea Jr and had tried – unsuccessfully – to rape him. Coincidentally, it was around this time that Reg first noticed how pretty Frank Shea's little sister Frances had become.

Although by then Ron was openly acknowledging that he was gay, Reg never really did – despite the fact that, as his brother's twin, they shared an identical genetic make-up and their inherited sexual orientation was of course identical. In their teens they had gone for much the same young boys and had had similar affairs. But then had come the period when, with Ron first in prison and then in the mental hospital, Reg had started to enjoy the company of women. He might or he might not have slept with them but as far as Frances was concerned it didn't matter. Frances was very much her own person and had no intention of losing her virginity before there was a wedding ring on her finger.

Even as early as August 1960, when Reg was briefly back in prison, he and Frances seem to have taken it for granted that one day they would marry. But as she made very clear to Reg in one of her letters, she was an old-fashioned girl and had no intention of being hurried.

'I've made up my mind when I want to get married – not next year but the July afterwards. That will give us enough time to get a house built and get the wedding organised properly. We don't want to rush anything, because it's got to last a lifetime.'

This was typical of Frances and from prison Reg had gone along with her – although he used to fantasise about her and what they'd do together after his release. In the letters I have seen, the only hint he gives of anything unusual in his attitude to sex is a casual reference to bondage. 'I have been thinking of a new way of tying you – Ha Ha! – and then tormenting you. Is there anything you are particularly looking forward to?' he asks.

That year, after Reg's release, the two of them had gone to Spain. But Frances hated the sight of blood and didn't care for bullfights, which had always fascinated him. Another year Reg took her to Milan where they spent an evening at La Scala holding hands throughout the most romantic of Puccini's operas, *Madame Butterfly*. One odd feature of these holidays together was that, as Frances made a point of telling her father afterwards, Reg always insisted that they slept in separate rooms. 'I respected Reg for that, and saw him as a good clean-living fellow who looked after my daughter,' Frank Shea Sr remarked. More worldly-wise, his wife Elsie, who had been told by Frank Shea Jr of Ron's behaviour, had formed her own suspicions about Reg from the start.

For the moment, however, in the excitement of the Twins' acquittal, all this seemed unimportant and the Krays had much to celebrate. Back in Bethnal Green they were being hailed as local heroes for their victory over the police. The Twins had bought the Hideaway Club from Hew McCowan at a knockdown price. And Boothby had written to congratulate them as only he could. 'In a way I feel that we have both been vindicated,' he wrote, although it's hard to see how this could have applied to him. This was, in fact, the last that the Twins would ever hear from him, for his life too was changing. He might even have learned his lesson, for soon he would be marrying Wanda Sanna, the convent-educated daughter of a Sardinian import-export dealer. According to Boothby's biographer, his bride, who was thirty-three years his junior, 'realised that there could be no question of children' and they are said to have stayed happily together until his death in 1986. (Rhodes James, p. 408.)

As for Reg's marriage, even Ron appeared to have accepted the idea of it by now. Only a few months earlier, when Reg had brought Frances to Esmeralda's Barn, Ron had been so abusive that a fight had broken out and the Twins had needed to be dragged apart or they might have killed each other. But that was all behind them now and Ron was cheerfulness itself. Apparently delighted with the idea of his brother's marriage, he behaved to Frances like some old gay uncle. 'So you're joinin' the family are you, Frances dear? Hope you'll enjoy it,' he would say whenever he saw her now.

In spite of this, Frances told Reg that she found Ron 'creepy' but he told her not to be so silly. 'Ron has his little ways, but once you get to know him you'll see he has a heart of gold.'

The one member of the family who couldn't hide her feelings was the Twins' mother Violet. Even several years later, after Frances had died, she confided to me that 'Frances was never good enough for my Reggie. When he brought her round to see me she'd just sit there, polishing her nails, and you know what? She couldn't even make us all a cup of tea.'

However, with the rest of the family, especially Grandpa Lee and Auntie May, assuring her how much they loved her, Frances was not particularly concerned about the feelings of her future mother-in-law. What did worry her was the sheer determination of both the Twins to make the wedding such a grand occasion. She knew that her Reggie was famous but until now she'd never realised just *how* famous, and when he promised her the East End's wedding of the year she always said it wasn't what she wanted. 'Reggie, dear, I just want you,' she'd say. But seeing how much he'd set his heart on a grand wedding she finally gave in, as she usually did with Reg, and went along with it.

The one setback to the wedding that did occur was completely unexpected. Without discussing it with Frances beforehand Reg had booked the big red-brick church of St James the Great for the wedding, and she knew how much he wanted Father Hetherington, the priest in charge, to marry them. The Twins had known Father Hetherington since childhood, but when they asked him to officiate he refused. To make matters worse he told them that he hoped they'd not go through with it.

Frances was surprised at how calmly Reg accepted this. All he said was, 'Why, Father? Tell me why.'

'Because I don't think either of you has any notion of what marriage is about. Nor can I see the faintest chance of you finding lasting happiness together. Worse still, if you insist on getting married I fear you'll end up causing lasting harm to each other.'

Frances had never heard anyone talk like this to Reg before and had it been anyone but Father Hetherington there would certainly have been trouble. But Reg controlled himself.

'What do you mean, Father?

'I'm sure you know what I mean, Reg, but I'll say no more.'

'Are you telling us we can't get married, then?' said Frances.

'Not at all. I'm sure Father Foster will be happy to officiate, if you insist. But I cannot.'

When they asked Father Foster, he did agree. Being younger and very friendly with the Twins, he was possibly more broad-minded than Father Hetherington and there was no question of him refusing.

From what Reggie told me later, I'm sure that he saw marriage to Frances as his last chance to escape – from the ties of twinship, from any slur that there might be upon his sexuality and from being taken over totally by Ron. Certainly to start with he thought that pretty Frances would provide a magical escape to a normal life, and he honestly believed that Father

Hetherington was wrong. Like Frances, he might even have thought that love would conquer all.

But, like Father Hetherington, Ron knew quite well that it wouldn't, and because he knew Reg through and through he simply smiled the contented smile of somebody prepared to wait. I'm sure he knew exactly what would happen and was determined that it would. Nothing could ever come between him and Reg, especially not a silly girl like Frankie Shea. Just give Reg time. He'd learn.

In the meantime, in the midst of the excitement following their acquittal, something that would be of considerable significance to the future of the Twins now made its first appearance. Through the publicity created by the wedding, change was in the air.

During the aftermath of the Boothby scandal, followed so swiftly by the Twins' acquittal at the Old Bailey, the news media had found itself in something of a quandary. It was widely known and accepted that the Krays were among the most powerful and dangerous criminals in London. But because of the establishment cover-up, and because Lord Goodman, as he now was, had gagged the press so thoroughly, no one in the media dared say so. It was certainly not possible to describe how the Twins had used Boothby's money to fix the McCowan trial, let alone to hint at the protection rackets, the long-firm frauds, the violence and the Twins' connections with the Mafia. So when, after the acquittal, two smart young journalists, Lewis Chester and Cal McCrystal, interviewed the Twins for an article in the *Sunday Times* they had a problem. Because of the newspaper's fear of libel, they could not refer to the Twins as criminals, still less could they even mention what they did.

Instead, with considerable ingenuity, the two journalists wrote a full-page human interest piece about the Twins, avoiding any reference to crime. Instead, they always referred to

Ron and Reg as 'the two famous sporting twins' who were 'part of the culture of the old East End'. There was no explanation of what the Twins' favourite 'sport' might be but from now on 'East End sporting twins' became the phrase the press invariably adopted when describing them. Equally important, Chester and McCrystal were the first writers to use words like 'myth' and 'legend' when describing why the Kray Twins were suddenly so popular.

This popularity spread to other writers on the *Sunday Times* and a few days later Francis Wyndham, novelist and feature writer in the paper's colour magazine, wrote to the Twins asking for an interview. Never ones to miss a chance for self-promotion, the Twins turned up next day at the *Sunday Times* offices to meet him. It was then that their adventures in the world of upmarket publicity really started.

From the beginning, Wyndham and the Twins got on famously together. They invited him to Vallance Road to meet members of the family, who reminded Wyndham of characters out of Charles Dickens. There was some truth in this and while he was preparing his article for the magazine, David Bailey, who had worked for the paper in the past, was commissioned to take the accompanying photographs.

As an East Ender, born and bred in Leytonstone, Bailey knew about the Krays and got on well with them, so much so that he arranged the photo shoot in the West End studios of *Vogue* fashion magazine, where he often worked. As well as using the studio for his fashion photographs, he sometimes shot his celebrity portraits there as well so at the time it seemed no big deal to him to be taking the Kray Twins there. But something remarkable did happen that day in the studios of *Vogue* magazine when Bailey used his camera to record the moment when the Swinging Sixties came face to face with the two most dangerous criminals in London. The result was one of the most memorable photographs of Bailey's whole career. His portrait finally became the Twins' monument, and forty years on there is still something terribly disquieting in that tortured image of the Twins.

But Bailey's role in the story of the Krays was not over. The *Sunday Times* never used Wyndham's article and rather than waste that double portrait Bailey decided to include it in his 'box of pin-ups', an impressively boxed and packaged limited edition of his prestigious portraits of key celebrities of the 1960s. These included pop stars like the Beatles and Mick Jagger, actors like Peter Sellers and Michael Caine, and models and starlets like Jean Shrimpton and Marianne Faithfull. To include that image of the Twins among such figures enrolled them in the ranks of accredited Sixties celebrities. For the benefit of anyone who was not too sure about the Kray Twins' claim to fame, Francis Wyndham wrote a fulsome piece about them which was printed on the back of their portrait.

The so-called celebrity culture really started in the Sixties. It was very much the product of what Marshall McLuhan called 'the electronic media' and unlike fame, which rested essentially on achievement, celebrity was primarily concerned with image – on being, as Henry James first put it, 'famous for being famous' – hence the importance of so many young photographers in the culture of the Sixties. Hence also the importance of the Bailey portrait at this point in the Twins' rise to fame. It didn't matter that, with the hush-up of the Boothby scandal, nothing of real importance about them could be stated in the press. To go with Bailey's virtuoso portrait of the Twins all that was needed was Francis Wyndham's explanation not of what they did but of why they were celebrities.

Starting from the premise that the East End was like the American Wild West, Wyndham went on to describe the twins as cockney versions of famous outlaws such as Jesse James, and there was a lot of talk of myths and legends and folk heroes. 'To be with the Twins is to enter the atmosphere (laconic, lavish, dangerous) of an early Bogart movie'.

All this was fairly harmless and the Twins of course loved it. For them it was invaluable publicity and it set a very large ball rolling. It was this that worried another photographer who also worked for the *Sunday Times* and who wielded considerably more influence than David Bailey. This was the Queen's new brother-in-law Lord Snowdon. As a young photographer he had lived in the East End where he'd learnt enough about the Twins to strongly disapprove of turning them into Sixties heroes. It was largely thanks to Snowdon's influence that David Bailey's box of pin-ups never found a US publisher.

By now it was time for Reg's wedding. As one might have guessed, Reg had got his way and this really did turn out to be the East End's wedding of the year. And suddenly the Twins were on display, surrounded by a fascinating mix of criminals and celebrities.

They were observing the first law of celebrity which states that 'a celebrity is celebrated for being a celebrity' and they can usually be spotted in the presence of other celebrities – in this case Diana Dors, Joan Littlewood and Tom Driberg, who were all at the wedding.

Another telltale sign of true celebrity is the presence of photographers, in this case the crown prince of Sixties snappers in person who, dressed in a blue velvet suit, drove up in a matching blue Rolls-Royce. David Bailey had recently left his best-known model and girlfriend, Twiggy, and confirmed his own position as a celebrity by marrying a film star, the French actress Catherine de Neuve.

This was the only time since his rise to fame that Bailey condescended to become a wedding photographer, together with Francis Wyndham as his assistant.

But as far as the wedding was concerned, only one person and one alone was in command. As the organ started up the marriage hymn 'Oh Perfect Love, All Love Excelling, the response from the congregation was far from perfect. It was the sort of awkward situation when nobody felt like joining in, and suddenly Ron showed what he really felt about the marriage as he started marching angrily up and down the aisle.

'Sing, fuck you, sing!' he shouted. And as usual when 'the Colonel' gave the orders everyone obeyed.

The reception that followed was at the now notorious Glenrae Hotel in Seven Sisters Road, where not long before the Twins and Mad Teddy had been arrested. But now it was crammed with starlets, gangsters, members of the two families – and Tom Driberg. As for pretty, nervous Frances, she was caught in a situation that she would never understand and a nightmare that she was never going to escape. Because of that unforgiving bond that ruled the Twins, the conflict between them would end up destroying her.

The marriage was a nightmare almost from the start and even the honeymoon was doomed. From his schooldays Reg remembered pictures of the Acropolis overlooking Athens so, wishing to impress his bride, he picked on Athens for their six-day honeymoon. What he didn't know was that the Athens of the 1960s had barely recovered from Greece's civil war and it was not the place to take a girl like Frances. There were no smart shops, no sexy nightclubs, nowhere interesting to go, and naturally the couple didn't speak a word of Greek. Since Frances found it hard to hide her disappointment, so did Reg, and instead of a romantic beginning to their marriage every evening Reg left her in their hotel bedroom while he went out on the town and got completely drunk.

When they returned to London, Reg continued to get everything wrong. Wanting to spoil Frances with a smart West End existence, he rented an apartment in a luxury block near

Marble Arch, but almost from the start Frances hated it. Violet had been right about one thing. Her new daughter-in-law couldn't cook. She also missed her friends. The West End was unfamiliar and she felt lonely and homesick for Bethnal Green. Although he kept telling her he loved her, Reg was miserable and lonely too and was soon drinking more than ever to disguise his inadequacy. He was ten years older than his bride, a homosexual gangster who preferred neat gin to making love to her, and despite all the fuss about the Wedding of the Year the marriage died before it even started.

Somehow they endured four wretched weeks together, staring at the traffic around Marble Arch before they realised that their only hope lay in getting back to the East End. Even now this just might have worked had Reg chosen any other place to live than in the empty flat directly under Ron's at Cedra Court.

I always wondered why he did this, for Reg wasn't totally naive and must have had some idea of what would happen. One can only suppose that, as usual, he was being torn between his longing to escape from Ron and his awareness that he couldn't live without him.

Also, Ron's power as the dominating twin was getting stronger by the day and since the unhappiness and strain of his marriage were simultaneously weakening Reg there was little he could do against him. Every evening Reg and Frances had the same routine. Just before seven Reg would pour himself his first neat glass of Gordon's gin, followed by another, after which he'd disappear upstairs leaving Frances to watch television and go to bed alone. Instead of sleeping, she was often kept awake by the sound of music and male laughter from the flat upstairs.

When Reg finally did return, sometimes as late as three or four in the morning, he was often paralytic and could even be sadistic. He would shout obscenities at her and she told a friend that on one occasion he was actually foaming at the mouth. She insisted that he never hit her but he certainly threatened her with violence. He also warned her that he would hurt members of her family. Knowing how much she feared the sight of blood, he cut his hand and let the blood drip over her. Also knowing how she dreaded guns, he threatened her with one. Sometimes he sobbed and blamed her for the fact that their marriage was unhappy. Once she awoke in the dark in the middle of the night and knew that beside her was her husband and another man.

By now Reg was reverting to a Jekyll and Hyde existence and effectively becoming two quite separate people. In the morning when he woke the husband of the midnight hours had gone and in his place there was the gentle Reg who was once more kind and thoughtful, and for whom nothing was too much trouble. He never seemed to have a hangover, and in the morning he was always sober. As for Ron, although Frances sometimes recognised his voice shouting from above she rarely saw him now except when he passed her on the stairs. Every time this happened his greeting was the same. 'Cheer up, Frances dear. You're lookin' worried.'

In fact she was terrified of Ron by now and understood the power he had over her husband. To one girlfriend she confided her belief that Ronnie had bewitched him. 'Ron possesses him,' she said.

Frances endured eight weeks of misery before returning to her parents. She told her mother that the marriage had become a nightmare. When her mother asked her what she meant, Frances sobbed that her husband was a pervert and was unable to make love to her. The only time he tried to was by pretending that she was a boy and attempting to take her from behind. 'I feel defiled,' she sobbed. 'What can I do? No one else will ever want me.'

I once asked a cousin of the Sheas why Frances didn't leave Bethnal Green, and start a new life somewhere else. 'How could she?' he replied. 'Bethnal Green was the only place she knew and her family was all she had. Besides, Reg had warned her that if she ever ran away from him he'd always follow her and find her.'

I'm sure that this was true, but I'm also sure that there was more to it than that and that both she and Reg had now become dependent on each other. In years to come she would continue to obsess him from beyond the grave. Otherwise it's hard to understand what happened next. No sooner was Frances safely back in Ormsby Street with her family than Reg started coming round to see her as he used to do when they were courting. And since her parents wouldn't have him in the house, he'd stand patiently outside on the pavement until Frances opened her bedroom window. Then they'd talk, often for an hour or so. Before long this was becoming something of a habit and hardly an evening passed without it happening. But the marriage itself was clearly over, and with it vanished any hope Reg ever had of escaping from his fate. As for Frances she was henceforth at the mercy of the Twins.

15

Killing Cornell

WHILE REG'S MARRIAGE was collapsing, crime was booming and the summertime of 1965 was full of promise for the Twins. The police were keeping clear of them, no other gang would challenge them, and having benefited so dramatically from the cover-up of the Boothby case the Twins had finally become what they liked to call themselves – 'the untouchables' of the London underworld.

To begin with they appeared all set to take advantage of this chance that fate and the Establishment had given them. They already had their network of protection throughout London, bringing in steady money from the clubs and casinos that they 'minded'. Their long-firm frauds were set to bring them in much more. Fresh rackets were increasing, and no other gang in London cared or dared to tangle with them. By now the name of Kray had taken on a more specific meaning. What other criminals had ever done what they had done, seeing off Scotland Yard, winning a major trial at the Old Bailey, and boasting influential friends in parliament?

The Boothby case had also given them extraordinary prestige within the underworld, not only in Britain but also in America and on the Continent. It was there for the taking. In Britain organised crime was in its infancy but with this boost from the Establishment and effective freedom from interference by the law no other gang in London was remotely like them. Thanks to the threat contained within that one commanding syllable, the name of Kray had suddenly become the most important logo in the underworld.

It was rather like a franchise, and since they were its undisputed owners the Twins really didn't need to do a lot themselves. No longer was there any need to court unnecessary risk, either from the law or from other criminals. Their reputation alone was so impressive that others would pay for their support. If they lacked experience they had advisers who could help them.

The most important of these was still Leslie 'The Brain' Payne, the king of the long-firm frauds, who was as anxious as ever to work with them and build his empire based on fraud. In conjunction with his ever-faithful accountant Freddie Gore, he'd recently set up Carston Securities, with smart new offices in Portland Place. Payne was an interesting case on his own account, as part of the new breed of dedicated entrepreneurs that the enterprise culture of the Sixties had thrown up. In different circumstances he could easily have been mixing with equally plausible but outwardly respectable financiers of the day whose own versions of the long-firm fraud, politely known as asset stripping, had given birth to so many of the bloated fortunes of that wonderfully corrupt decade.

One of the more intriguing aspects of organised crime is the way it mimics global capitalism (and sometimes vice versa) so that a crime in one country can have repercussions in another. At around the time that Reg had been making his marriage vows before Father Foster in St James the Great, an armed gang was staging a successful raid upon the Royal Bank of Canada in Montreal. It was a professional job, and the gang had known exactly what they wanted. Along with over thirty thousand dollars in cash, fifty thousand dollars' worth of instantly negotiable bearer bonds had also disappeared. Six weeks later the same gang struck again, lifting a hundred thousand dollars' worth of debentures and bearer bonds from a bank in West Ontario. During that summer further bank raids with a similar trademark followed in other parts of Canada, as a result of which over a million dollars' worth of securities (worth around ten million dollars today) had vanished. For criminals the joy of these securities lay in the fact that they were easily and instantly negotiable, but although the Canadian police and the FBI had spent a lot of time and effort watching for somebody to cash them somewhere in America no one did.

It didn't take much brainpower to work out that the bank raids had been masterminded by the Mafia and that the stolen securities were being held by a Mafia-backed syndicate in New York that specialised in laundering large quantities of hot capital. By now they had several million dollars' worth of stolen bearer bonds on their hands but knowing that they were under observation, they were wary of marketing them in North America.

The previous autumn Ron's visa trouble in New York which stopped him meeting Meyer Lansky had been unfortunate. When Ronnie failed to turn up for his appointment the Mafia's boss of bosses lost interest in the Krays, which had repercussions on their standing with the Mafia in London. But for the support of their old friend George Raft, the Twins might well have lost their monthly pension 'minding' the Colony Sporting Club in Mayfair.

But now the Twins' triumphant outcome of the McCowan case had changed all that and none of their Mafia friends had missed the way they fixed their trial and blackmailed Lord Boothby into pleading for them in the House of Lords. Even in America it would have been hard to find two gangsters with such influence in politics. From now on the Twins could do no wrong, as far as London-based members of the Mafia were concerned. There could be no argument over who should deal with those stolen bearer bonds in Europe.

Not that either Ron or Reg could do this on their own, but they had their ideal character who could, their 'man with the briefcase', Leslie Payne. Following the collapse of his big Enugu scam and what he saw as the unnecessary loss of Esmeralda's Barn, Payne had been unusually pushed for money and, master fraudster that he was, had been using the Twins' name and reputation as backing for a series of elaborate long-firm frauds. As always seemed to happen with Payne 'The Brain' these frauds had worked without a hitch and had brought in badly needed cash when he and the Twins both needed it. But humdrum long-firm frauds, however profitable, were beneath a man of Leslie Payne's sophistication and he enjoyed the challenge of dealing with stolen international bearer bonds on behalf of the US Mafia.

Within a day or two of getting clearance from America Payne was on a plane to Montreal, returning with a sample of $80,000 worth of stolen bonds in his famous briefcase for the Twins to process. Such was the magic of the name of Kray, combined with the silver tongue of Leslie Payne, that the representatives from the New York syndicate had been happy to accept a mere $5,000 on account and a few days later Payne cashed the bonds through a friend in a London broking house at their face value – less a discreet discount for the Twins' services.

For the Twins all this was easy money, and as further deals followed the Mafia began regarding them as trusted associates. More than ever now, the Twins' name could guarantee that Mafia-backed clubs and gambling junkets would be free from interference by the law. As for rival competition, no other gang in London would have risked trouble from the Twins.

More European business with Payne followed, and the Mafia regarded the Krays as the gang they did business with. They could rely on them to ensure there'd be no trouble for their plans to put more money into investments in new clubs and bring more gamblers flying in from all over America.

Ron had more grandiose ambitions. Together with his paranoia went the instincts of a genuine tycoon – the love of power, the passion to control everyone around him, and above all the monomaniac's obsession with himself. Like the true psychopath he was, for him reality and fantasy were one and the fact he was working with the Mafia and entering the league of big-time international racketeers was simply an expression of his uncontrolled ambitions, as were the other trappings he was planning – the private plane, the widespread foreign interests, and a house like Billy Hill's in southern Spain.

So what went wrong? In the first place Reg was diverted by his guilt and worries over Frances. In the second place, Ron suddenly made up his mind to ditch Les Payne, which proved a serious mistake. Payne knew too much to have around them as an enemy and, more dangerous still, he was not afraid of them. Having survived the battle of Monte Cassino in the infantry he was not particularly concerned by anything the Krays could do to him, and so he retired, lay low, and waited for the wind to change – as he knew it would.

To compound their error over Leslie Payne there was the man the Twins adopted in his place. What had happened was that after several months of trouble-free profit from the sale of bearer bonds throughout Europe there had been problems with the certification of some of the stolen bonds. Someone had suggested that Alan Bruce Cooper might be able to assist them and they had agreed.

Instead of rational Reg it was rampant Ron who now began to take control and whose ideas increasingly dictated what would happen. The Twins had London in their grasp. The mob needed them – and in their eyes the Krays had proved themselves the best in London.

★

At this time Ron was relying more than ever on his favourite clairvoyant, fat Dot Brown of Walthamstow, wife to the Firm's strongman, the even more enormous Tommy 'The Bear' Brown. According to Dot Ron was Attila the Hun reincarnated. Once a week he'd visit her and she would put curses on any new name on his hate list.

Dot also reassured him that, with his spirit guide protecting him, he was not only untouchable but unkillable as well. But instead of making him feel more secure this actually increased his chronic insecurity. At the same time his mental state was worsening, with psychotic mood swings alternating with days of black despair and periods of grandiose excitement. It was then that he truly felt invulnerable, as indeed he almost was. In his lucid moments when he was being driven by his voices he could be particularly dangerous. As a homicidal maniac his sense of freedom from the attentions of the police had increased his wilder feelings of omnipotence. But these were matched by those periods of black despair, particularly once he started drinking. To remain stable he should have stayed off alcohol and adhered to his prescribed intake of Stematol. 'If you take drink and drugs together on the scale you're doing you'll either kill yourself – or someone else,' Doc Blasker warned him.

Because of the twins' shared psychology, Ron's growing schizophrenia increasingly affected Reg. In the past, throughout their constant fights and disagreements, Reg had always managed to control him in the end. But now the strain and worry over Frances were seriously affecting Reg as well and upsetting whatever balance still remained between them. Reg did all he could to stop Ron's growing madness interfering with their business. The Hideaway Club, renamed El Morocco, continued to make good money, the Mafia connection prospered, fresh rackets were increasing, and no other gang in London cared or dared to tangle with them. So as the new year dawned in 1966 it looked as if everything could still work out. The Twins appeared not just untouchable but immoveable as well, so firmly embedded were they in the London underworld. And there they would have stayed – if Ron's inner voices hadn't started telling him that the time had come to kill someone.

Until now, Ron had practised almost every known form of violence except murder. He had branded Lenny Hamilton on the face, he had shot Teddy Berry and Albert Donoghue in the legs, he had cut more people in more parts of their anatomy than even he could possibly remember. He had smashed opponents on the head with iron bars and disfigured them with broken bottles. The only thing he hadn't done was kill – until the evening of 9 March 1966 when he decided to repair this ultimate omission.

For one of the most celebrated murders of the century, which three years later would earn Ron thirty years in prison, it is strange that the killing of the minor East End gangster George Cornell should still be something of a mystery.

The Twins had first met him in a military detention centre back in 1954 when they were all trying to get out of the army. In those days Cornell was still called Myers and he came from one of the poorest Irish-Jewish families in Watney Street who had always been the chosen enemies of the Krays. Over the years he had become a big, bald, bull-like man who still enjoyed a fight with anyone but a few years earlier, when he had changed his name from Myers to Cornell, he'd made it clear that he'd left Watney Street behind for good. Although he continued in the world of minor villainy he 'ducked and dived' to make a living.

For the last few days Ron had been in the middle of a serious depression and Reg persuaded him to stay at Vallance Road where Violet could look after him. As often happened when he was depressed Ron was soon ignoring Doc Blasker's warnings about mixing alcohol with medication, and since Reg couldn't stop him drinking he asked two of their recently recruited young Scots gangsters from the Gorbals, Ian Barrie and 'Scotch Jack' Dixon, to look after him. They were doing this in Reg's absence late one afternoon when somebody turned up with the news that he had just seen George Cornell drinking in The Blind Beggar, a nearby pub on the far side of Whitechapel High Street.

This was not of any great importance. The Beggar was Cornell's local and he was probably waiting to meet someone for a drink. But in the desperate state that Ron was in, even this scrap of gossip was enough to fire his suspicions. Had Reg been there he would have told Ron to forget it and not be stupid and that would have been an end to it. But since Reg was not around, Ron saw his chance – and took it.

He always kept his favourite gun, a 9 mm German army Luger automatic, concealed beneath loose floorboards in his bedroom and he knew that Barrie was also armed. Since Dixon's car was parked outside in Vallance Road the three of them could be at The Blind Beggar within ten minutes. Then, while Ron and Ian Barrie went inside to do what needed to be done, Scotch Jack could be waiting outside at the wheel to guarantee their getaway. No sooner had Ron worked all this out than he put it into practice.

When the three of them drive up to The Blind Beggar it is shortly after opening time and the pub is all but empty. The barmaid, who to guard her anonymity will always be referred to as 'Mrs X', has just served Cornell his first pint of the evening and stands behind the the bar, polishing glasses, when the street door opens and Barrie enters, firing two warning shots into the ceiling. Mrs X dives for the cellar but her colleague, Patsy Quill the barman, is caught by the open door as Ron Kray pushes past him. Gun in hand, Ron marches in that jerky zombie-like walk of his in a straight line to where Cornell is sitting. All this happens so swiftly that there is nothing that Cornell can do except remark, 'Well, look who's 'ere' as Ron lifts the gun towards him, his finger on the trigger.

Either from vanity or haste Ron hasn't thought to bring his spectacles, and since he is near-sighted he needs to get in close before he fires the single shot at point-blank range into the centre of Cornell's forehead that kills him. For a moment Ron stands where he is, staring at Cornell who slides slowly off his chair. Then he turns on his heel and, zombie-like as ever, marches back the way he came, leaving Cornell dying on the floor with his final glass of beer untasted.

Only when she's sure that Ron has gone does Mrs X emerge from the cellar to see if there is anything she can do to help her former customer. But all that anyone can do for Cornell now is call an ambulance. By the time it arrives Ron is safely back at Vallance Road with his two accomplices, neither of whom, to tell the truth, has the faintest notion why Ron did it.

As murders go, almost everything about that killing was distinctly odd, even Ron's choice of weapon. The Luger automatic he had kept beneath the floorboards was not the gun that any self-respecting gangster would have chosen for this sort of operation. A field weapon of the German military in the second world war, the Luger is both cumbersome and difficult to conceal, but it has always been popular with collectors who make a fetish of weaponry and guns, as Ron did himself. ('I like the feeling of guns, although I am usually happier with fists or a knife,' he confesses somewhere in his memoirs.) Being essentially a military weapon it also gives a sense of soldierly importance to those who use it, which probably explains why Ronnie, 'the Colonel', liked it. It was also the weapon of choice for Nazi execution squads engaged in killing Jews in Eastern Europe, and much about that cool, robotic killing of George Cornell suggests an execution. There had been no preceding fight or disagreement, the victim put up no resistance, and in his role of executioner Ron placed himself at no greater risk than a hangman at a hanging.

The *Oxford Dictionary* defines an execution as 'to put to death in pursuance of a sentence', which sounds like a fairly accurate description of Ron's behaviour as he pumped that single risk-free bullet into the brain of George Cornell. And from then on everything he did became increasingly macabre. If what he told his nephew Ronnie Hart is true, while standing watching Cornell's lifeblood jetting from his forehead he experienced an orgasm, and during the journey back to Vallance Road he was also physically sick. He got back to find that Reggie had returned, and on discovering what had happened Reg was beside himself with fury.

'You silly useless bastard, what the fuck d'you think you're up to? shouted Reg. It was a question to which, on this occasion, Ron could make no answer.

But despite his anger Reg was cool enough to know that something needed to be done before Ron's behaviour brought disaster to everyone concerned. Just how stupid could his idiotic brother be? After all that he and Ron had been through in the last few months, and then to play into the arms of the law with a pointless, idiotic crime like this – and in broad daylight too.

But Reg also knew that unless he acted quickly he and Ron would be spending their foreseeable future in prison. Ron would go down for murder and the police would have no problem framing Reg as an accessory. And all this aggravation just to kill George Cornell, who was causing no trouble to anyone.

One of many useful arts that Reg had learned from all the years he'd been looking after Ron was damage limitation, thanks to which he acted now with great efficiency. Ron is ordered off to have a shower and a change of clothing – 'and for fuck's sake make it quick.' Violet, who has emerged from her kitchen, is told exactly what to say to the police if they come round, as they're sure to do. ('You know nothing and have seen nothing.') Finally a reminder to Ron to not forget his pills.

One thing Reg knows for certain is that in his present hyper-active state Ron must be kept firmly out of everybody's way. Luckily Reg knows an understanding publican in Walthamstow with a flat in a run-down house in the Lee Bridge Road where Ron can stay for a few days without anyone knowing.

The publican promises to look after him, and this is where Ron stays in hiding for the next few days with members of the Firm in constant attendance, drinking heavily and reliving every moment of the killing. To keep his courage up he plays the wartime speeches of his hero, Winston Churchill. This must be one of the weirdest scenes of all Ron's homicidal fantasies but it can't seriously explain why on that evening in early March it suddenly became so desperately important for him to murder George Cornell.

Various motives were subsequently produced, few of which made any sense The explanation from the prosecution at the Twins' Old Bailey trial in 1969, encouraged by admirers anxious to endow Ron's action with at least a smattering of glory, was that the killing was Ron's belated contribution to the gang warfare that had been going on for quite some time between the Kray Firm and the Richardsons. There had been a number of 'incidents' between the Twins and the Richardsons' henchman 'Mad' Frankie Fraser, including a late-night con-frontation at the Astor Club in Mayfair that nearly, but not quite, ended in violence.

But neither the Twins nor any members of their Firm had been involved in the so-called 'fracas' at a club in Catford which had ended in a shoot-out between the Richardsons and a local gang in which several of the Richardsons were wounded and one of the local men was killed. Nor was George Cornell involved.

All that *had* happened was that on one occasion George Cornell was supposed to have shouted out to Ron that he was a 'fat poof'. Ron told me this himself, but in fact this wasn't the real reason why the murder happened and it was not until many years later when Ron was safely locked away in Broadmoor that he finally explained why, all those years before, he had felt he had to kill Cornell. During a visit his close friend Wilf Pine asked him why he did it and received the nearest that Ron ever came to giving anyone a proper answer.

From what Ron told Wilf Pine, the killing really had its origins in an incident that had happened many years before when the Twins had been 'minding' an illicit card game in an upstairs room at the Green Dragon pub in Hackney. That evening Ron, for once, was on his own. He also admitted he was drunk, and when he arrived to find Cornell was there all the old antagonism between Watney Street and Vallance Road flared up between them. After the insults came a fight, which ended with Cornell giving Ron what he himself described as 'the hiding of my life'.

'I'll be honest with you, Wilf,' he said. 'Cornell kicked the shit out of me that night.' If Reg had been there too, or if Ron had not been drunk, this could not have happened. But since it did, and since it was one of the very few occasions when Ron received a beating rather than inflicting one, it stayed in his memory for ever.

'Afterwards, of course, I wanted to go after him, like next morning, but Reg put a block on it. "Don't go getting involved," he said. We were getting a good pension from the place from Bill Ackerman who ran the Green Dragon at the time. So Reg told me, "Ron, don't fuck it up by going for Cornell. It just ain't worth it."

'So I didn't do anything about it. But over the years, every time I saw Cornell he gave me a sneer and said something sarcastic. Yeah, once he did call me a fat poof, and a couple of other things I won't repeat. But it was always a case of wrong place, wrong time for me to retaliate and it meant that Cornell was somehow always on my mind. I don't know if I was afraid of him or what, but as the thought of that beatin' kept on coming back to me I suppose I might have been. Fear can make you do funny things. Then, after I heard about the Richardsons' fight at Catford, I wasn't at my best. I know now that my pills weren't working, And when I was told that Cornell was just around the corner at the Beggar, I could see him coming round to Vallance Road and making a name for himself by trying to kill all of us unless I stopped him. Luckily, I had a gun and Reg wasn't there to stop me, so I took the chance and was away and did it and was back again, just like that.

'And that was how Cornell got killed. And you know, Wilf, the funny thing is that it worked. After that I didn't have to remember being beaten by him any more. Even now when I think about him, all I can see is his fucking head spurtin' blood instead.'

This account of Cornell's killing matches what we know, and certainly by early 1966 Ron was becoming increasingly deranged. Later he would admit as much in his memoirs. 'I didn't know it then, but I think it was my mental illness, my paranoia. I just couldn't stop myself hurting people, especially if I thought they were slighting me or plotting against me' – which also applies to Ron's obsession with Cornell as he described it to Wilf Pine.

In practical gangland terms the killing of Cornell accomplished less than nothing, and was little more than a textbook killing by a homicidal schizophrenic. But by giving the Twins a new and authentic role as murderers it became important in their rapidly developing mythology.

It was now that murder took its place in the Twins' ongoing narrative and linked up with the myths that those they knew had been spinning round them for so long. From now on a veneer of homicidal glamour started to obscure the banality of the Twins' everyday existence.

All this was very different from the succession of highly profitable and efficiently organised crimes that Reg had hoped to build around the fact that they were untouchable. But from now on the two of them would be involved in a round of crazy killings that would do little for their criminal careers but would guarantee their places in the world of myth and legend as their real world descended into nightmare.

Had the Twins wanted further proof of their status as 'untouchables' they only had to witness Scotland Yard's attempts to catch Cornell's killer. By now it was an open secret, whispered in the pubs of Whitechapel and Bethnal Green, that Ronnie Kray had done it. Finally this reached Scotland Yard and led to a visit from its star detective Commander Tommy Butler who summoned the Twins to an identity parade before Mrs X at the Commercial Road police station.

But Reg by then had been in touch with the East End's own Mr Fixit, 'Red-faced' Tommy Pumley, who had had a word or two with Patsy Quill and Mrs X, explaining that if they knew what was good for them and so on. They were both East Enders so he didn't have to spell out the consequences.

It must have been a harrowing experience, particularly for Mrs X. After seeing one of her customers killed in front of her she now found herself face to face again with the man who did it. Confronted with those dead black eyes of Ron's she found it hard to stop her tears but she never faltered. Drying her eyes, she told Commander Butler that she was sorry but this had been a dreadful time for her and she had never had a memory for faces. And no, she couldn't recognise anyone among the six men before her as the one who murdered George Cornell.

After which the great Commander Butler saw no further point in remaining in the East End any longer and was driven back to Scotland Yard, leaving the badlands of Bethnal Green and the Twins who ruled them to their own devices

Soon after this Billy Hill decided that the Twins might be unwise to push their luck too far and that the time had come for them to take a little holiday. As usual he had plans for them – but not if they were going down for murder. So he suggested that they might enjoy a few days as his guests in Morocco.

Billy Hill had been getting to know Morocco rather well. From his house in southern Spain it was easy to take the ferry over to Tangier where he had made a lot of friends. Some were criminals and some were not, but one thing that never failed to impress him in Tangier was the availability of heroin and marijuana. In Morocco they had always grown it and called it hashish, and almost everyone he knew either smoked it or enjoyed it in one way or another. He didn't care for it himself but he had discovered that already there was quite a lot of hashish being smuggled from Morocco over to Europe via southern Spain, and thence to London where the craze for it was only just beginning, particularly among the younger set who already frequented Marrakesh.

As for the Twins, it was during this holiday in Tangier that they became involved in one of the most surreal encounters of the Sixties. Whilst they were there three of the Rolling Stones – Mick Jagger, Brian Jones and Keith Richard – had also been on holiday in Morocco with Anita Pallenberg, Marianne Faithfull and the Twins' surprising fan, the fashionable art dealer Robert 'Groovy Bob' Fraser. This was the occasion when Anita had suddenly abandoned the Stones' guitarist Brian Jones in favour of another member of the group, Keith Richard, and during the first days of their new romance the loving pair had driven off from Marrakesh to Tangier with 'Groovy Bob' as chaperone. Anita described what happened in her diary.

She, Keith and Robert would go off on their own, wandering around the Kasbah and on the beach. One day they encountered two men walking along the beach in suits, looking like the Blues Brothers. It was of course the Kray Twins. Anita recounts how Tangier was a place where everyone went to get away, including gang members. In those days she'd heard all about the people the Twins had nailed so immediately imagined something horrific had occurred. Robert knew them both and approached them to ask why they were there. 'Oh, we're on holiday,' they replied. But Anita Pallenberg was closer to the truth than she imagined.

16

Exit the Axeman

B Y NOW THE Twins had reached a point where their lives were changing fast and, as Ron's madness grew, Reg's problem was to keep so many different shows upon so many roads. First and foremost came what Reg was good at, 'doing the business' and keeping the money rolling in from the rackets he'd been busily creating, like the long-firm frauds, the currency scams and the European sales of stolen securities, not to mention the 'pensions' from the clubs and businesses that they protected.

As well as keeping all this business going, early in 1966 Reg became actively involved in acquiring a fresh interest in various West End gaming clubs to take the place of Esmeralda's Barn. Had Reg been left to get on with this in cooperation with Leslie Payne things could still have been fine. And had he not merely listened to the advice of Billy Hill but been able to build on what he told him, who knows what Reggie might have done. There was just a chance that he might have even sorted out his life with Frances instead of stuffing her with yet more pills from Doc Blasker and leaving it too late to get her into hospital.

All of this could just have happened if it hadn't been for Ron. But then, if it hadn't been for Ron and his erratic bouts of madness there'd have been little to recall about the Twins today: no legends, no iconic photographs, no British gangster movies, none of the myths surrounding these two celebrity criminals to liven up the image of the Swinging Sixties. Without Ron's madness and the ensuing killings it would have been like Jack the Ripper without *his* murders. Which gives the strange, sick tale of Frank Mitchell, also known as 'The Mad Axeman', a special place in the twisted saga of the Twins.

Much of the fascination of this whole disastrous affair comes from the way it started off as one of those highly publicised good deeds that the Krays made such a meal of. But, as Gore Vidal once said, 'No good deed goes unpunished,' particularly a good deed by the Krays, which in this case ended up killing the recipient.

It was Ron's combination of homicidal arrogance with his abject fear and bouts of wildest fantasy that had a way of leading him and those around him up so many dangerous paths. And what marked him out from most other paranoid schizophrenics and made his flights of fantasy so memorable was not only the determination with which he pursued them but the way he ended up imposing them on Reg and the rest of the Firm by force of will. In the process it was Ron's unpredictable behaviour that became the source of much of his charisma, together with the positively Gothic shroud of mystery that dangerous madmen often weave around them. Certainly in the Mitchell case it was the strange psychotic mess of one of Ron's wilder excursions into wilful unreality which lay behind the waking nightmare that he imposed not only on himself but on all around him in the closing days of 1966.

If you compare what followed with the Twins' artful exploitation of the Boothby scandal just two years earlier, not to mention the fixing of the McCowan trial soon after that, it's clear that things were going very wrong indeed in Krayland as Reg began to lose control and crazy Ron took over.

The Twins had known Frank Mitchell for almost a decade, ever since Ron met him in Wandsworth Prison back in 1959 and fell

in love with him. Knowing Ron, it's usually assumed that there
was some sort of homosexual relationship but I've seen no
evidence for this and it would seem unlikely. Mitchell was
strongly heterosexual and Ron was attracted to teenage boys,
not to grown men. But what did arouse Ron's deep devotion
was that Mitchell represented almost everything he dreamed of
being – tall, good-looking, and so strong that he could lift up
two men by their belts until they touched the ceiling. There was
also much about him with which Ron could identify. Like Ron
he had a way of turning violent when threatened. But in
Mitchell's case there had been no Reg around to look after him
and from his earliest teens Mitchell had been in and out of
Borstal. Thereafter he had been confined almost continually to
one institution or another, ending up in Broadmoor. It was
when he escaped and threatened an elderly couple with an axe,
that the press gave him the title that had dogged him ever since
– 'The Mad Axeman'.

Not that it was that far wrong. Mitchell had been certified
insane while still in Broadmoor, but when his case came up for
trial the judge ruled him fit to plead and promptly sentenced
him to indefinite life imprisonment as a danger to society. By
the time Ron met him at Wandsworth he had become
thoroughly institutionalised and was a menace to everyone,
himself included. His strength made it impossible to restrain
him. He was impervious to pain and had been birched – and
later flogged with the cat-o'-nine-tails – for violent attacks on
prison staff.

All of which impressed Ron greatly and he insisted on
making Mitchell the star beneficiary of the Twins' 'Aways
Society' which had been looking after him with money and
attention ever since. When Mitchell was accused of the
attempted murder of a fellow prisoner in Wandsworth, the
Twins arranged for Reggie's own barrister, pretty Nemone
Lethbridge, to represent him and their London tailor made him

a suit so that he looked his best in court. Thanks to this – or, more probably, to the way the Twins put the frighteners on any prisoner who might have testified against him – Mitchell was acquitted. None of this brought him any closer to the one thing he had set his heart on – a definite release date – but from now on Mitchell worshipped both the Twins, especially Ronnie, as his salvation.

Sometime after his trial an important change in Mitchell's status did occur. He was moved to Dartmoor, and while he was in the prison that had always been regarded as the grimmest in the country he seems to have been as happy as he ever would be. Dartmoor Prison had been changing and a sympathetic governor took an interest in Mitchell's case, promising him that if he behaved himself he would do what he could to get him the release date that he craved.

So Frank Mitchell became a model prisoner. He was given the blue armband of a 'trusty' and ended up with other prisoners working on the moors. The prison staff humoured him, his fellow prisoners admired his physique, and the officer in charge turned a blind eye when they visited a pub on the moor when their work was over and Frank spent money from the Krays to buy them all a drink. Part Romany, Mitchell had a way with horses and used to ride the moorland ponies. He also had a way with women and did much the same with the young school-teacher from a nearby village who became infatuated with him. But he was still existing in a penal limbo, and when the Governor's promises about a release date failed to materialise he began complaining in his letters to the Twins.

Then, in the spring of 1966, something unexpected happened. Reg and Frances went on a weekend trip to Devon, which suggests that something of their old relationship survived and they still cared for one another. But inevitably the trip was also an excuse to visit Ron's old friend Frank Mitchell. The meeting went well, with Reg giving Mitchell news about his hero Ron and the other members of the family, and Mitchell going on at Reg about his one obsession – his release date, and the time the governor was taking to obtain it.

Reg did his best to reassure him, saying that he and Ron would not forget him and would do everything possible to further his release. Above all, Frank must keep his spirits up and stay out of trouble. In the meantime, he and Ron would make their friends visit him regularly.

'But what about Ron? When will he come and see me?' Mitchell asked.

'Soon. But you know what Ron is. Always something different on his plate.'

'But promise he will come.'

Reg promised, and the visit ended with Mitchell giving Frances a velvet-lined jewel box that somebody had made for him in the prison workshop. Afterwards Reg was happy with the way that Frank and Frances seemed to understand each other.

Afterwards, of course, Ron never kept the promise that Reg had made on his behalf but several members of the Firm did make the four-hour drive from London down to Dartmoor in the months that followed. These included 'Scotch Jack' Dixon, who had acted as Ron's chauffeur when he shot Cornell, and 'Big Albert' Donoghue, a powerful and taciturn Irishman whom Ron had recently recruited to the Firm. And, as ever, Mad Teddy also went, getting on so well with Mitchell that they started up a regular correspondence. This continued all that summer, and in all Mitchell's letters one theme and one alone emerged. The governor was not sticking to his promise over his release date, and he couldn't stand the situation any longer.

On hearing this, Ron became distressed and told Reg that something must be done. Reg advised doing nothing, saying that anything they did do could only make the situation worse. Like many prisoners before him Frank must be patient and do his time like anybody else. At first Ron seems to have agreed. Then, as often happened now, he changed his mind. Without telling Reg he sent Mad Teddy down to Dartmoor with a message. For the time being Frank should keep his mouth shut, but the Twins had a plan. When the time was right they'd tell him what it was. Whatever happened, Frank would soon be free.

I once asked Reg how he and Ron reached this disastrous decision but he instantly clammed up, which was understandable. Still, various reasons for the springing of Frank Mitchell were subsequently suggested. Albert Donoghue, who was to play a key part in the escape, was convinced that Ron wanted Mitchell out to deal with a former ally of the Richardsons called Terry Swayling but this struck me as improbable. The Twins never had a problem getting people hurt – there was no need to get Mitchell out of jail to do it for them.

When I wrote *The Profession of Violence*, I suggested that the freeing of Frank Mitchell started as an attempt to offset unfavourable underworld publicity following the Cornell murder, and I still think there was something in this. Around this time the Twins were becoming unusually aware of their public image and from watching all those Warner Brothers gangster movies they had picked up the notion that gangsters don't desert their buddies when they land in trouble. I know that Ron felt this about Mitchell. But the truth is that their motives for this whole affair have long remained a mystery and it's only recently that I've discovered what I now believe to be the answer.

One must remember that freeing Frank Mitchell was essentially Ron's idea, and that he had often been reminded of the similarities between Mitchell's plight and his own in the Long Grove mental hospital ten years earlier. The similarities were indeed quite striking. Like Ronnie, Mitchell had been certified insane and was having to endure the fate that Ronnie had always dreaded while in prison – imprisonment without a release date. And what struck me over Ron's plan to release him was that it turned out to be a virtual carbon copy of what happened after Ron's own escape from Long Grove which Reg had organised back in 1958.

Ron had convinced himself that all Frank had to do was to copy his example. Since Frank was working on the moors it would be easier to spring him than it had been when Ron and Reg had swapped places to escape from Long Grove. And as soon as Frank was free there'd be no problem.

Ron and Reg could easily arrange for members of the Firm to look after him once he was safely tucked away somewhere in the country, as they had when Ron himself had been hiding up in Geoff Allen's caravan. If Ron could do it so could Frank – lie low, take things easy, and cause no trouble to anyone. Then after several months in hiding, when he'd proved his sanity by keeping out of trouble, Frank could peacefully surrender to the authorities and get a release date, just as Ron had done. If it worked for Ron, why not for Frank?

Knowing that Reg was sure to disagree with his idea, as he often did these days, Ron talked it over first with Teddy Smith who, as usual, eagerly supported him. Since Teddy saw himself as the Firm's self-appointed writer in residence he also promised to organise a media campaign and help Frank write letters to the press to ask for a release date. Teddy had an even brighter notion. He was still very much in touch with his old lover Tom Driberg. With his Labour government in power, Tom was more influential now than ever and he owed the Twins a considerable favour for their discretion in the Boothby business. With the support of the media and a helping hand from the influential Driberg, Frank's troubles could be over sooner than anyone expected.

The more Ron thought about it, the more convinced he was that the time had come for him and Reg to do all they could to get their old friend out of prison. When finally he told his brother, Reg, as he'd expected, disagreed strongly. But one can see how weak Reg's position had become and how difficult he was finding it to stand up against Ron's inescapable obsessions. Not for the first time, for the sake of peace Reg ended up agreeing. In essence the plan was based entirely on what Ronnie had done when faced with the authorities over *his* mental problems – help Mitchell to escape, keep him at liberty long enough to get him decertified, and finally, at some future date, persuade him to surrender. Who knew, people might even praise the Twins, and Ronnie in particular, for acting so public-spiritedly to right a wrong inflicted on a badly treated friend.

What nobody seems to have pointed out to Ron was one important difference between the two cases. Ron had been virtually unknown when Reg got him out of Long Grove, and six months later he was able to surrender and return to prison with minimal publicity. With Mitchell this would clearly be impossible. By christening him the 'Mad Axeman' the media had made him one of the most notorious prisoners in the country. Once he had escaped he would terrify anyone who came in contact with him and when he surrendered there would be vast publicity. Those involved would find themselves charged with a serious offence and would almost certainly end up in prison. Far from helping Mitchell this would leave him further than ever from release and might well ensure that he stayed inside for ever. For what Ron failed to understand was that the outside world – and in particular the world of judges and policemen – did not think and feel as he did, and that what he saw as a good turn to a badly treated comrade others would regard as a serious criminal offence, releasing a dangerous psychopath upon the public.

Reg did tell me some years later that he tried his best to

dissuade Ron but, as was happening more than ever now, he found it hard to get through to him and soon gave up. When their brother Charlie learned about the plan, he was even more emphatic in his opposition. When Ron asked for his assistance, he refused to get involved.

'You don't care about your friends like I do,' muttered Ron. 'You don't believe in loyalty to your own. Frank is one of us, and you won't risk anything to save him.'

During these arguments Ron often brought Mad Teddy in to back him up. 'I'll help him write the sort of letters that will get results. What Frank needs is publicity. Make everyone understand what the poor guy's suffered. He's been birched. He's had the cat-o'-nine-tails. He's been inside for eighteen years, and they treat him like an animal.'

Against arguments like these Reg didn't stand a chance. He could only go along with them, particularly now, for he had too much on his mind with the way his personal life was going. He was becoming deeply worried about Frances, and rather than argue he left Ron and Teddy Smith to worry over Frank Mitchell.

Early that November, Teddy Smith paid one last visit to Dartmoor, with a message from Ronnie. Frank was not to to worry about his release date any more. His escape was fixed for 12 December. Which meant that two madmen, Ronnie Kray and Teddy Smith, had finally decided on a half-baked plan to save another madman, Frank Mitchell.

With Ron effectively in charge, arrangements were chaotic. Ron had originally hoped to hide Mitchell after his release in a flat belonging to a friend in Shoreditch but at the last minute the friend backed out and they were forced to make do with Lennie 'Books' Dunn, purveyor of second-hand books, blue films and cheap pornography, whose wife had had enough and had left him to his own devices in their dreary ground-floor flat in suburban Barking.

Ron then chose Albert Donoghue and middle-aged Billy Exley to drive down to Dartmoor to collect Mitchell, but at the last minute it was discovered that neither Donoghue nor Exley had a valid driving licence and they had to borrow driving licences from two other members of the Firm so they could rent a clapped-out green Vauxhall for the journey. Then Reg pointed out that Mitchell would need a change of clothing from his prison garb, and since the ex-wrestler Tommy Brown, 'The Bear', was the only member of the Firm as big as him they persuaded him to lend them a set of cast-offs that would fit Frank. With such problems it was clear that far too much was getting rushed, but everyone now went in fear of Ron and what he'd do if anyone dared to disappoint his old friend Frank. Frank was depending on them all. How could anybody let him down?

And then, to complicate yet further an already over-complicated situation, Ronnie, changeable as ever, switched all his erratic energy into chasing yet another of his favourite will-o'-the-wisps – the police. And this at a time when, following the Boothby cover-up, the Twins were effectively invulnerable, and nobody at Scotland Yard wanted any fresh involvement with the Krays unless absolutely necessary.

But Ron had been informed that a police detective called Townsend was offering the Twins immunity from arrest for unlicensed gambling in one of their pubs for a mere twenty pounds a week. Had Ronnie not been so obsessional about the police he'd have known that the last thing he or Reg needed was to pay a corrupt police detective for anything. But Ron never was completely sane about the police and could not resist an opportunity like this to score off any member of the hated force. So once again he turned to George Devlin the private eye he and Reg had employed in the McCowan case, to fix him up with a miniature recorder. A few days later Ron met Detective Inspector Townsend at the pub, listened to his proposition and, having secretly recorded it, said he'd think it over.

Instead, he sent a copy of the recording to the Director of Public Prosecutions. So far, so good; Inspector Townsend was suspended pending investigations, and largely on the strength of Ron's recorded evidence he was sent for trial. Then something happened that Ronnie might have possibly foreseen – he was summoned to appear as a prosecution witness in court. Ron had always refused on principle to act as a witness in a court of law, and when he did so now the judge subpoenaed him to appear. When Ron still refused he was threatened with imprisonment for contempt of court. Which left Ron no alternative but to act exactly as he had after murdering Cornell – go into hiding. Since all this happened just a few days before the Twins were planning to spring Frank Mitchell it made everything more complicated still. Reg argued strongly that this meant the whole attempt should be postponed but still Ron wouldn't listen. Unlike the rest of them, he knew how Frank would feel. He knew how disappointed Frank would be. You couldn't disappoint a friend like Frank.

This meant that as the day of Mitchell's great escape approached, Ron had barricaded himself in a flat in the Finchley Road which he filled with weapons, medication, alcohol and his precious recordings of the wartime speeches of Winston Churchill. The curtains were kept permanently pulled, while favoured members of the Firm brought him food and drink and a regular supply of teenage boys. But as Ron slipped into one of his depressions his plan to free Frank Mitchell lost all hope it ever had of succeeding. And there was still much worse to come.

On 10 December, with only two days left before Frank

Mitchell's dash for freedom, Frances who had taken an overdose of sleeping pills a few months earlier, made a second serious attempt to kill herself. Her father found her just in time. 'Dad, you should have let me go,' she murmured. But Frank Shea called an ambulance instead, and got his daughter into hospital. When Reg heard the news and tried to visit her he was told she was too weak to see anyone.

With Reg unable to think of anything except seeing Frances, this provided yet another argument to postpone the freeing of Frank Mitchell. But still Ron wouldn't hear of it. Postponement now would have devastated Frank and had this happened Ron would have gone berserk as well. Which meant that out of fear of Ron, the Axeman's grand escape was set to go ahead, with Ron in a state of drug-induced depression in a flat in the Finchley Road, Reg distraught with worry over Frances, and a plan that hadn't got a hope in hell of ever working. Apart from which, everything was going swimmingly.

The twelfth of December dawned. The only hope for Mitchell now was that with everything going wrong, something was bound to happen which would stop the plan proceeding. There were, God knew, enough potential hiccups in it all for something untoward to happen. Mitchell could have got lost in the December mist. The green Vauxhall could have broken down. But since Sod's Law was now in operation, poor Mitchell couldn't even count on a disaster which might just have saved him.

Instead, for just this one key moment, everything went like clockwork. The green Vauxhall made it to Dartmoor. Donoghue and Exley didn't lose their way. And at the pre-arranged moment the morning mist lifted off the moors and, slap on time, there was Mitchell standing at the rendezvous on the Princetown Road, looking like a very large schoolboy on a holiday adventure and wearing a mask he'd made from his schoolmistress's black silk underwear. When Donoghue told him to take the damned thing off he sulked for a while but soon recovered his high spirits which lasted for the rest of the four-hour trip to London. Not until they reached their destination did the first cold douche of irredeemable disaster which would henceforth blight this whole appalling escapade wash over them.

Mitchell had been picturing this moment for years and expected a hero's welcome from enthusiastic members of the underworld, followed by a party with champagne and pretty girls and famous faces about whom he had heard so much but never met. The least that he expected was that the Twins would obviously be there to welcome him in person. But when the car pulled up outside Dunn's wretched flat in Barking there was no sign of a party, no sign of the Twins, no sign of anything that even moved until Donoghue, by dint of hammering on the front door, finally dragged out the miserable pornographer with the hangdog face and nervous twitch to greet the big escaping hero.

Whatever Frank had been dreaming of for all those years it was emphatically not this. But for him all that really mattered now was Ron — or rather Ron's non-appearance. Had Ron been there he would have reassured him. As soon as he saw his old friend again, he'd know that everything was fine. But with no sign of Ron, the big excited schoolboy had suddenly become a sadly disappointed schoolboy. 'Where's Ron?' he asked pathetically. Donoghue did his best to dispel Frank's disappointment but the reasons for Ron's absence weren't easy to explain. Try as they might, they couldn't make Frank understand why Ron couldn't be there to look after him in person as he'd always said he would.

'He'll soon be here,' Donoghue told him. 'Be patient. Ron will come. You have my word for it. He'll come.' But Ron never did.

★

In the meantime Donoghue and Exley did their best – which clearly wasn't much – to look after Frank and keep him happy. Exley cooked him steak and chips, but they didn't like to give him alcohol in case it made the situation worse.

It was a situation that would have driven any sane man crazy, and Mitchell wasn't very sane. He had passed within half a mile of where his parents lived and suddenly felt homesick. 'If Ron's not here, I'm going home,' he abruptly announced.

'Frank, be sensible. You can't go home. Your mum's house will be the first place the Old Bill will think of searching for you.' So to divert him they spent the afternoon teaching him simple card games like snap and pontoon. When he started getting bored they humoured him as best they could. 'Show us how you can pick up two men, Frank,' said Exley, which he did. 'Tell us about that bird you had on the moor,' said Donoghue,

But Frank was prudish and he didn't want to talk about his schoolmistress, and as darkness fell and the hours ticked by he was already starting to get suspicious.

'If Ron can't come, why can't I see Reg?'

'You will, Frank, but Reg is a very busy man. He'll come later.'

At last nine o'clock arrived and they watched the news on television. That cheered Frank Mitchell up at once and he rocked with laughter when he saw Royal Marine commandos on the moor, trying to find him. What the announcer did not say was that the marines were armed and under orders to shoot on sight.

'They'll never catch me alive,' he said.

'No, Frank. They never will,' said Exley.

It was nearly midnight before Reg came at last, but he was clearly jumpy. What was really on his mind was not Frank Mitchell or his problems. He'd been trying all that evening to see Frances in hospital but when the doctors said it was too early he blamed this bitterly on her family.

'I'll kill the lot of them,' Reg muttered. 'Killing's too good for scum like that.'

Soon the hours were turning into days, and nothing happened. Everyone was running short of conversation. Shifts were arranged and 'Scotch Jack' Dixon was brought in to change places with Exley. But there was still no sign of Ron – nor, for that matter, any sign of the police or even any indication that they had an inkling of Mitchell's whereabouts. Which meant that at this moment, had they wanted to, the Twins still had a chance to organise something that would have saved Frank Mitchell's life. Somehow they might still have sent him abroad. Failing this, they could have got him to a safe house in the country. They might just have found someone more suitable to look after him. But nobody thought of anything like this.

Ron was still drugged out of his mind in a drunken stupor in the flat in the Finchley Road, and Reg was trying to control his fury over his in-laws. The only member of the Firm who was still trying to work out what to do with Mitchell was Teddy Smith and on arrival at the flat next morning he had the unenviable task of organising Mitchell to write the all-important letters to the press, which was now their one slender hope of a happy outcome to the situation.

It was heavy going. Mitchell had been taught to write in prison but was desperately slow, and lacked what Smith considered the proper style for a letter to the press. So after some disagreement they ended up with Smith dictating and Mitchell laboriously penning two letters on which his future – and his life – depended. One was to the editor of the *Daily Mirror*, and the other to the home secretary, care of the editor of *The Times*.

The home secretary's letter went went as follows:

Sir,

The reason for my absence from Dartmoor was to bring to your Notice my unhappy plight. To be truthful, I am asking for a possible Date of release. From the age of 9 I have not been completely free, always under some act or other.

Sir, I ask you, where is the fairness of this. I am not a murderer or a sex maniac, nor do I think I am a danger to the public. I think I have been more than punished for the wrongs I have done.

Yours sincerely,

Frank Mitchell

There was no reply and two more days passed with nothing happening. It was now a week since Frank's escape and it was Donoghue who had the sense to realise that something must be done or Mitchell would go berserk. Donoghue had heard him groaning in his sleep and he was threatening to leave the flat and go out and find himself a woman. After this, Donoghue sent Reg a message saying that if Mitchell didn't have a girl as soon as possible they'd all be in for trouble.

This time Reg did come, and since there was no point any more in telling him that Ron was just about to come, he promised him a girl instead. At last this seemed to cheer him up.

'What sort d'you like, Frank? Blonde or brunette?'

'I don't care as long as she's nice. And very sexy.'

'Fine, Frank. I'll remember.'

'And Reg. Don't be long. I'm getting lonely.'

Reg wasn't used to finding girls so he consulted Tommy Cowley, a member of the Firm who specialised in looking after the West End clubs, and Cowley recommended Churchill's Club in Bond Street. Early that evening Reg and Cowley visited the club to see what talent was on offer. It didn't take them long to pick a shapely blonde with a ready smile called Lisa

Prescott. Since the Twins were 'looking after' Churchill's at the time, Reg seemed to think that they didn't need to pay her. Nor, more important, did he feel obliged to tell her anything about her 'duties'. Had he done so, no hostess in her senses would ever have accepted.

Instead, Reg talked to her about this rich Arab friend of his who had just arrived in London and was feeling lonely. He asked her if she liked Arabs.

'If they're rich,' she said, and reluctantly agreed to come.

When she reached the flat and saw that the 'rich Arab' was Frank Mitchell she recognised him at once but had the good sense not to say so.

Few girls, however keen or desperate for money would have gone through with it but Lisa knew that there was no alternative. At the same time she was a professional, and made it clear that she wasn't doing anything until there was money on the table. And she stood her ground.

She was a small woman and Mitchell could have forced her had he wanted to. But in the face of her refusal he showed a sort of battered decency which, combined with the way he still trusted those who were going to betray him, makes the end of the story seem more sick and sad than ever.

Reg reluctantly returned to Vallance Road and came back with £100 in a paper carrier bag. After pocketing twenty for expenses, Donoghue gave the rest to Lisa, and she started work. It was heavy going. After each session making love Mitchell supposedly leapt out of bed, did fifty press-ups, then started off again.

But although Lisa helped staved off disaster for a while she also raised the stakes. Not only was she trapped like all the others. To make her situation worse she was also an outsider as well as a potential witness.

It wasn't long before she too was becoming frightened, particularly when Reg made it clear that it was out of the question to think of returning to her little flat in Marylebone. When he told her, 'This is like the war. You're in this for the duration,' Lisa understood that she'd be lucky to get out of it alive.

In the intervals between sex and press-ups, she and Mitchell started talking. They talked about the country. Ronnie had promised he would take Frank to his house in the country. 'Promise you'll come there with me, Lisa.'

The only excitement came when the papers published both of Frank Mitchell's letters. *The Times* did it straight, without comment. The *Mirror* also published theirs and the editor added some words of exhortation to Frank. 'Wherever you are, Frank, be a man and give yourself up.' Had it been left to Frank, by now he would have done so. But when he suggested this, Reg made things clear that it would be over their dead bodies. And to make things worse, after the publication of the letters there was no further news from anyone.

Since there was no response from the police, let alone from the Home Office, it was clear that Ron's plan wasn't working and they had landed in a mess to which there was no solution. Or rather, there was one obvious solution which nobody in that airless bed-sitting room, with the the curtains pulled and the electric fire permanently on, cared to think about, let alone discuss. It's hard to know when everyone realised that the game was up and the whole hopeless enterprise was doomed to failure. But if anybody did, no one dared to say so.

This meant that the atmosphere within that stuffy little flat was becoming tenser by the hour as hopelessness set in, and even Mitchell must have understood the truth — that he had exchanged one prison for another. The room had become a prison for them all, for if Mitchell was trapped within it so were his captors who were now utterly involved in keeping this large dangerous human being fed, watered and sexually serviced.

Once they had come to realise how all of them were now involved in what had started so light-heartedly, the suspicions and the fears began to form around one all-important question that no one dared to ask. Who would be the first to break? Would it be Reg, whose desperate worries for his wife were constantly distracting him? Or homicidal Ron who, having initiated this whole crazy caper, had apparently opted out and was leaving everybody in the lurch?

But the biggest danger now was Frank himself who was growing more suspicious by the hour. Who wouldn't have been suspicious in his situation? But his obsession with his precious Ron was getting on everybody's nerves. So were the questions he was always asking. 'Why does Ron stay away from me? I thought Ron was my friend. Why can't he come and see me?' It was a good question and since Frank was getting so upset Donoghue suggested that Reg should bring Ron over in disguise, as he used to bring him to The Double R at night after his escape from Long Grove.

Reg simply answered that this would be impossible.

But why was it impossible? What was Ron up to in his Finchley Road hideaway? All too predictably he had started drinking and as he floated in and out of sanity the intricate psychology of the paranoid schizophrenic was being triggered off by its surest motivator – fear. It would not be long before those volatile emotions of Ron's rickety stability would be overwhelmed in a flood of panic at the thought of what was happening.

This meant that the only person Frank Mitchell could really trust was Lisa, and inevitably he fell in love with her.

Whatever she was, she tried to be honest with her clients. Girls like her knew better than to fall in love with anyone and she didn't like to lie to him. She also knew that if it came to it she was expendable, particularly to people like the Krays. She hadn't taken long to work out the situation, and while she knew there could be no way out for Frank she also knew that her own chances weren't much better. With only a few days left to Christmas, Frank was getting still more restless and was saying that he wanted to spend Christmas with his family and take Lisa home to meet his mother. For by now he had decided that he was in love with her. She knew that she could never be in love with him. But if it made Frank happy to believe they were in love, she'd go along with it. By now she was desperately sorry for him. He talked a lot about his mother.

'I know she'll love you, Lisa. She's never seen me with a girl like you. So promise you'll come with me, Lisa.'

'I promise,' she replied.

Meanwhile Mad Teddy Smith had still not given up and made one last attempt to sort things out by contacting his old lover Tom Driberg. But when he went to a public call box and rang the number he had always used to speak to him in the past, whoever answered pretended not to know him and hurriedly rang off. The same thing happened when he rang again that evening. This left him one last hope – to persuade Francis Wyndham, the Twins' former contact on the *Sunday Times*, to act as a go-between with the Home Office over Frank's surrender.

But Wyndham understandably refused to get involved. When Teddy reported this to Reg it briefly jolted him from his worries over Frances into doing something practical. He finally took charge as he had after the Cornell murder to save everyone, himself included, from arrest. If he didn't make a decision nobody else would.

He realised that there were just two possibilities. The first was to persuade Mitchell to surrender to the authorities, which would inevitably land the Twins in trouble followed by immense publicity, a sensational trial and lengthy prison sentences for all involved – and Mitchell's situation would be worse than ever.

And the second possibility? It didn't take much imagination to work that one out.

Had there been any further doubt about his fate, it was now that Mitchell wrote his own death warrant in the form of a note he laboriously composed to Reg spelling out a threat which placed a dagger to the heart of both the Twins. Unless they did something soon he would leave the flat and go round to Vallance Road to talk to Violet. Once he started threatening their mother they knew that they would have to kill him – or have him killed. Mitchell's behaviour left them no alternative. At first Ron wouldn't hear a word against his friend until Reg mentioned Ron's earlier fear which had triggered off his murder of Cornell, when he became obsessed with the idea that Cornell would come to Vallance Road to murder him and Violet.

The threat to their mother had restored Ron to some sort of sanity, and he sent a message round to Freddy Foreman to arrange a meeting.

One gets some idea of the state the Twins were in when one realises that faced with this mess that Ronnie had created neither of the Twins nor anybody else in the Firm could clear it up.

The arrival of Freddy Foreman – who liked to call himself the managing director of British crime – on the scene signalled the arrival of the professionals in the madhouse. They simply had a job to do and, as with most things Foreman set his mind to, it was done with maximum efficiency.

The time for pity or softness or any sentimental nonsense was over. He acted in the only way that one can do this sort of thing – swiftly, efficiently, pitilessly. For the first time in many months an action that involved the Twins would not be bungled.

Why couldn't they kill Mitchell themselves? Ron was too drugged and unreliable. Mitchell could easily break free, and anyhow, he still had the gun he'd taken from Exley.

Besides, too many people were involved, which meant that there would be too many witnesses.

It was a very simple plan but, when it comes to killing, simple plans are usually the best. And with Mitchell showing every sign of preparing to escape from the flat it had to be done quickly if it was to be done at all. Which meant making arrangements for the following evening, 22 December.

Reg, of course, was in on it, and since Donoghue had always got on well with Mitchell he was the one he chose to tell him the glad tidings that Ron was staying in the country with Violet and wanted Frank to join them both for Christmas. Some friends would drive him down and Donoghue would travel with him. To avoid arousing suspicions they had an unmarked van which would be waiting for them down the road at six o'clock. Ron sent his love and said he couldn't wait to see his old friend Frank at last, and they'd have a great old time together. Happy Christmas.

Then, as they waited for six o'clock to come, everybody in that bleak suburban dungeon acted out the gruesome tableau of deception round the figure of the lovesick Axeman.

'No, Frank,' they told him. 'Lisa can't go with you in the van. She'll come on later. Imagine what would happen to her if you were stopped by the police.

'Yes, Frank. Ronnie's in his house in the country. He's there now with Violet getting it ready for you and Lisa. Lisa will love it, won't you, Lisa? The two of you will soon be there together.'

Mitchell had already asked someone to buy him a Christmas card and he gave it to her now. She read it.

'For Lisa, the only one I love,' he had written.

'Lisa, don't be long. I'll be waiting for you,' he said.

'I know you will,' she said, and gave him one last kiss.

'Happy Christmas, Frank,' everybody said, 'Enjoy yourself.' And as he followed Donoghue outside to where a van was waiting just along the road with its headlights dimmed, everyone knew that the nightmare they had lived through for so long was over, and that no one in that room would have to see any more of Frank Mitchell this side of eternity.

Donoghue always claimed that when he and Mitchell left the flat, and he led him down the Barking Road to where the van was parked, he, like Mitchell did not know what fate awaited him and genuinely believed that they were going somewhere in the country. This was, to say the least, unlikely. Donoghue knew the Twins well enough to know that they had never had a country house. But he also knew that if he gave the slightest hint of trouble, he also would be dealt with later.

Sometime afterwards Donoghue described what happened. How the driver of the van got out to meet them, opened the van's rear doors and told Mitchell to get in. Two men, Foreman and Gerard, were already sitting on the floor and he heard one of them tell Mitchell to make himself as comfortable as possible on one of the rear wheel casings. With which the driver shut the doors, told Donoghue to get in beside him, and started off.

When he glanced back, Donoghue could see what happened next. Foreman was holding an automatic, Gerard a revolver, and as the van gathered speed the shooting started. Mitchell, of course, didn't have a hope in hell. Something like twenty rounds entered his body and his head, and although he made one last despairing lunge to reach his killers two shots behind the ear finished him off for ever.

As he was now a witness Donoghue imagined he was next and was preparing to make a fight of it when the van stopped and the driver signalled to him to get out. Not a word was spoken and as he started walking back towards the flat, half expecting a bullet in the back, he heard the van accelerate away. The last he saw of it were its rear lights vanishing around the corner.

Less than five minutes had elapsed since he'd left the flat but by the time that he returned Reggie had arrived with several members of the Firm and had already started clearing up, destroying any evidence of Mitchell's presence, down to the faintest sign that he had ever existed. Even the beret he had worn was burned and when it was all over everyone went on to a party at Walthamstow. Donoghue and Lisa stayed on drinking until almost all the other guests had gone. It might have been exhaustion or relief or simply the drink, but Lisa suddenly became upset so, as he put it later, Donoghue 'did the honourable thing, and spent the night with her as she needed comforting.'

All of which left the question open of what subsequently happened then to the unusually large body of Frank Mitchell. Donoghue always said he didn't know and didn't want to. The Twins, on the other hand, undoubtedly did know but kept the secret to themselves until their death. And the stories started. The old tales about the body being stuck in the concrete of some distant flyover reappeared. Perhaps it had been placed in someone else's coffin by a dodgy undertaker. Perhaps, ultimate indignity, it had been cut up for animal feed and fed to pigs.

In fact it was Foreman himself who finally decided he would spill the beans on prime-time television. Relying on the double-indemnity rule of British justice, which ruled out anyone being tried for the same crime twice,[1] he had already confirmed Donoghue's account of Mitchell's killing in his memoirs. Now he went on to give the answer to the final mystery of the Mitchell case, in the process revealing one of the best-kept secrets of the London underworld, the story of what he called the 'Little Facility' at Newhaven.

Just along the coast from Brighton, the port of Newhaven on the estuary of the River Ouse serves a dual purpose. On the left bank is the harbour for the cross-Channel ferry to Dieppe, and on the right its west quay has long been home for the trawlers of the fishing fleet. In the past Newhaven also had another role, as a centre for smuggling along the coast, which continued on and off for years. Sometimes there were bitter confrontations between Customs men and smugglers. Sometimes smugglers were betrayed, and sometimes Customs men were killed. And from time to time it was useful for the smugglers to be able to dispose of an unwanted body – which was when Newhaven's best-kept secret started. None knew better than the local fishermen that a human body dumped in the English Channel rarely disappeared for good and that the swift Channel tides would usually wash it up somewhere in the end. But a few of the old trawlermen had also learned that there were certain places where the water was deep enough to ensure this didn't happen.

In an emergency it could be very useful to know exactly where a weighted body wrapped in chicken wire and canvas could be sunk for ever. It was a piece of knowledge passed on from one generation of fishermen to the next. And it was knowledge that whatever smart old sailor ran the 'Little Facility' at Newhaven on behalf of the London underworld in the 1960s must have made the most of. For according to Freddy Foreman, Mitchell's body was driven down to Newhaven late at night and the 'Little Facility' became the final destination for the 'Mad Axeman's' bullet-riddled corpse. So far it has not resurfaced.

17

Invitation to a Sacrifice

THERE WAS A deceptive calm between the Twins in the aftermath of the Axeman's murder. For Reg there must have been considerable relief in having Ron still in hiding from the court order naming him as a witness in the Townsend case. Wherever he was now, Ron would always be an unpredictable liability for Reg who could never be certain what would happen next. With Ron safely out of harm's way – at least for the time being – and being looked after by someone from the Firm, Reg and the family might even have a chance to come to some decision over what to do with him. But this wasn't easy.

There could be no argument over the seriousness of Ron's condition and, far from quieting his fears, the cool extinction of Frank Mitchell by Fred Foreman seemed to have intensified Ron's nightmares. Since the killing he'd been haunted by the fear that friends of both Mitchell and Cornell were now out for their revenge. It was up to him to kill them first, and to keep his courage up much of Ron's time was spent preparing lists of those who had to go – and how he'd deal with them.

This occupied his time, but once he'd finished the nightmares started, nightmares in which he, and not his enemies, was the victim. There was no escape from his imagination: it kept returning to the death scene at the murder of Cornell, which he had relived so compulsively after shooting him. The only difference now was that, since Ron had become the victim, he had condemned himself to watch the bullet entering his own head, not Cornell's.

This was when his nightmares started up in earnest, as the tortures he was planning for his enemies turned on him and gave him no relief. After one of these attacks he was usually delirious and would lie immobile on his bed, drunk or drugged with Stematol, for days on end, with Reg or one of his boys beside him till his fears abated.

Once, in the middle of the night, his terrors were so frightful that he tried to kill himself by slashing both his wrists. If it hadn't been someone in the next room who heard his groans and summoned Reg, Ron would have bled to death. Later there were times when Reg would wish that he had. Instead, he found himself telephoning Doc Blasker and once more dragging the old man from his bed. Not that there was much for the accommodating doctor to do when he arrived, except dress Ron's wounds and warn him yet again against taking large quantities of alcohol with his medication. But when he was alone with Reg the doctor warned him that his brother was seriously sick. He needed far more expert treatment than Blasker could give him and ought to be in hospital.

But how to get him there? At the best of times, Ron was terrified of hospitals and at a time like this, with a manhunt going on for Mitchell and his bullet-riddled body only recently consigned to the English Channel, too much depended on keeping Ron safely under wraps and as far away as possible from the eyes of the police. As it was, Ron had already convinced himself that Scotland Yard knew where he was and had his flat under constant observation.

In fact of course they hadn't, for by now the Mitchell search had stalled and the police had not the faintest inkling where he was. No one had talked and so far no one had connected his disappearance with the Krays. Still less had those searching for him heard the faintest whisper of what had taken place in Lennie Dunn's drab flat in Barking, of all unlikely places.

Smart as ever, Reg had made arrangements for postcards to be sent at intervals from France to fellow prisoners at Dartmoor in Mitchell's handwriting, wishing them all the best and signed 'Your old friend, Frank'. Thanks to this, the police, ably assisted by Interpol, would soon be switching their attention to the Continent.

Not that this did anything to reassure Ron, who by now was spending all his time peering through the curtains at the road below, convinced that anyone he spotted waiting at the bus stop had to be a plain-clothes detective. Like all his other fears this soon became obsessive and rapidly reduced him to a state of misery. Finally Reg was able to persuade him that he needed help but, as he still refused to enter a hospital or even a doctor's surgery, this was difficult to arrange. So Reg explained the situation to a psychiatrist he trusted and arranged for him to be picked up in Reg's car by the traffic lights in Trafalgar Square. Reg would be sitting in the front seat by the driver and Ron, heavily disguised in wide-brimmed hat and dark glasses, would be in the back.

This was the only way that Reg could think of to convince Ron he was safe from the police and from his enemies – and surprisingly, it worked. For the next three-quarters of an hour as the car drove slowly round Hyde Park, Ron was sitting in the back, anxiously discussing his problems with the psychiatrist. Not that there was much the man could do, apart from prescribe fresh medication and suggest a change of scenery from the Finchley Road. But, for whatever reason, after meeting him Ron started to recover.

Reg found him another smaller flat above an antique shop in Chelsea. Quite suddenly Ron no longer felt that he was under observation. He stopped drinking and the deep depressions lifted. A few days later, heavily disguised, Ron ventured out with Reg beside him, and for the first time since his hibernation had started, Reg felt safe in bringing Violet to see him.

Until now, Reg had always stopped their mother seeing Ron in hiding, knowing how much it would upset her. He'd told her that since Ron had to hide from the police, it was best that she remained in ignorance of his whereabouts. This seemed to satisfy her, but now that she had seen her precious Ronnie once again she began to worry. At this point she had no idea of the truth about Frank Mitchell, but she certainly knew what had happened to Cornell. She also knew her Ronnie well enough to spot the signs of what was happening.

What did upset her was less the harm that he might cause to others than the thought that he could end up on his own in some dreadful institution like Long Grove mental hospital, where he had been so lonely and unhappy. Some time later, when she and Reg met for a serious discussion over what to do with Ron, she produced an idea of her own to solve the problem. In the next few months all the houses in Vallance Road would be demolished, so what was to stop her and old Charlie moving to the country? They were both getting on, and she thought she might enjoy it. It would need to be somewhere nice with a bit of peace and quiet so that she could make a home for Ronnie and look after him. Ron had often told her that he'd like to live in the country, like a country gentleman, and he could have his own apartment and feel free to come and go. Violet knew this would make all the difference to poor Ronnie and she wouldn't have to worry herself sick about him any longer. Couldn't Reg do something about it?

Reg said he'd think about it, and the more he thought about it the more he felt it might not be a bad idea.

In the meantime Reg continued to keep business ticking over until better times returned. The only trouble was that they didn't and all of Reg's self-control was needed to hold things together.

Brother Charlie was a help when it came to 'doing the milk round' – collecting the weekly protection money from the West End clubs they 'looked after' – but even here there were problems. The truth was that the murder of Cornell had not been good for business. News of what had happened had inevitably reached the underworld, and the Mafia-backed owners of the Colony Club were becoming nervous of the Kray connection. Reg had just managed to smooth things over, thanks largely to the intervention of the Twins' old friend and loyal ally George Raft, when a few weeks later came the news that Raft had been expelled from Britain by order of the Home Office. Even then, Reg kept his nerve. Then, late that April, something happened which, if the rumours were correct, must have added a forbidding burden to his already over-burdened shoulders.

By now it appeared as if Ron was miraculously back on track to recovery. This often happened after one of his attacks. His stamina was remarkable and he could emerge apparently unscathed from periods when he had seemed close to death. If it had not been for the court order still having three months more to run, there was nothing to prevent him coming out of hiding and starting life anew as if nothing had happened. But something did happen on that April day which has never been explained and probably never will be. Instead, I imagine it will join the other mysteries that the Twins have left behind to tantalise the curious. The Twins enjoyed doing this in life and now that they're dead we must rely on what evidence there is to make up our minds about what occurred.

What we do know is that on that fine spring day the Twins, together with their brother Charles and Teddy Smith, took a day off from their troubles and drove to one of their favourite seaside haunts where they could enjoy the sea air and relax – Steeple Bay in Suffolk, where they had a caravan. Even at the height of summer it was never crowded, but at the end of April they would almost certainly have had it to themselves. In retrospect, what made this particular day important was that this visit to the Suffolk coast was the last time that anyone ever heard of Teddy Smith. Indeed, for all intents and purposes, during that day at Steeple Bay Mad Teddy somehow vanished from the face of planet Earth.

So what happened to him? The strict answer is that no one knows for sure and that one or two survivors from that period are stubbornly convinced that he is still alive. Frankie Fraser claims to have heard from him in Australia, and Danny la Rue's former minder Frank Kurylo insists that he once spotted him in a cinema queue in Leicester Square. So if all we had to go on was the fact of Teddy's sudden disappearance he would have to be consigned to the ghostly band of other possible victims of the Krays, including Ron's gay driver Charlie Frost, and another Scottish gangster, Jock Buggy, whose battered corpse was found floating in the sea off Brighton.

Apart from adding to the cloud of mystery which still hangs around the reputation of the Twins, it is important to remember that, long before they murdered anyone, many who had known them well were thoroughly convinced that they were murderers. Anita Pallenberg, for instance, that time when she was on holiday with Keith Richards, and met the Twins on the beach at Tangier 'looking like the Blues Brothers', took it for granted that they had long been killers, as did most of her friends in the Chelsea 'Popocracy'. Certainly by then all of them would have heard persistent rumours that the Krays were in the habit of disposing of their victims in the concrete pillars of the recently completed Chiswick flyover.

This was also quite untrue[1] although one of the reasons for the persistence of this particular rumour was the way that it connected with one of the less appealing tales of the US Mafia and how they encased *their* victims in 'concrete boots' before dumping them in the Hudson River. So powerful was the image that connected concrete with the Krays that even today I can't drive past the Chiswick flyover without a sense of lurking apprehension.

Despite this there are several reasons to suspect that Teddy Smith *was* murdered by Ron Kray. The first is that he vanished from the scene so swiftly and completely. Previously he'd been something of a fixture in the Firm and suddenly he just vanished, which is a fairly commonplace phenomenon in gangster circles where an unexplained disappearance signifies an untoward demise.

The second reason is that, for all his Sunny Jim qualities, Mad Teddy always had an unappealing way of screwing up and nowhere more so than during his participation in the Frank Mitchell fiasco. The fact that the real cause of the disaster was entirely Ron himself had only served to make Mad Teddy's situation that much more precarious. For someone as emotionally unbalanced as Ron, particularly with his mind fuddled and bemused by solitude and alcohol, there would have been an irresistible temptation to offload the blame for the death of his previously much-loved friend, Frank Mitchell, onto the pathetic shoulders of a subordinate as silly as Mad Teddy.

I personally believe that this is almost certainly what happened, but if this were all the evidence we had we would still be in the misty realms of supposition. I have, however, recently discovered one further, more conclusive reason for believing that Mad Teddy Smith met his death quite literally at the hands of Ronnie Kray at the caravan site at Steeple Bay sometime in April 1967.

Many years later when Ronnie was in Broadmoor and described to his friend Wilf Pine how he killed George Cornell, Wilf ended the conversation by asking Ron if he'd ever murdered anybody else. Apparently Ron paused and thought a while, as if uncertain whether to continue, then replied;

'Yes, one.'

'Who?' Wilf asked.

'Mad Teddy Smith.'

'How?'

'I got his head in an armlock and broke his neck. That's all. It was easy.'

However, when Wilf asked him why he did it Ron became evasive and muttered something about 'trouble with a boy'. When Wilf asked what sort of trouble he wouldn't say.

Although I realise this still isn't proof I'm tempted to believe it. In the first place, by the time they talked Ronnie and Wilf Pine had become close friends, and Ron had no incentive to lie to Wilf about something that had happened all those years before. On top of this there was another piece of evidence that totally convinced me that he told the truth. Early in 1968, less than a year after Mad Teddy disappeared and the Twins were still at liberty, I was seeing quite a lot of them while I was working on my book *The Profession of Violence*. I remember how, as part of my research, Ron said he'd show me how to kill a man. A macabre demonstration followed in which, before I could refuse, he had placed his boxer's arms around my neck and, with practised expertise and undisguised enjoyment, started squeezing. It happened very quickly. The blood rushed to my head, and just as I was on the point of passing out Reg intervened with the memorable request, 'Ron, for Christ's sake stop. He's got to write our fucking book.'

Fortunately for me, Ron did as he was told. But I'm pretty well convinced that poor Mad Teddy Smith was not so lucky.

Since it is unlikely that we will ever know much more about events that day at Steeple Bay it's fairly pointless speculating on the effect that Mad Teddy's death would have had upon the Twins. We know that following his nice day out Ronnie returned to his hideaway over the antique shop off the Fulham Road, and there he stayed until his court order expired at the end of that July. We also know that if, following a hard day's work, the Krays had found themselves with an unwanted corpse on their hands, this would not have been an insurmountable problem. If nothing else, the neat disposal of Frank Mitchell's body by the 'Little Facility' in Newhaven had shown exactly how this could be done and the absence of a body following Mad Teddy's murder is no proof that it had never happened.

One thing we do know is that, during the weeks following the trip to Steeple Bay, Reg suddenly began to show an unaccustomed interest in his now estranged wife Frances. Whatever else might have caused this it was clearly no longer because of her lively sense of fun or the cockney starlet style of her glamour which originally attracted him. After two unsuccessful suicide attempts Frances was in a fairly pitiable condition. One of her old friends described her as 'looking like a ghost of her old self' but in spite of this Reg had recently been seeing more of her than at any time since the marriage foundered.

There could be several reasons to account for this. One was the fact that Frances had recently moved from the strongly anti-Kray regime of her parents' home so close to Vallance Road to the more relaxed family of her brother Frank in Wimbourne Court, a modern block of flats in Walthamstow. Another possibility was that Reg and Frances had both been going through a lot of nervous strain and were simply finding comfort in each other's company. But I am convinced that for Reg there was one further, more compelling reason now for seeing her.

As we saw in the run-up to his marriage, one of his most important reasons for marrying Frances in the first place had been his desperation to break the bonds that tied him so inescapably to Ron. Somewhat naively, he had been envisaging marriage leading to a relatively normal life that would include a settled home, sociable hours, new friends and even children. And, as we have also seen, this profoundly serious attempt by

Reg to use his marriage as an escape route from the nightmare situation with his twin had failed before it really started. The sexuality he shared with Ron had been against it, as had the all-embracing life of crime they also shared. But the overriding reason for Reg's marital disaster had undoubtedly been Ron himself, who had looked on Reg's marriage as a battlefield on which he had to struggle for his own survival.

For Ron his need for Reg had always seemed far deeper and more desperate than that of 'that useless silly girl', as he referred to Frances, and he employed all his ruthlessness and cunning to defeat her. In the process he had all but destroyed her – until now, when I believe that Reg suddenly saw her as his last chance of fleeing from the nightmare that was starting to engulf him.

For whatever else he was, Reg was realistic. Unlike Ron whose life was dominated by the fantasies and fears of schizo-phrenia, Reg was still relatively sane, and ever since the murder of Cornell in every crisis it had been Reg who had protected him. He had always done this in the name of the twinship that united them. But more than ever now Reg realised the truth. By tying him so tightly to his twin, those twin bonds did not merely bind him to a brother. They also tied him permanently to a homicidal madman. But must these terrifying bonds last for ever? If they were destroying him, why not break them while there might be still a chance – by going back to Frances?

During this period, Reg and Frances certainly increased the time they spent together and afterwards Frances told a friend of her surprise at how much Reg had changed. It could almost have been the old Reg she remembered from the days when they'd been courting. He was so gentle and so understanding and he had actually apologised for what had happened. He had even been in tears as he swore to her that he realised his mistakes, and had vowed that all he wanted was to make amends for the sadness he had caused her. When she asked him if he still loved her, he said he loved her more than ever. He also said he longed to have her back and promised her that she could trust him.

And, after all, legally she was still his wife. He would find another flat, this time as far away from Ron as possible, and he would abandon his old life, becoming a successful businessman instead. One thing he'd learned from crime was that there wasn't that much difference between straight business and the other kind, and he was sick to death of the life that he'd been living.

I can remember that Reg often spoke like this, but to prove to Frances that he was serious he now suggested they should go on a foreign holiday together, as they had done in the days before they married. He would spoil her and make a fuss of her as he always did, and they could start enjoying life again. It would be like a second honeymoon, and he suggested going to Ibiza at the end of June. As usual, Reg was so persuasive that he ended up by convincing himself, as he was inclined to. Whether he convinced Frances is another matter, but they got as far as calling at the local travel agent's there and then, and booking tickets for Ibiza.

Reg kept those tickets for the rest of his life and the memory of that day haunted him for ever. It was a long time since he'd seen Frances so excited as when they talked about that holiday together. When finally he took her back to Wimbourne Court and they kissed goodnight, they promised they would meet again next day.

Reg firmly believed in premonitions. He claimed to have known when Ron had his first attack of madness all those years before at Winchester, and it would be the same years later, after Violet died. Now the same thing happened to him over Frances. I remember him telling me how he woke in the middle of the night and knew for certain that something terrible had happened. After this there could be no question of going back to sleep, so as soon as it was light he drove round to Wimbourne Court intent on seeing her. But as he was about to ring the bell he realised it was far too early for anyone to be awake, so he drove away.

An hour or so later, when Frances's brother Frank got up, he took her in a cup of tea. Thinking she was fast asleep, he left it by her bed and went off to work. But something about his sister worried him and at lunchtime he returned to find her still in bed, just as he had left her, with the cup of tea untasted on the bedside table. It was then he realised she wasn't sleeping but had died from an overdose of sleeping pills.

Usually when someone dies in a family, it ushers in at least a brief period of peace in which old enmities can be forgotten and the bereaved can draw together as they mourn the dear departed. But this could not happen with the Krays and the death of Frances marked the beginning of a period of rapidly ascending bitterness, self-pity, black revenge, and ultimately bloody murder.

The first to set the tone for much of what ensued was the dead girl's father, Frank Shea Sr, who arrived at Wimbourne Court around lunchtime in response to a desperate phone call from his son. He had driven instantly to the flat and, seeing his daughter lying there so peacefully, his first thought, like his son's, was that she must be sleeping. It was only when he took Frances's hands in his and felt how cold they were that he knew the truth. Twice already he had had to deal with false alarms when he had found her after a suicide attempt and dragged her back to life. Now it was too late for that.

'I could feel her arms already stiffening and there was nothing we could do. She'd been dead for hours. It is a terrible thing to say, but at that moment all I could think of was how those bastards had destroyed my daughter, and how much I hated them.'

Wisely, his son Frankie waited until his father left before

informing Reg at Vallance Road that he had bad news for him. He didn't say what it was but Reg always claimed that he had guessed the truth, and he drove to Wimbourne Court at once. Just as her father had at first failed to realise the truth, so it was not until Reg held Frances's hands in his and felt how cold they were that he knew for certain she was dead. And as with Frank Shea, Reg's first reaction was a wave of bitter hatred which entirely engulfed him.

'I could only blame her parents for everything that happened. They didn't want her to be happy with me, and they kept on and on at her until she killed herself. It was as simple as that,' he muttered.

This is the point at which the body of sad, wraithlike Frances Kray becomes the centre of a funereal extravaganza which was something of a dress rehearsal for the mammoth East End funerals that the Krays would one day give themselves. As for Reg, throughout this period there are times when his performance as the grief-stricken husband seems so theatrical that one gets a glimpse of the natural actor concealed beneath the sharp blue suiting of the East End gangster.

First comes the show of grief when visiting the mortuary to identify his wife. As Ron's period in hiding still has several weeks to run, Reg goes accompanied by his young good-looking cousin Ronnie Hart, who has recently joined the Firm after a spell in the merchant navy and who does his best to console him. But for Reg this is not the time or the place for consolation as he stands beside his wife's lifeless body, with tears streaming down his face, calling 'Frankie, darling Frankie. Come back to me, my darling Frankie.'

Answer, unsurprisingly, comes there none but once Frances's body has been shifted from the mortuary to English's funeral parlour in Whitechapel High Street Reg still visits three and sometimes four times every day to see her lying in her silk-lined coffin. In death she looks so peaceful that one might have thought that something of that peace might spread to Reg. But as he stands before the open coffin, all his thoughts are turning not to peace but to revenge. As he stands there mumbling to himself, Hart hears him saying, 'I'll get even with those bastards, even if it takes the rest of my life to do it. They took her from me and I'll make them pay.'

'Who took her from you?' Hart inquires.

'The Sheas, of course. Her fucking family. They were jealous of our happiness together, so they poisoned her mind against me, and I'll kill them. I'll kill the lot of them.'

In his current state of mind, Reg means what he is saying and only one thing holds him back – the superstitious fear that, wherever she may be, Frances may be watching and would not forgive him if she knew he had harmed anyone she loved.

So he vents his hatred by fighting her parents every inch of the way to the churchyard.

Since he is still legally their daughter's next of kin, he insists on being shown where she died, and on removing all her personal possessions, including her correspondence, her lipstick and her underwear. The Sheas beg him to allow them to bury her as she wanted – under her own name and somewhere of their choosing. He refuses angrily. Her name is Kray, not Shea, and he'll bury her where and how he pleases. He also insists that she'll be buried wearing the white satin wedding dress he bought her. Even in death she's still his wife and he's in charge of her funeral, as he is with everything else concerning her.

What happens next is fascinating, offering the first clear intimation of how the cult of Krayhood is already forming in his mind. First comes the purchase of an expensive plot of land in Chingford Cemetery, where not only Frances but he and other close members of the family can be buried when they die. This will become their place of permanent memorial, and in time, in imitation of Poets' Corner in Westminster Abbey, people will start calling it 'Kray Corner'. By burying Frances there already, in a plot large enough for him to join her later, Reg will also be giving both of them one final chance to do in death the one thing they could never do in life – lie peacefully together.

As for the funeral itself, it was certainly a great production. As Reg boasted later, 'I'd given my wife the East End's wedding of the year. Now I was giving her the East End's funeral of the year.' As if in compensation for her wretched death, Reg was posthumously giving her everything that he and his money could buy to express what really mattered to him now – his all-consuming sorrow – in a lavish show of conspicuous bereavement.

If anyone was proved right by these events, it was their old priest Father Hetherington who had so resolutely refused to marry them three years earlier 'because of the damage they would do to one another'. But since the damage had been done, Father Hetherington saw no point in still refusing when Reg asked him to bury Frances. He said he would conduct the funeral in St James the Great, the church where they were married.

The Shea parents did score one sly victory, which they made sure that Reg would not discover until it was too late. Elsie Shea persuaded the undertaker to let her clothe her daughter's wasted body in a white slip and tights, so that as little as possible of her flesh was touched by her hated wedding dress. Elsie also claimed that, just before the undertakers screwed the coffin lid down, she removed Reg's wedding ring from her daughter's finger and replaced it with a simple ring that she had given her as a child. Such was the spirit now presiding over the 'East End's burial of the year' in which poor haunted Frances Shea was laid to rest.

For the burial at Chingford Cemetery was clearly more in honour of the Krays than in memory of Frances. It was also clearly patterned on what Reg had read about the way the Mafia

staged its funerals in America – the dozen or so statutory black
limousines packed with large men and celebrities, the most
expensive highly-polished coffin Messrs. English's, the undertakers, could provide, and the avalanche of flowers which
carpeted the graveside. Every member of the Firm had been
ordered to send a wreath, suitably inscribed with personal con-
dolences. (Reg told Donoghue afterwards to check the cards to
see if anyone had disobeyed.) Ron, who was still dodging the
police, sent a mammoth bunch of pink carnations, and yet more
flowers cascaded in from every quarter of the underworld. Not
to be outdone, Reg remained the undisputed winner in this
graveside battle of the flowers, with three major floral tributes
of his own.

His final gesture was to throw a five-pound note onto the
coffin for the gravedigger as he strode off, ashen-faced, through
a sombre audience of silent mourners.

Reg's bitterness was in fact more complicated than it appeared,
for it wasn't only Frances he was mourning but himself. Of
course he was fooling himself – as he often did – if he seriously
believed the marriage could have worked. His genes, like Ron's
had been against it from the start, and if anyone knew this it
would have had to be Frances. In the loneliness of her bed on
the night she killed herself she must have faced the fact that,
however considerate Reg now appeared, she and her marriage
were both doomed together and she couldn't face a repetition
of that first disaster.

This was something that Reg never could or would admit.
For him the death of Frances had destroyed all his hopes of that
brave new life he had convinced himself that they were just
about to share, and much of the bile and bitterness boiling up
inside him came from the thought of the lost paradise which 'all
those bastards' had destroyed. It was for this that he never could
or would forgive them. But there was more to it than that. Like

Ron, at times like this when the rage and tension deep within him threatened to become unbearable he found his only real relief in alcohol, which he started to consume in devastating quantities. A few months later, when I was seeing quite a lot of the Twins, Reg was drinking straight Gordon's gin from a half-pint beer glass and managing to stay upright and more or less coherent until the bottle was empty, when he'd order another.

Had this been all, he could probably still have coped and started easing off the drinking as his misery and rage subsided. But this wasn't all. Between his rage and wretchedness, the booze was making him profoundly vulnerable.

As we have seen, thanks to the accident of their birth the twins were unique genetic rarities. They had always been abnormal, and with Ron's advancing madness the tension between them had become unbearable. To understand the nightmare now beginning to engulf them one must imagine a pair of Siamese twins reaching maturity, only to discover that one of them is a homicidal schizophrenic.

Although, of course, the Twins were not joined together physically, there were close parallels between this scenario and the nightmare that Reg was facing. Now on the edge of an alcohol-induced breakdown, his genetic legacy had caught up with him as the true nature of the Twins' discordant twin relationship revealed itself in earnest. Ron was already mad and indulging in a homicidal orgy, while Reg was getting close to joining him.

Much of what passed between them now was actually a repetition of the teenage battles in which they had fought for dominance, and which Ron had always won by taunting Reg until he lost his self-control and the two of them united in a splurge of all-consuming violence. What never failed to bring the Twins together was one thing and one alone – violence, either against each other or, better still, against their enemies. It was then that the addictive frenzy of a fight transformed them into one terrifying creature with four legs, four fists and one identical intelligence. That summer, after Frances died, this creature was increasingly in evidence as Ron's madness spread and threatened to engulf them both.

Mayhem reigned that summer with the Twins egging each other on in a rampage of continuing terror. But now, in contrast with the past, it was often Reg not Ron who led the way, urged on by his hunger for revenge not just for Frances but for the life he might have led if fate had not betrayed him. When the rage was on him and the red mist once again descended, the Twins were united in a way that they had not been since they fought their teenage battles with the rival gangs from Watney Street, merging their separate identities in the shared intoxication of untrammelled violence.

For Reg, alcohol fuelled this madness by destroying any feeling of restraint as he stumbled round the East End streets searching out targets for revenge. But inevitably it was Ron who found him his first victim, an old friend of theirs called Frederick. A would-be villain, Frederick had been with the Twins in the days of the billiard hall, and although since then he'd settled down and started a family he kept in touch with them and often drank with them. Out of the blue one evening, Ron casually remarked that he'd overheard Frederick saying something out of order about Frances.

'What did he say about my wife, the bastard?' muttered Reg.

'I'm not repeating it,' said Ron. 'It would upset you.'

And although Reg kept on at him Ron would say no more, knowing he had said enough to start his brother brooding. For the rest of that night, Reg remained awake, drinking steadily and planning his revenge. Early next morning he summoned two members of the Firm to 'come over with their van and bring a shooter'. There was work for them to do.

It was just after seven when the van drew up outside the flat in Hackney where Frederick lived. He was still in the bathroom, shaving, and his wife was giving the children their breakfast when Reg, with his two heavies, rang the bell. Frederick's wife answered it.

'Tell Frederick that Reggie's here and wants a word with him', said one of the heavies.

By now the children had joined their mother at the door to see who had arrived and Reg had to push through the group, gun in hand, shouting for the kids' father. Frederick appeared at the head of the stairs, his face covered in shaving soap.

'Filthy bastard,' shouted Reg. 'You've been saying things about my Frances. I thought you were my friend.'

Tears were streaming down his face as one of the heavies stumbled up the stairs and struck Frederick such a blow that he came tumbling down. Then, as the children started screaming, Reg started shooting. Luckily he was so drunk that all his shots went wide, except for one that hit Frederick in the leg. He lay there, groaning.

At the sight of blood Reg seemed satisfied. The heavies helped him back into the van and off they went with Reg beside the driver, sobbing.

'That bastard had it coming to him, saying things about my wife, my lovely Frances,' he kept muttering.

This time it was brother Charlie's turn to call Doc Blasker in to see to Frederick's injuries, along with Red-faced Tommy Plumley to make sure that no one talked to the police. So no one did. But when Reg told Ron what he'd done, Ron went ballistic.

'Drunken slag,' he shouted. 'Here we are, trying to earn ourselves a living and you risk the lot by gunning down a friend. Anyhow, you couldn't kill anybody if you tried. You're too fucking soft. When I did my one I made a proper job of it and Cornell couldn't walk around no more – not like your friend, Frederick.'

So after shooting Frederick Reg's state of mind grew worse, instead of better. Time passed him by like a dream, which always ended with him feeling utterly alone and scared of what was happening to him. At times like this the only person he could talk to was Father Hetherington, who never failed him.

'I used to feel better after seeing him,' he told me once, and he'd usually start thinking of a different life. What about the Foreign Legion? Or, better still, a long, tough African safari? What was stopping him? But even as he asked himself these questions, he always knew the answer – Ron. 'How could I leave my brother? How could Ron ever cope without me?'

This was the point at which Reg's dreams returned as nightmares and his rage began in earnest and he started drinking once again.

Ron's court order lapsed at the end of that July, leaving him free to emerge from hiding. He seemed madder now than ever, and once he was back on the scene the Firm's activities became madder too. Many of the old financial standbys, like the income from 'respectable' protection and money from gambling and stolen securities, dwindled. Now that Les Payne and his sidekick Freddy Gore had gone, the elaborate long-firm frauds that had always brought in large amounts of money had all but vanished too. In their place the Firm was getting into more downmarket rackets like pornography and dealing in the amphetamine pills called purple hearts. Then at one stage there was talk of taking over all the fruit machines in London, which came to nothing.

But for Ron there were also the paranoid illusions of the schizophrenic, which Reg believed that some outsider had to be encouraging since so many way-out projects were suddenly obsessing him. On his own, would Ron ever have hit on the idea of taking over a diamond mine in the Congo or assassinating the African leader President Kaunda? For that matter, why should he suddenly think of trying to release the Congolese leader President Tshombe who was under house arrest in Algiers?

But Ron was in deadly earnest about all this. After claiming to have met some of Tshombe's followers in London he was talking of a task force from the Firm flying to Algeria, where they'd use helicopters and nerve gas to storm his captors' villa. Once freed, Tshombe would make his getaway by hovercraft. Ron had also plans to mastermind an international forged-currency syndicate with the printing plates manufactured in New York by a master forger, the notes mass-produced in Switzerland and Europe swamped with quantities of fake currency under the firm direction of the Krays.

Needless to say, none of these James Bond-like schemes came remotely near fruition. The only one that did was an idea which Ron had picked up for himself during that visit to Nigeria in 1964. He'd never forgotten what he had learned about the leopard men, the secret brotherhood of dedicated murderers who terrorised the country and indulged in ritual murder in their initiation ceremonies. Before anyone could join the leopard men he had to prove himself by killing someone so that murder would form a bond of loyalty at the centre of this brotherhood of murderers.

Ron was particularly excited by all this and talked a lot about turning the Firm into something similar. The Mafia required any candidate for membership to 'make his bones' by killing someone. Within the Firm he had passed this test himself by killing George Cornell. Now the time had come for Reg to join him. Others could come in later, but not before Reg had shown them the way. Murder was what mattered now. Only when Reg had killed could the Twins be totally united.

So Reg was at his twin brother's mercy, and, with Ron's encouragement, his shootings started up in earnest. But so far nobody had died, for Reg's aggression took the form of acts of random violence in which he indulged for their own sake, like the night he arrived at the Starlight Club in Highbury so drunk that he made little sense to anyone, himself included. Spotting a businessman called Field whom he thought he knew, he staggered over to him, waved a gun in his face and asked him for a thousand pounds. Field answered that he hadn't got a thousand pounds. Reg shot him through the leg and ordered a member of the Firm who was acting as his bodyguard to smash his face in. Which he promptly did. But these actions accomplished less than nothing except to leave a lot of trouble and expense behind which needed to be cleared up later. Once again Ron was furious. 'You drunken slag,' he said on learning what had happened. 'Ain't it time you got your fucking act together?'

When he tried to do so, Reg got so drunk that he no longer cared if Frances was watching him through some heavenly spyhole, and ordered Albert Donoghue to bring her brother Frank to the Carpenters' Arms as he wanted to talk with him. In fact, he had decided that the time had come to kill him, but when Frank appeared he looked so uncannily like Frances that Reg started weeping and bought him a drink instead before sending him packing.

After this Ron started taunting Reg unmercifully, as he had when they'd been children. But now the taunts were all about his brother's cowardice when all he had to do was murder someone. What could be easier?

'I've done mine, Reg,' he kept repeating.' You know it's time that you did yours as well.'

For Ron in fact was now so paranoid, and so obsessed with the thought of traitors in their midst, that he wanted Reg to play his part in killing them. But when sober, Reg was still reluctant; so one night when they were out drinking together at the

Green Dragon, Ron decided that the time had come to show Reg how to do it.

Among those standing at the bar was a tough old villain called George Dixon. The Twins had grown up with him and had known him for years. But recently Ron had been hearing things about him which he didn't like. Ron was particularly upset about certain things that Dixon had reportedly said about Cornell. He needed to be taught a lesson, and since Reg wouldn't do it Ron would have to. There was no time like the present, and the sooner it was done the better.

So, there and then, in full view of everybody in that crowded bar, Ron drew an automatic from a shoulder holster, brought the muzzle up to Dixon's head and pulled the trigger. There was a click and nothing happened.

The gun had jammed but, unpredictable as ever, Ron took this very coolly.

'Hey', he said, taking the bullet from the chamber and throwing it across to Dixon. 'It's just saved your fucking life. Wear it on your watch chain as a souvenir.'

As for persuading Reg to murder someone, Ron wasn't particularly worried any more. He knew that Reg would do the business when he had to. There was always somebody around who needed killing.

Although he had a reputation as a fearless fighter and a bit of a womaniser, there was something just a touch pathetic about Jack 'The Hat' McVitie. Perhaps it was the hat he wore to hide his baldness. Why bother? And why was he always getting beaten up? A few months earlier, a gang of hooligans he'd offended tried to teach him a lesson by smashing his hands with a crowbar. But Jack wasn't one for lessons, and he showed everyone he didn't care by starting brawling once again, long before his hands were healed. But obviously Jack *did* care, just as he cared about his baldness and the threats of violence. For the truth about him was that he was a drunk, that his nerves were shot to pieces, and that his courage came from monster pep-pills called 'black bombers'. Jack was also far too eager to be of service to anyone who would employ him and that summer, when the Twins started wholesale dealing in purple hearts, he came in useful.

As with the trouble concerning Frederick, it was Ron who was responsible for carrying the Twins' involvement with Jack the Hat further. By doing this, was he already seeking to set him up? Probably. Certainly it was Ron who set things rolling by making the original deal with Jack to murder another of the Twins' former friends turned enemy – the man with the brief-case, Les Payne. Ron had been hearing yet more rumours, this time that Payne had joined forces with enemies of the Krays who were anxious to betray them to the law.

This was simply one of countless rumours that both the Twins were all too ready to believe and which found a ready home among Ron's paranoid suspicions. So Ron paid Jack the Hat £100 on account to kill Les Payne, promising him a further £400 when Payne was dead.

Reg didn't fancy the idea of this, and in the old days would have had no difficulty persuading his brother to forget it. Reg had liked Les Payne when things were going well and wouldn't think badly of him now. But these were not the good old days, and ever since Frances died Reg seemed to have lost the ability to oppose his brother. So the contract went ahead, and Jack the Hat did his best to murder Leslie Payne by shooting him outside of his home in Purley – but even here Jack failed, and by failing offered Payne a warning, which made Jack's task doubly difficult thereafter.

Jack still did his best. But the man with the briefcase was a hard man to kill, and Ron started worrying about his money. When he heard that Jack had made a scene in Freddie Foreman's 211 Club in Balham, he started shouting that Jack's behaviour was 'a diabolical liberty' and he would pay for it. Jack should have known that Foreman was a friend and ally of the Twins, and there and then Jack's name went to the top of Ron's private list of candidates for murder.

So great was Ron's fury that when he told Reg what Jack had done, for the sake of peace Reg weakly agreed to drive over to the Regency Club in north-east London where Jack usually hung out to 'sort the fucker out'.

This sort of thing was happening all too often now, with Reg ending up doing whatever Ron told him to; and when he arrived at the Regency that night he definitely intended to kill Jack the Hat. But once he saw him there was something so pitiful about this threadbare villain, moaning on about his debts and his nervous troubles and his sick baby daughter, that once again Reg's heart was touched and instead of shooting him he gave him fifty pounds.

'I s'pose you'd've sent five hundred quid to George Cornell,' said Ron when he heard what Reg had done. Ron also sent a threatening message to Jack McVitie, giving him one more chance. Either do the business with Les Payne or face the consequences. It was a simple enough message but inevitably it caused a fresh misunderstanding, which rapidly led on to everything that followed. For on receiving it Jack instantly thought that Reg had double-crossed him, got roaring drunk, swallowed several more black bombers, and appeared in the upstairs bar at the Regency waving a sawn-off shotgun. Then, in front of everyone, he started shouting threats against the Twins.

Human nature being what it is, there were several people standing in the bar that night who could hardly wait to pass the news of Jack the Hat's behaviour back to the Twins. Then the trouble really started.

All this happened on a Friday night and the following evening the Twins took over the Carpenters' Arms for what they called a 'Ladies' Night'. The wives and girlfriends honoured with an invitation to these painfully polite affairs were careful to behave exactly as the Twins expected – particularly with Violet present, as she was that evening. On such occasions Violet was very much East End royalty and all the women knew their places in her presence. None of them would have dreamt of sitting at the bar, still less of ordering herself a drink or speaking out of turn. There was something very Japanese about these villains' women as they sat together like geishas with their elaborate hairdos and expensive dresses, sipping their Babychams and chattering together.

The men, who were likewise on their best behaviour, also kept strictly to themselves. Dress on such occasions was strictly formal, in the style of the so-called 'gangster chic' favoured by the Twins – snow-white shirts with tightly knotted slim silk ties, and sharp blue suits with narrow trouser legs and knifelike creases. Newer arrivals in the Firm tended towards highly polished black winkle-picker shoes.

On these occasions the men went easy with the drinking. (The time for serious consumption would follow closing time.) They were also careful with their language, particularly with Violet present since she couldn't abide swearing. For the Kray Twins' ladies' evenings took their cue from Violet and were essentially polite affairs, the East End on its best behaviour, which in the circumstances made that evening at the Carpenters' a surreal beginning to the horror that would follow.

To make it stranger still, Reg was in an unusually good mood, drinking little, showing no sign of whatever strain he might be under, attentive to the ladies, and perfectly at home as he played the part that he enjoyed: the perfect host. The rest of the Firm appeared to take their lead from him and the solitary fly in the ointment was, as usual, Ron, who remained at the far end of the bar with an expression on his face like thunder.

When Reg inquired what was up, Ron said he had the hump

with Jack McVitie. He would have to be dealt with, and since
no one else would do it he would have to. That was what was
pissing him off. Why was he left with all the dirty work while
all the others ponced around like women? But fucking McVitie
was completely out of order, and if Reg wouldn't deal with him
Ron would have to, just as he'd dealt with fucking George
Cornell.

Nobody appears to have heard Reg's reply, but several
members of the Firm at the Carpenters' that night did notice a
change come over him as he started drinking heavily again.

In those days pubs still closed at ten-thirty but that night there
was an open invitation for any members of the Firm, together
with their partners, to go on to a party at Blonde Carol
Skinner's place at No. 71 Cazenove Road, Stoke Newington.
And many of them did, Ron included, which in the circum-
stances was surprising, especially as there was no sign there of
Reg. But just before eleven Reg did appear at the Regency
Club, with a gun and two members of the Firm, searching for
McVitie; but they couldn't find him.

This was a key moment in that evening's rapidly unfolding
drama. For at that moment, drunk as he was, Reg was clearly of
a mind to murder Jack McVitie when they found him. Instead
they were greeted by a friend of theirs, the young and highly
got-together owner of the Regency, John Barry. As landlord of
a popular North London drinking club, one of Barry's many
skills lay in averting trouble on his premises and the last thing in
the world he wanted was a murder that night – or any night –
at the Regency. So, using all his powers of persuasion, he set
about trying to convince Reg not to murder Jack the Hat; and,
surprisingly, he succeeded.

Late though it was, and drunk though he was, when faced
with the reality of killing someone as pitiable as Jack McVitie,
Reg faltered. And he did not merely falter. Even when Barry

tactfully suggested that it might be best if he left his gun with him, Reg actually agreed to that as well. After watching Barry lock his .32 automatic in a drawer in his office, Reg went off calmly to join Ron and all their other friends and acquaintances drinking their heads off at Blonde Carol's party.

Had that been the end of it, and had Reg's automatic stayed safely locked away in Barry's drawer, all the guests at Carol Skinner's party would have thoroughly enjoyed themselves and the whole story of the Twins might well have had a very different ending.

But thanks to one person and to one alone, this didn't happen. For as soon as Reg turned up at the party and admitted that Jack the Hat was still alive, Ron became positively transfixed with rage. This was not one of Ron's customary rages – which were frightening enough – but the implacable fury of a total madman. Without a further word, he brushed Reg aside and in his madness instantly took charge of what rapidly became a battle not only for the life of Jack McVitie but also for the soul of Reggie Kray.

No sooner had Ron heard that Jack McVitie was alive than he cleared the decks for action, and with the abrupt announcement that 'this is going to be no place for women' packed all the women and the younger men off to join another party which was conveniently in progress down the road. It's hard to imagine that anyone was terribly upset by this, for by the sound of it Blonde Carol's party can't have been much fun, with Ronnie in the state that he was in; and apart from the Twins, the only males left behind were a fresh recruit to the Firm called Ronald Bender, two young Cypriot brothers, John and Chrissie Lambrianou, who had set their silly hearts on entering the Firm, two gay brothers called Mills who had spent the evening dancing with each other, and Reg's cousin and companion in mourning, the ex-merchant navy sailor Ron Hart.

At this point in the evening Reg must have seemed completely useless compared with Ron who now took total charge. Mad though he was, there was not a hint of wavering or weakness about him now. The Colonel was back and firmly in command as he gave his orders to set the trap to deliver the unsuspecting Jack McVitie to his killer.

First, Ronnie Bender was to drive immediately to the Regency with an urgent message from Ron Kray to Barry, telling him, on pain of death, to come at once to Carol Skinner's with the gun that Reg had left in his possession.

Next the two young Lambrianous were given their part to play. Ron had heard that they were friends of Jack McVitie, so it was up to them to follow Bender to the Regency, find McVitie and, without arousing his suspicions, invite him to join them at the party in progress at Carol Skinner's – all this, of course, without mentioning a word about the Krays.

Finally, the Colonel had an important role for his cousin Ronald Hart who was to go to the empty flat upstairs and from one of the windows keep a sharp lookout for Jack's arrival. As soon as he saw him he must scoot downstairs as fast as his legs would carry him to warn the Twins.

Throughout all this, Reg made no contribution whatsoever to what was going on – apart from drinking heavily to calm his nerves. In the state that he was in he must have found it hard to know quite how he felt about McVitie – or anything else. Not that it mattered any more what Reg was thinking. The Colonel, and he alone, had taken over and was in command.

A few minutes after midnight, from his lookout point in the upstairs room, Ron Hart saw a beaten-up Ford Zodiac draw up outside the house, and three occupants get out: the two young Lambrianous and a man in a hat – Jack McVitie. He was clearly in the best of spirits, for Hart stayed long enough to hear him laughing as they walked towards the house, at which point he followed orders and dashed down to the basement to raise the alarm.

It can't have taken long, but for those waiting in the room it must have seemed an age before the door burst open and in came Jack the Hat in party mood.

'Where are the birds and the booze?' he shouted. Then he saw Ron sitting on a sofa in the middle of an empty room. What Jack didn't see was that Reg was standing, gun in hand, behind the door, and before Jack had even realised that he was there Reg had tried to shoot him through the head. But this was a rare occasion when the history of the Twins was going to repeat itself and the same thing happened as when Ron had tried to shoot George Dixon in the bar of the Green Dragon a few weeks earlier.

Reg's automatic jammed.

When he realised what was going on Jack seems to have thought he had a chance, for he remembered what had happened when Ronnie's automatic had jammed and how Ron had let Dixon off with a warning and nothing more was said. So even if the Twins were angry and felt that he deserved a beating for not killing Leslie Payne, fair enough. Jack was perfectly prepared to take even a kicking without complaining. But Ron wasn't going to give him the chance.

Jack must have recognised the warning signs on Ronnie's face as those dead-black eyes of his began to bulge and incoherent grunts began emerging from his lips. By now the two gay brothers, sensing trouble, had made themselves scarce along with Chrissie Lambrianou who had wanted so desperately to be a gangster and who, seeing what was happening, was sitting outside on the stairs, weeping.

Although Reg had thrown away his useless automatic, those remaining in the room must have known by now that Jack would die. He must have known it himself. The only question that remained was how. Reg was still grappling with him from behind, and Ron was screaming curses at him and ordering Reg to kill him. But Jack was strong, and with the strength that comes from total desperation he suddenly broke free and dived for the window in the corner of the room which overlooked the garden.

He nearly made it. His chest and arms had actually passed through the window and the rest of him was just about to follow when his legs got stuck in the broken glass as he made one final lunge for freedom. But Jack was not to cheat death so easily and someone pulled him back. Who did this would always be a matter for dispute. It might have been Ronnie or it might have been Ron Hart, although Hart was always going to deny it.

'Be a man, Jack!' screamed Ron.

'I'll be a man, but I don't want to die like one,' said Jack. But he was not being given the alternative. For by now it was Ron who held him pinioned from behind and Reg had replaced his useless automatic with a carving knife that someone had found in the kitchen. But even now Reg hesitated.

'Kill him, Reg, Do him!' hissed his brother. 'Do it now!'

In his final dive for freedom through the window Jack had lost his hat. It would later be discovered on the windowsill where it had fallen as he struggled to escape. He stood there looking very bald and gaunt, with all the resistance out of him.

'Reggie, why are you doing this to me?' he asked pathetically. Reg answered with a thrust from the carving knife into his face below the eye – and the butchering of Jack McVitie started. It soon became more an orgy of rage than a cold-blooded murder as Reg lost all control and set about him like a maniac, stabbing repeatedly at his chest and stomach with the knife. 'It ended with Reg standing astride him and raising the knife until the point rested on his throat as though he was taking aim. Then, using all his strength, he shoved the knife down so hard that it impaled Jack on the floor.'

Later Reg would claim that Ron Hart joined in the killing, but this is unlikely. Hart had always been a friend of McVitie's and Ron had been determined that Reg should do the murder on his own. Undoubtedly Hart did witness everything that happened, and later admitted to having pushed a handkerchief into McVitie's mouth 'to stop the flow of blood and the gurgling noises he was making.' Hart also claimed that when Reg's victim stopped breathing it was Ronnie Bender who put his ear to Jack McVitie's chest and finally pronounced him dead.

According to Hart, Bender was also given the job of disposing of Jack's remains, which he rolled up in a bedspread and dumped in the bedroom on the bed next to the one where Carol's children were sleeping. He also gathered up the rest of the incriminating debris in the flat, including Jack's dangerously recognisable hat which Reg discovered on the windowsill, then started cleaning up the room with a mop and a bucket of water. But the killing had been so frenzied and chaotic that blood was spattered all around the room. Where Jack had been killed a pool of blood was already soaking into the carpet and the floor beneath.

While Bender did his best to deal with this, Blonde Carol and Hart's girlfriend Vicki returned from the party down the road and were ordered by Ron to take over and do their best to scrub the carpet, while Bender disposed of Jack McVitie's body. According to Hart, the Twins had made no plans to deal with this, and Bender propped the corpse up, still wrapped in the bedspread, in the back seat of his car. He then drove it over London Bridge and parked the car outside a church near Foreman's pub, the Prince of Wales, in Lant Street and left it there for him to deal with. But having already murdered Frank Mitchell for the Twins, Foreman's patience with Ron and Reg was wearing thin – and he wasn't an undertaker.

So all that Sunday the car was left where Bender had parked

it, with the body in the back barely covered with the children's bedspread and one of the feet poking out. Later that afternoon there was a wedding in the church, but although the car was covered in confetti no one can have looked inside or noticed anything unusual. Next day it was only when someone complained to Foreman about the smell that he reluctantly became involved .

Apart from complaining that when he removed McVitie from the car, he was covered in some sort of slime, Foreman never did say anything more about how he disposed of yet one more unwanted body. One presumes that once again he relied on the underworld's surest way of 'vanishing' a corpse for good and that Jack McVitie now joined Frank Mitchell in that invaluable 'little facility' of his at Newhaven.

Not that McVitie's final destination mattered very much. What was important was the place his murder would assume in the story of the Krays that before too long would start to dominate the media, obsess the law-abiding public and enthrone the Twins in their position as murderers for ever.

If Charlie Richardson was right and the killing of Cornell was Ron's 'necessary sacrifice', then McVitie's murder did much the same for Reg. For whatever else it might have been this was no ordinary gangland murder. There were much stranger and more compelling reasons why Jack McVitie had had to die than that.

18

The American Connection

TOP POLICEMEN may sometimes be idle but rarely where their prospects for promotion are concerned, and among the higher ranks at Scotland Yard few can have ignored the dismal lessons of the Boothby scandal and its cover-up, followed by the disaster of McCowan.

Even more than had been the case with the politicians and the members of the media involved, individual policemen and detectives had actually witnessed what was going on and had drawn their own conclusions. Some had done their best to deal with the Twins in the past and knew the threat they represented. Members of C11, the Yard's own Intelligence Section, had spent some months keeping Boothby and Ron's questionable friends under observation and had helped to write reports that had later been suppressed. Those without direct contact with the affair had been told what happened by their colleagues and had seen what had followed – with the Commissioner himself denying that an investigation into the Twins had taken place, and police activity against the Twins ceasing with the failure of the McCowan prosecution.

With the Twins still basking in their status as 'untouchables' it was widely assumed among the police that Ron and Reg had access to information from the upper reaches of the Yard itself, which increased the sense that no one could be trusted. The effect of this on morale at Scotland Yard had been disastrous. A subsequent Chief Commissioner, Sir Thomas Mark, called Scotland Yard in the 1960s, 'the most routinely corrupt organisation in London', with the Flying Squad riddled with corruption, several senior officers regularly receiving bribes from criminals, and the head of the Yard's Vice Squad (improbably named Inspector Virgo) sent to prison for wholesale dealing in pornography.

Simultaneously the rumour mill at Scotland Yard was grinding out the message that the Twins would never be arrested while Sir Joseph Simpson occupied the chair of Chief Commissioner. But Sir Joseph was a tough old bird. Despite two heart attacks and serious warnings from his doctors, he was hanging in there and as long as he was Chief Commissioner he had no intention of permitting his part in the Boothby cover-up to be revealed – or any of the secrets that went with it.

So far, so obvious, but despite the disastrous effects the cover-up had been having on law and order by making the Twins 'untouchable', they could hardly have gone on killing people without someone in authority making at least some effort to stop them. In 1967 two separate operations started, aimed at doing precisely that.

The strangest and most unlikely of these operations originated from an office in the US embassy in Paris occupied by a shadowy figure called Admiral John H. Hanly. The Admiral's job description on the contemporary diplomatic list was brief to the point of anonymity. It described him simply as 'Chargé d'Affaires from the Treasury Department, attached to the US Embassy,' which didn't get one very far. The truth was that Admiral John H. Hanly was a very senior agent in the US Secret Service and a highly influential member of the American intelligence community.

Originally created as an offshoot of the US Treasury after the assassination of President McKinley in 1901, the US Secret Service was the oldest and most prestigious law enforcement agency in America. Its first priority was, and still is, the safety and security of the President and its responsibilities extended to intelligence gathering on a range of serious federal offences, including nationwide organised crime, narcotics, counterfeiting, serious fraud and currency offences.

With Hanly the title of admiral was deceptive. During the first world war, and later in Korea, he reached the rank of rear admiral in the Naval Reserve through distinguished active service. But in character, aptitude and training Admiral Hanly would always be a secret serviceman having started his working life before the war as an undercover agent with another branch of the Secret Service, the Bureau of Narcotics, in its struggle with the US Mafia. He had been a friend and protégé of the celebrated Chief White, the man President Roosevelt chose to head the bureau, and in 1939, when war in Europe started, Hanly enlisted with US naval intelligence.

Through his work with the Bureau of Narcotics, Hanly had already made himself the foremost authority on the man believed to be 'the most important Italian-American gangster the USA ever produced', Charles 'Lucky' Luciano. During the early 1930s Luciano was responsible for ruthlessly creating the 'national syndicate' which formed the basis of the modern Mafia; and when the law caught up with him and gave him fifty years in prison for organising prostitution, he still maintained his undisputed hold on the Mob from inside prison.

In 1939 the US Navy was concerned about the risk of waterfront sabotage and someone suggested that, as a patriotic American, Lucky might be asked to use his influence with the labour unions to prevent it from happening. In principle, Lucky agreed, and the result was the so-called Luciano Project on which Hanly worked for many months, visiting Luciano regularly in his cell in the Albany State Correction Centre and helping him coordinate waterfront security through Mafia members of the dockyard labour unions throughout America.

The result was a great success and helped establish Hanly's reputation. Maritime sabotage virtually ceased throughout the USA. But Luciano didn't get his nickname 'Lucky' accidentally and there had to be a pay-off. When the war ended, Luciano was paroled for 'services to his country' and deported to Sicily – where he rapidly began reorganising the power of the Mafia on the island. Almost simultaneously Hanly joined the US Secret Service.

The Service had offices across America and for several years Hanly was employed as an 'agent in charge', directing operations against organised crime in Baltimore and later in Chicago. Then in January 1961 came his proudest moment when he headed the Secret Service detail responsible for the security of President Kennedy at his inauguration. Three years later Hanly had a double stroke of luck. Late that summer he received the assignment of his life when he was granted diplomatic status at the US embassy in Paris and was put in charge of the operations of the Secret Service throughout Europe and the Middle East. This meant that he had no involvement in the blackest day in the history of the US Secret Service when three months later President Kennedy was assassinated at Dallas and the Secret Service was inevitably blamed.

By then the Admiral had discovered much to keep him busy in Europe. In Sicily the Mafia, which Luciano helped to re-establish, was flourishing, with its laboratories working round the clock to satisfy heroin demand in Europe. In France the famous French Connection was growing richer still from the narcotics traffic with the States. And as the Mafia began shifting more of its activities to Europe, London became a target for the Mob with its octopus-like control of this most inviting new gambling capital of Europe.

★

The first that the Admiral heard about the Twins came at the end of 1963 when his London agents reported them 'protecting' Mafia-controlled casinos like the River Club and the Sporting Club in Mayfair. At first the Admiral treated this as routine information and it was not until the Boothby scandal suddenly erupted in the European press in 1964 that he first began to take them seriously. The case fascinated him, as it fascinated many foreign observers, and he was particularly intrigued by press reports describing Ronald Kray as 'King of the London Underworld'.

One of the responsibilities of the US Secret Service was to check on undesirables entering America and the monthly list of visas issued by their London embassy showed that 'the King of the London Underworld' had just received a tourist visa. When further checks revealed that he was on the point of flying to New York it was easy to ensure that one of the Admiral's agents was there to greet him on arrival, cancel his visa, and give him the bum's rush back to Britain.

After this the Admiral became still more intrigued by the news that Lord Boothby had been in touch with the American ambassador in London, begging him to use his influence to overrule the cancellation of Ronald Kray's visa. As we have seen the ambassador not only refused but he felt it his duty to report the incident, which was how news of it found its way into the file marked 'Kray' in the Paris Bureau of the Secret Service. When media reports of Boothby's intervention in parliament on the Krays' behalf, a few weeks later, were added to the file, they confirmed what the Admiral had suspected all along about the Boothby scandal. He wasn't convinced for a moment by Lord Goodman's cover-up and the twins appeared suspiciously like certain criminals he had known in America – godfather figures with powerful connections in politics and a dangerous ability to blackmail politicians.

From then on Admiral Hanly started doing something that Scotland Yard refused to do, and instead of shying away from the Twins he kept them under observation. When their names came up again in connection with the marketing of the Mafia's stolen bearer bonds in Europe, first through Leslie Payne in London and then on a larger scale through Alan Bruce Cooper's contacts in the bank in Hamburg, he checked on that as well. Concerned that the Mafia was turning to Europe as a large-scale market for such stolen bank securities, it was the US Secret Service that stepped in and stopped the traffic, and the Twins backed off. But when the Admiral passed this information on to Scotland Yard they took no notice, and Cooper disappeared below the radar.

With several of the Admiral's familiar old enemies from the Mafia – like Meyer Lansky and the Gallo brothers – now controlling some of the richest gaming clubs in London and attracting gamblers by the plane-load from the States, he made a special trip to London in an attempt to persuade the authorities to crack down hard on infiltration by the Mafia. He met Sir Joseph Simpson who promised action. He met serious top officials from the Home Office who also promised action. But in the end all that happened was that the Twins' friend George Raft, who was Meyer Lansky's highly paid front man at the Mayfair Sporting Club, was peremptorily expelled from Britain, leaving everything exactly as it was and the Admiral feeling thoroughly frustrated .One of the few characters he met on his trip to London who shared in his frustration was the then head of Scotland Yard's Murder Squad, Commander John du Rose. Both were in their mid-fifties and, like the Admiral, John du Rose had also started his career as something of a star, with the press hailing him as 'Four-day Johnny' because of the time he took to solve a murder. But now, as head of the Murder Squad, he was feeling thwarted by the Commissioner's refusal to allow either him or his detectives to pursue the Krays for involvement in Cornell's murder. The fact that Four-Day Johnny personally failed to get on with Simpson didn't help the situation, and like the Admiral he believed that there was no excuse for such behaviour. 'But that's what happens when policemen get involved in politics,' as he told the Admiral.

The Admiral sympathised and promised he would find a way to deal with the Twins and their friends in the Mafia. In the meantime, to show that he meant business, he instructed one of his agents in Morocco to inform his friend, the police chief in Tangier, that Ronnie Kray was in his city. A few days later Ron received his marching orders from the Governor of Tangier and found himself for ever banished from his favourite hunting ground for teenage boys.

It was early in 1967 that the Admiral's patience was rewarded and he got the lucky break he needed. A report came through from Washington DC that a drug trafficker called David Nathan had been arrested with a shipment of LSD that had come from Marseilles. It had been sent by his son-in-law who was resident in France, and the Admiral recognised the name at once. It was Alan Bruce Cooper.

Had the Admiral been a policeman he would have played safe, ordered Cooper's extradition to stand trial with Nathan in the States, and congratulated himself on having struck a further blow against the growing traffic in narcotics between Europe and America. But the Admiral wasn't a policeman. He was a secret serviceman, and secret servicemen have different mind-sets from policemen. All the Admiral's instincts told him that once he relinquished Alan Bruce Cooper he would lose the hottest contact he would ever have between the Kray Twins and the Mafia. It was most unlikely he would ever get a chance like this again and he felt that it was up to him to grab it while he could.

One can see the Admiral's point of view, but one can also see that he was now in danger of believing that the Twins' involvement with the Mafia was far greater than it really was. This led him to believe that once he had Cooper under his control he would hold the magic key to a whole range of Mafia-backed operations, not just in Britain but throughout the rest of Europe. Mistakes like this occur in the fluctuating world of criminal intelligence, but in spite of this, like the old spymaster that he was, the Admiral was unable to resist having Cooper brought to Paris and offering him a deal. Either face extradition to America, with a twenty-year stretch in prison at the end of it, or work for Uncle Sam. To nobody's surprise, Alan Bruce Cooper chose Uncle Sam.

Cooper always insisted that narcotics really weren't his thing and that the LSD parcel he dispatched from France was sent purely as a favour to a member of the family. This might have been true, for Cooper really was a much bigger fish than he appeared. Physically he was not impressive. He was very small, with a worrying stutter, thin parchment-coloured hair and a faint moustache like a child's eyebrow painted on his upper lip. But his lack of inches might have been the reason for his remarkable survival. A bigger, more dominating character would have probably attracted enemies in the macho world of big-time crime. But people tended not to notice Cooper, and across the years he'd grown rich from several major deals involving gold smuggling, arms dealing and, more recently, from milking the ever-growing international trade in stolen securities. For him all this was just as well, for if Cooper had a weakness it was a liking for the good life, which had left him with expensive tastes – as the Admiral soon discovered when he tried deciding how to use him.

The Admiral's plan turned out to be the sort of undercover operation you find in the pages of 1960s secret-service thrillers by Len Deighton and John le Carré, and landed Cooper with the role of a double agent working closely with the Krays and reporting back to the Admiral in Paris. This meant there was a lot at stake and the Admiral, who had learned his trade by dealing with no less a character than Lucky Luciano, was treating this as yet another major operation. In return for all the trouble he was taking he was counting on the Krays becoming an invaluable source of information over the whole range of the Mob's activities in Britain, including gambling, counterfeit currency and the large-scale marketing of stolen securities in Europe. So this was not the time to cut back on expenses. Since the US Secret Service was a branch of the US Treasury, it could call on almost limitless resources, which the Admiral decided he would use to set Cooper up in London in the style to which he was accustomed and that the Twins expected of him. He would have to take his time to gain their confidence and slowly gather all their secrets. The Admiral knew that this would not be easy.

Before Cooper moved to London, the Admiral realised that he would need support in London from someone in authority. So he invited John du Rose to Paris, explained what he proposed for Cooper, and suggested making it a joint operation against the Twins and the Mafia in London.

Du Rose was clearly flattered by the idea and when the Admiral introduced him to Cooper they got on well together. Later, when I got to know him, Cooper always spoke warmly of du Rose, as 'the straightest copper I have ever met'.

Du Rose's attitude to Cooper was more realistic. 'Sooner or later he'll end up in a ditch with a bullet in the back of his neck,' he told the Admiral. But in the meantime he was perfectly prepared to make the most of Cooper's undoubted talents and cooperate with him in any way he could. He and John Hanly trusted one another and if, through Cooper, he could gain entry to the closed world of the Krays and destroy their power for good, what had he to lose? As an old detective John du Rose had schooled himself not to let a lot excite him. But when he was offered Cooper on a plate, together with the full support of the US Secret Service, something must have told him that this just might be the chance of a policeman's lifetime.

Of course it was risky, and not just for Cooper. But at this point in the game none of them realised quite how mad and dangerous the Twins could be; nor could they foresee where the Admiral's plans would lead them. During this meeting both Hanly and du Rose were particularly insistent on the need for secrecy, and emphasised that Cooper was answerable solely to Hanly in Paris and du Rose in London. The two of them would do everything they could to help him, and while he was in London he would be working closely with du Rose and keeping him informed of all he did. In return, du Rose promised Cooper his full support, including concocting bogus Scotland Yard reports in order to impress the Twins and, wherever possible, mislead them.

After the meeting Cooper knew that he could count on their support, but he also knew the rules. However much they were prepared to help him, if anything went wrong John du Rose and Admiral Hanly would both drop him like a very hot potato.

Despite this, Cooper couldn't quite believe his luck. Just a day or two before he had been facing twenty years in prison, and today he was being bankrolled by the US Secret Service. He had always been a chancer and wasn't one to quit in the middle of a winning run. Besides, for all his charm, the Admiral wasn't offering him a viable alternative. So Cooper decided he would make the most of the situation and next day flew to London.

In London in the 1960s life for rich Americans was good. The Admiral had arranged for Cooper to have a London office in the European Exchange Bank at 101 Dean Street, which had originally been set up as a front by the US Secret Service. At the same time Cooper was informed that a luxurious apartment near Kensington Palace had been placed at his disposal, together with an authentic English butler, a well-stocked cellar and a Rolls-Royce Silver Cloud.

A few days later he was joined by his wife Beverley, their young daughter Leslie, and Sam, their Yorkshire terrier. Before long the family was displaying all the effortless assurance that one might expect from very rich Americans in Europe.

This was intelligence-gathering *de luxe*, on a scale that Britain's MI6 could never have afforded. Only someone as important in the US Secret Service as Admiral John H. Hanly could have ever mounted such an operation. But with the US Treasury there to meet the bills, no one seemed to worry. Certainly nobody ever questioned the Coopers' way of living. So while Admiral Hanly was pursuing his obsession back in Paris, the Coopers made the most of their life of luxury in the line of duty. Before long it would be serving to disguise the fairly hideous risks they soon discovered they were taking.

To start with, Admiral Hanly's plan worked perfectly and when Cooper made contact with the Twins they were obviously impressed by all the signs of Cooper's new prosperity. Ron was particularly taken with him now and during the summer of 1967, when Ron was making such determined efforts to persuade Reg and other members of the Firm to murder someone, he was often meeting Cooper every day. When Cooper overcame his stutter, he could be a strangely mesmerising talker and Ron started to depend on him for information and advice. Certainly Cooper seemed to have an encyclopaedic knowledge of organised crime in Europe and America – and what he didn't know, he could always make up from his fertile imagination.

At the same time Cooper made fresh contact with du Rose and kept him carefully informed about whatever he was up to. In return, du Rose arranged to let him have bogus documents from Scotland Yard so that he could feed the Twins with misleading information. Most of Ron's wilder flights of fancy during that long hot summer came from Cooper. He took a lot of trouble over the Tshombe escape, the whole idea of which came entirely from Cooper. As did another way-out plan which impressed Ron for a while – a fully worked-out scheme for kidnapping the Pope.

In the end Reg became cynical and poured cold water on most of these ideas while Ron was going off his head with fantasies of bloody murder. Most of the crazier ideas that Ron came up with in the months before McVitie's murder were being fed to him by Cooper.

At the same time Cooper was discovering much more about the Twins. He realised that Reg was comparatively sane and didn't trust him, and that Ron had become a death-obsessed psychotic who was concerned with one thing only – killing people.

All the talk about freeing Tshombe and kidnapping the Pope was fine but it was soon becoming clear that there needed to be more to their collaboration than this. Since Reg didn't trust him, he played along with Ron's homicidal fantasies about his murder syndicate. He even suggested calling it Murder International. But Ron wanted further proof of Cooper's seriousness, which was when Cooper made a serious mistake that could have been disastrous. When he inadvertently let slip that he had been an arms dealer, Ron instantly started asking him for weapons.

Some months later, when I was learning more about McVitie's murder, something puzzled me – the way that Reg's gun had jammed when he tried to shoot McVitie, after a similar gun belonging to Ron had jammed a few months earlier when he had tried to shoot George Dixon. Modern automatics are specially designed not to jam. And yet here, not one but two .32 automatics belonging to the Twins had jammed within a few weeks of each other.

When I mentioned this to Cooper some months later he finally admitted that both the guns had come from him. He said that at the time Ron was constantly demanding weapons for Murder International and after discussing this with John du Rose, the police commander had reluctantly agreed to Cooper supplying the Twins with a pair of .32 automatics to prove that he meant business – provided that both the guns were immobilised beforehand.

Presumably that summer the Twins had too much on their minds to have noticed the coincidence when both the guns had jammed. But by now, with Ron increasingly obsessed with his dreams of killing people, Cooper must have understood the full extent of the nightmare he was in. If the Twins had suspected that he was a spy, he'd have had it; and if the Admiral suspected that he'd lost his nerve, he'd also have had it. As he told me later, 'It was then I realised that I was like the man on the high wire in the circus doing my act without a net – and facing death whichever way I fell.'

Meanwhile, to add a further complication to a nightmare situation, barely a month before the Twins killed Jack the Hat Scotland Yard had finally started their own investigation of the Krays under the former chief inspector 'Nipper' Read. He owed his appointment to Sir Joseph Simpson's deputy, Assistant Commissioner Peter Brodie, who had set up the Kray unit on his own authority. And, rather than risk trouble from the Commissioner, or betrayal from his colleagues, Nipper Read had arranged to have it safely tucked away in total isolation from the rest of Scotland Yard in Tintagel House, a faceless block of offices on the far side of the river. To show how seriously Brodie took the need for secrecy members of the team were actually provided with false cover stories. (Interestingly, the line they chose, just to make sure that no one else in Scotland Yard would question it, was that Nipper and his men were busily investigating a number one docket – a corruption charge against other members of the police. This would not arouse anyone's suspicions with so much corruption going on around them.)

The way that Read was summoned back to take charge of the first investigation of the Twins in more than three and a half years was in itself an illustration of what was happening.

Since Nipper always felt that the McCowan case was the one disaster of his career he was not best pleased to find himself having to face the Twins again; and since he'd had no contact with them now for over three years, his first action was to put in a request for all the files on their activities in the meantime. Back came the reply that there were no files.

No files, no information in the whole of Scotland Yard on the two most dangerous criminals in London? Surely some mistake.

But stranger things were still to come.

Since Commander John du Rose was the Head of the Murder Squad, he had overall responsibility for what went on in Tintagel House, and Nipper regularly reported back to him. At this point, relations between the pair of them were perfectly amicable, with du Rose very much the senior officer in charge, smoking his cheroots, discussing progress and offering the younger man his experienced advice.

But while he was apparently assisting Nipper Read, du Rose never felt obliged to tell him of his own quite separate freelance efforts to entrap the Twins. Still less did he explain his relations with a former arms dealer turned gold smuggler who was in close touch with them, and that with the backing of a senior agent in the US Secret Service, he had recently authorised him to supply a pair of .32 automatic pistols to the Twins.

19

Murder For Two

ONE OF THE strangest consequences of the McVitie murder had been the subsequent behaviour of the Twins. Far from them showing any signs of revulsion or remorse, the killing left them in the best of spirits and had clearly brought the two of them even closer together. Whatever the rights or wrongs of Jack McVitie's slaughter, it had been so badly bungled that it would be hard to imagine even the most hardened killers wishing to be reminded of it later and one might well have thought the Twins would have wanted to forget about it too. But not at all.

The necessary sacrifice had been made. The joint credentials of both the twins as murderers had been established and, in Mafia language, Reg had 'made his bones' at last – or rather, Jack McVitie's bones, which were now wrapped in chicken wire and firmly weighted down in one of the deepest stretches of the English Channel.

After the killing the Twins' first thought was to get Ron Hart to drive them to the house in Walthamstow belonging to their father's lifelong friend and fellow deserter Harry Hopwood. Later Hart described how he ran a hot bath for them and helped them to perform a sort of ritual cleansing, scrubbing beneath their fingernails and washing their hair, and getting rid of everything connected with the killing, down to their shoes and every scrap of clothing, all of which Hopwood later burned. He also threw Reg's useless .32 automatic into the Grand Union Canal near the Queensbridge Road (where police divers found it, still jammed, a year later). Someone arranged for fresh clothes to be brought over from Aunt May's house in Vallance Road, and members of the Firm who saw the Twins next morning remember them as bright as sunshine, laughing and joking and in the best of spirits.

One might have thought they'd just accomplished some heroic deed. Hearing about this later, I was reminded of Ron hiding in the flat in the Lea Bridge Road after murdering Cornell, and playing those wartime records of his hero Winston Churchill. Something similar was happening to Reg. For the rest of his life he would always speak with pride about killing Jack the Hat. He had 'done society a service' by getting rid of him. (Ron was content with simply stating that he was 'scum'.) But there was more than this to the killing, and to the Twins' subsequent behaviour. It took a while to work out what it was.

One thing at least was obvious. Whatever else had been accomplished, Jack's death had served to reunite the Twins. At long last, Reg 'had done his one'. Honour, if that was the word for it, had been satisfied between them, and their endless arguments and rows over Reg's need to murder someone were behind them.

The following afternoon Hart drove them up to Cambridge where they were booked in under another name at the University Arms Hotel. Cambridge was an odd destination for the Twins. They'd never been there before and it was hard to imagine them in that stuffy old university hotel, less than twenty-four hours after butchering McVitie – which was presumably the point of their going there at all. For if by any chance the police had been pursuing them the University Arms Hotel in Cambridge would have been the last place on Earth they would have thought of looking.

Not that the Twins had any need to worry. Sick he may

have been but Sir Joseph Simpson was still Her Majesty's Commissioner for Police and as determined as ever to avoid any further confrontation with the Twins. As for John du Rose, as Head of the Murder Squad he was in a quite alarming situation. He couldn't have known it yet but the .32 automatic that he had recently sanctioned Cooper to pass on to Reg as part of Admiral Hanly's plan to catch the Twins had actually been involved in Jack McVitie's murder. Had Four-Day Johnny not insisted on having it immobilised Reg would undoubtedly have used it to shoot McVitie through the head, and in due course John du Rose might well have found himself in court as an accessory to murder. Instead, as things turned out, by making sure that the weapon didn't work, du Rose had saved McVitie from a speedy death by bullet only to condemn him to a slow and bloody death from Reg Kray's carving knife instead.

But at this stage Four-Day Johnny didn't know about McVitie's murder. Nor did Cooper, and nor did Admiral Hanly. The police knew even less, for the morning after Jack was murdered his anxious wife had gone to her local police station to report him missing but no one had seemed particularly concerned. Jack often went missing and since Nipper Read was still trying to work out how George Cornell had met his death the fate of Jack the Hat would have to wait. However, for the Twins it looked as if McVitie's murder was about to open up a new, exciting chapter in their lives.

One of the more attractive members of the Kray menagerie was the 'property developer' Geoff Allen, whom we last encountered looking after Ron in the caravan on his Suffolk farm following Ron's escape from the Long Grove mental hospital. Geoff was a man of parts – card sharp, gambler, con man and womaniser – but in the underworld he was known as the most successful arsonist in Britain. He had been burning down properties for years and growing rich and happy on the proceeds, while the insurance companies seemed incapable of catching him.

He still had a soft spot for the Twins, which he put down to what he called 'a streak of devilment in my nature'. Others ascribed it to his lack of inches. Geoff Allen was extremely short, although this didn't seem to interfere with his success with women, and he might have felt a little bigger with the Twins around. Certainly with them he behaved like a sort of underworld godfather, acting as their private banker, helping them to solve their problems, and giving them advice as and when they needed it. This was a moment when they needed it.

After McVitie's murder, which they described to him in detail, it had been Geoff's idea to hide them away for a night or two in Cambridge, just in case of trouble. He made the hotel reservations for them, and afterwards he paid the bill. When Monday came and there was still no sign of trouble, it was Geoff who collected them in his blue Rolls-Royce, and drove them to an even more unlikely destination – the Lamb Hotel in the picturesque village of Lavenham.

Anyone not knowing who they were would certainly have wondered what these three suspicious characters were up to in that sleepy Suffolk village in mid–October. But just for once all three of them were doing something absolutely legal. They were house-hunting.

Remembering Violet's desire for a place in the country, Reg had as usual turned to Geoff for help. But now it wasn't only Violet who had dreams of moving to the country. So, in theory, had the Twins, since everything in Vallance Road was soon to be demolished. Once again Geoff had come up trumps and picked a winner. For £12,000 he'd found them a house over-looking the village green in the tiny village of Bildestone – and that afternoon all three of them drove off in Geoff's Rolls-Royce to see it.

'The Brooks' turned out to be an elegant cream-painted Edwardian villa, with a paddock and a private drive and a garden which reminded one of tea on the lawn and games of croquet – except that Ron had rather different things in mind. Still on a high after murdering McVitie, he was very much in favour of buying the house at once. Reg was as usual slightly doubtful and no one mentioned Violet or old Charlie. But what was secretly exciting Ron was the thought of transforming The Brooks into the sort of fortified stronghold he'd recently been dreaming of, complete with guard dogs, searchlights and the machine guns that he was nagging Cooper to get him. Here he could be safe at last and, as usual now, Reg went along with the idea. But having found their dream house the Twins were up against a problem that hadn't worried them for years: money – or, to be precise, their lack of it.

They weren't exactly broke but their flush days as criminal tycoons were over. During the last year they'd been spending too much time on murder and far too little making money.

After all the easy profits Reg had been milking from the frauds and rackets and gaming clubs in years gone by there was now something ridiculous in the mere idea of the Kray Twins being forced to ask Geoff Allen for a mortgage. But, ridiculous or not, Geoff obliged as usual. Since I can't imagine many building societies welcoming the Twins as customers I would guess he paid for it himself. In return the Twins were promising swift repayment from a new and exciting source of income that they seriously believed was in the offing.

Since they thought, correctly, that at present there was no real threat from the police, they were anxious to return to London. But before they did they still had one thing to attend to – a meeting at Geoff Allen's stately home of Gedding Hall near Stowmarket. The Twins had personally arranged this in advance for 5 November, which was in two days' time. Geoff was lending them Gedding Hall for the occasion, and the Twins were very anxious to impress their all-important guest by pretending that the stately pile was theirs.

Frank Taylor was a gay, gregarious, very tall New Yorker, who was working as editor-in-chief at McGraw-Hill, the New York publishers. Since he had little experience of criminals he was not to know that the famous lawyer who had rung him recently at his New York office had connections with the US Mafia. (He was actually a friend of Alan Bruce Cooper who had given his name to the Twins as someone who might help them.) The lawyer was extremely charming and Frank was flattered when he made it clear that he realised Frank was no ordinary publisher but had also been a film producer, with one of the great movies of the 1960s to his credit – *The Misfits*, based on a story by Arthur Miller and starring Marilyn Monroe, Montgomery Clift and Clark Gable.

Having mentioned this in passing, the lawyer then explained that he was calling on behalf of friends in London who were looking for someone to produce a film about their adventures. They were identical twins who'd been involved in some of the most sensational recent crimes in London, and since they were thinking of retiring they felt the time had come to make a film about their lives.

The lawyer must have done quite a selling job on the Twins' behalf for real-life crime was not Frank Taylor's speciality. But, since the lawyer clearly knew a lot about him, he might have mentioned that these friends of his were gay, which could have added to their interest value and persuaded Frank at least to talk to Reg on the telephone. Frank did his best to make it clear that although he'd be in London on a business trip in late October, he was afraid they'd have no time to meet. Then Reg said something that made him change his mind.

As far as I could gather, this happened when Reg mentioned the house where he and his brother Ron were living in the country. Suddenly the thought of two gay twin cockney criminals operating from a stately home in Suffolk struck Frank as so bizarre that he simply had to see them. The upshot was that he said that he would set aside the last day of his trip to London to go and meet them.

Later, Reg and Frank had several fairly lengthy telephone conversations. Then, on the day before Frank left for London, Reg made one further call to his New York office to confirm his arrival and arrange the details of his visit. At nine o'clock on the morning of 5 November a friend of his called Tommy Brown would meet Frank at the reception desk of his hotel in Albemarle Street, then drive him up to Gedding Hall. He and his brother Ron were both looking forward very much to seeing him and he promised Frank he'd not be disappointed. Over lunch they could talk about the film they wanted and he assured him he'd be back in London long before the rush hour started.

Reg made this call to Frank Taylor on 19 October. Frank left for London the day after. Reg murdered Jack McVitie eight days later.

For a long time I was puzzled by this sequence of events. Why should Reg have fixed a date with a film producer to discuss a movie on his life with Ron, then murder someone just before the meeting? What, if anything, could be the link between these two events?

I knew, of course, that Reg's almost hysterical reaction to his wife's suicide, plus constant needling from Ron throughout the summer 'to do his one' had by that autumn brought him to the point where he was quite prepared to murder almost anyone. But was it simply a coincidence that the murder came so swiftly after he had fixed the date for Frank Taylor's visit?

One must remember that the Twins were movie mad, often identifying with the heroes of the gangster movies they had grown up with; and there were two new films that summer that had made a great impression on them both. One was the adaptation of Truman Capote's anatomy of a murder, *In Cold Blood*; the other was the story of the two young bank robbers Bonnie Parker and Clyde Barrow in Arthur Penn's award-winning movie *Bonnie and Clyde*.

Later the Twins would tell me how impressed they both had been by the way Faye Dunaway and Warren Beatty transformed these two young small-town killers into doomed romantic rebels battling against a hostile world. This was how they liked to see themselves and it wasn't hard to imagine what a film about *their* lives could be. As identical twin criminals, and with all the tales that they could tell, their story had to be unique. But one important fact was missing. At that moment only one of the Twins was actually a murderer. Had that been the case with either Bonnie or with Clyde no film about them would have worked, and the same applied to the two young murderers of *In Cold Blood*.

Even while Reg was finalising arrangements for Frank Taylor's visit Ron still wasn't letting Reg forget what he had to do, and that until he did his duty their legend would be incomplete. Without their legend there could be no film, and without their film their lives would be forgotten.

With Frank now due to visit them at Gedding Hall in two weeks' time there was no time to lose. If the one thing that their story still required was the sacrifice of someone as insignificant as Jack the Hat, the poor man never stood a chance.

The truth was that the Twins' entire performance, from their introduction to Frank Taylor to the murder of McVitie, had as much to do with image as with crime. It was also crazy. At a time like this the last thing they needed was another murder on their hands and only a madman would have dreamt of doing it. But then, Ron *was* mad, and during the ten years since he'd been certified insane his madness had been growing worse. Now that he'd started killing people, and Reg was effectively under his control, the two of them were sharing in Ron's paranoid illusions of invulnerability, coupled with his manic certainty that he was right.

They were also driven by the need to make some money and were genuinely excited by the thought that, once their image as twin criminal celebrities was established for the future, the earnings from the film would sort out their finances and pay for their retirement.

In fact, of course, they'd made a deal with the devil, and ultimately it would be McVitie's murder that was going to condemn them both to somewhat premature retirement. But late that autumn, in their first post-homicidal rapture, Ron and Reg both genuinely believed that they were doing what their destiny dictated. At last their bid for riches, fame and immortality had started.

Once the Twins were set on this determined course of action, one can but admire the single-mindedness with which they now pursued it. Before they even killed McVitie they had already decided to arrange the all-important meeting with Frank Taylor up at Gedding Hall. Had they suggested meeting him in some suitably discreet London venue to discuss their story he would probably not have even bothered to see them. But like the natural con man that he was, by also telling Frank that Gedding Hall was theirs Reg instantly converted what would have been a fairly humdrum business proposition into a genuine adventure. From then on, Gedding Hall would do the rest.

For Gedding Hall possessed a magic of its own. When Geoff Allen had acquired it a few years earlier he'd seriously intended treating it as he had treated so many other houses in his time. But when it came to it something stopped him, and instead of torching Gedding Hall he started living there instead. (Some years later he would sell it on to Bill Wyman of the Rolling Stones, who also fell in love with it and allowed Geoff to be buried in its grounds, following his death in 1992.)

For the truth about the house is that although it is almost entirely Victorian mock-Tudor, built in the 1890s by a former mayor of Leicester, what with its moat and drawbridge and its suitably romantic tower it is architectural showbiz of the highest order and manages to look more Tudor than the real thing. It would have made a perfect setting for a Gothic thriller and, whether consciously or not, the Twins could not have picked a better place to impress an American film producer. From the moment that Frank Taylor saw its rose-pink ramparts in the autumn sunlight and its black swans gliding on the murky waters of its moat, the Kray Twins had their famous guest on toast.

Little else was left to chance. Geoff Allen played the Twins' devoted side-kick to perfection. Brother Charlie, summoned specially from London to meet the great producer, needed little coaching for the real-life part of their worried older brother. Several of Geoff's old girlfriends, given the role of gangsters' molls, presided over a meal of salad and cold ham in the cavernous dining room. And while the Twins were drinking their accustomed Newkie Browns, a respectable bottle of cold white wine was produced for Frank Taylor. As for the Twins, with Ronnie on a schizoid high and a famous film producer in their midst, they must have been in seventh heaven,

I think the truth was that, largely thanks to Gedding Hall, Frank Taylor and the Twins were distinctly taken with each other from the start. Indeed, with Jack the Hat already decomposing in the English Channel, the Twins were so impressed with Frank that they probably did think that Jack McVitie hadn't died in vain. Whilst for Frank, the sight of these two gay cockney gangsters dominating London crime from this spectacular house deep in the English countryside was like a dream of gay empowerment come true. Knowing Frank, I can imagine him playing up to them with a lot of high-camp Hollywood gossip. Predictably they couldn't wait to hear everything that he could tell them about Marilyn Monroe, and in particular how she shared her lovely body with Jack and Bobby Kennedy and their old friend, the monstrous Mafia boss of Chicago, Sam Giancana.

Over lunch they continued with the ultimate film buff's ego trip of deciding who should play them in the film about their lives. Ron wanted his old admirer from Morocco, the actor Stanley Baker, but Reg picked on Albert Finney. Frank made it clear that he preferred Rod Steiger, and by now he was genuinely excited by the possibilities he was seeing in the film. It was early days, of course, but it wasn't every day that a film producer found himself being offered such a story. Think of what Hitchcock would have made of the combination of the Twins and Gedding Hall. Think of what Frank himself could do with it. Before he left he was already talking of sorting out an option on the film rights to their story.

This raised a subject which was still as yet unsettled. The Twins already knew that their chances of a movie would be considerably improved if someone wrote their biography and they had already asked Francis Wyndham, their old fan from the *Sunday Times*, to do it for them. But Francis had grown wary of them since they tried involving him in their plans after the Mad Axeman's disappearance. No longer seeing them as a pair of fairly harmless cockney Humphrey Bogarts, he had sensibly declined.

When Reg mentioned this to Frank on the telephone Frank told him that he knew Capote and would ask if he was interested. Capote rapidly replied that he was not, and when Frank explained this to the Twins they asked him if he had anyone else in mind.

This is the point at which I enter the story of the Twins. The previous year McGraw-Hill had published the American edition of my authorised biography of Ian Fleming which, thanks largely to the popularity of the earliest (and to my mind the best) James Bond films, had done extremely well. The Twins, of course, did not know me from Adam but, like everybody else, they knew all about James Bond. And when Frank suggested I should write their book, neither twin objected.

20

The Kingdom of the Krays

THROUGHOUT THIS TIME I had been living in Rome while researching a new book on the Roman Colosseum, and I was just finishing a late breakfast when Frank Taylor rang from London. He was still at Brown's Hotel – which, like many Americans, he loved – and was obviously excited.

'John, I must tell you that I've just had one of *the* most amazing days of my life. There's this pair of cockney twins running London crime from a stately home in Suffolk. They're desperate for a film about their lives and they need somebody to write a book about them. After that great biography of yours on Ian, I think that you should do it. But first you have to meet them.'

I thanked him and promised that I'd think about it, but that wasn't good enough for him. When Frank was on a high he was unstoppable.

'Now listen – and take this seriously. For you this book could be a winner, but you must get over here as fast as possible and meet the twins before they change their minds. If you're doing anything tonight, forget it. You're booked on the evening flight from Rome to London, and everything's been taken care of. There's a ticket in your name at the Alitalia desk at Fiumicino airport and tonight you're staying at the Ritz. Dinner's on me, and first thing tomorrow morning someone will meet you at reception and drive you up to meet the boys at this place of theirs in Suffolk.'

It was then that I realised there was little point in arguing. Besides, nothing much was happening for me in Rome around that time. 'It sounds fascinating,' I said. 'Of course I'll go. Oh, and by the way, what's the name of these twins of yours?'

'Kray. The name is Kray. But if you know anything about them don't let it worry you. Your safety's guaranteed.'

During the following few months I lost count of how many times I would remind myself of Frank's guarantee of safety. But at the time it sounded reassuring.

'I'm being serious about this, John. If there's a book in this I'll publish it. If there's a film in it I'll make it. And if doesn't work you'll have had a day you're never going to forget.'

Even in the Swinging Sixties, one didn't often get an offer quite like that.

To start with, everything went according to Frank's plans. As I soon discovered, I *had* been booked on the Alitalia flight to London, a room *was* awaiting me at the Ritz, and Frank had even kept his word and paid for the meal I ate in lonely splendour in the hotel's empty dining room.

Action started on the dot of nine the next morning when reception rang to tell me that two gentlemen were downstairs, asking to see me. One of them was very large, and one was very small, and both of them introduced themselves as Tom. Large Tom, as I discovered later, was Tommy Brown, the celebrated all-in wrestler known professionally as 'the Bear'. His wife, Dot Brown, was Ron Kray's personal clairvoyant. Little Tom worked with Reg on 'security' and doubled as a minder with an East End double-glazing company. Both were members of The Firm.

From the start, Big Tom was very much in charge and had

managed to park his monstrous Mercedes round the corner from the Ritz. We piled in, and with both the Toms in front we headed through the morning traffic to whatever fate awaited me.

It's often claimed that throughout the 1960s the Twins were such household names that everybody knew about them. But until their arrest in 1968 this wasn't strictly true. As I would soon be seeing for myself, in Bethnal Green and much of the old East End they had long been local celebrities – as they were in the underworld and in certain ultra-swinging parts of Chelsea. But as I sat in the back of the Bear's Mercedes, racking my brains to remember all I could about them, I realised that there was not a lot that I could recall. I had a vague memory of the Kray name in connection with the *Sunday Mirror* libel action, and that had been more than three years earlier. Otherwise forget it.

However, when I tried to pump the Toms about the twins they closed up like a pair of clams and the rest of the journey passed in heavy silence. The magical mystery tour that followed took us up past Lavenham, where I recognised the famous church. Twenty minutes later came park gates, a brief view of a deer park – and then Gedding Hall was there before me like a sudden flash of magic in the middle of a rich autumnal nowhere.

I've always been a soft touch for con men and from that moment when I saw Geoff Allen with his cheery smile and Rupert Bear-style checked trousers, coming out to welcome me to Gedding Hall I felt reassured. Here really was a ray of sunshine on a rainy day.

'Come and meet the Twins,' he said. 'Frank Taylor told us all about you. Great guy, Frank. The boys can't wait to meet you.'

I'm not likely to forget my first encounter with the brothers Kray. All three of them, including older brother Charlie, were lined up there to meet me in the big oak-panelled dining room, with their backs to a blazing fire. As all three of them were wearing the Kray uniform of dark blue suits, white shirts and tightly knotted dark silk ties – they must have felt stifled in the heat.

Geoff introduced me first to the Twins' older brother, Charlie.

There was something about Charlie that always made me feel sorry for him. With his blond good looks, which he had inherited from his mother, he was obviously the odd man out and I noticed that the Twins tended to ignore him.

As for the Twins themselves, what surprised me was not so much their similarities as the differences between them.

The memory plays funny tricks, but I've still got a clear impression of Reg as I saw him then. He was five foot ten or so, with the dark eyes and hair of some gypsy forebear, but there was something about him that I found disturbing. For much of the time his face had what seemed a tortured expression which he was trying to offset by projecting a sort of desperate charm. He did not look a happy man.

But the one who really fascinated me was Ron, and my first reaction to him was that he was mad. It was partly the voice, which sounded as though he had some mysterious speech impediment. He looked older and heavier than Reg and his movements seemed curiously uncoordinated. He and Reg even had a different handshake. Reg had a hard dry bony hand with the knuckles of the right pushed back a good half-inch from a lifetime of punching people on the chin. Ron, in contrast, had a limp and clammy handshake.

Here I must explain that ten years earlier Ian Fleming, when he was still an unknown columnist, had given me a job as his assistant on the *Sunday Times*. By then he had written the first three or four James Bond novels, which had yet to make his fortune, and from working with him I must have picked up the

The Boothby case – Lord Boothby and Ron Kray at Boothby's flat in Eaton Square, together with rent boy and burglar Leslie Holt.

House of Lords

April 7, 1965.

Dear Ronnie.

Warmest congratulations. I never doubted it.

They gave me a pretty rough time in the House of Lords.

But they have been proved wrong; and I have been proved right.

So, to some extent, I share your triumph; because I don't think this kind of thing will happen easily or often again.

Yours ever,
Bob Boothby.

Please give my regards and congratulations to your mother.

(*Left*) The letter of congratulation sent by Lord Boothby to Ron Kray after the twin's acquittal at the McCowan trial.

The photograph that Ron Kray kept as evidence of his friendship with Lord Boothby. From left to right: Charlie Clark, cat burglar, Boothby's butler, Goodfellow, Boothby, unidentified teenage boy, Ron Kray, and Billy Exley, gangster, with his wife, dining together at the old 'Society' restaurant in Jermyn Street, London.

The Twins' necessary sacrifices: (*top left*) George Cornell and (*top right*) Jack McVitie, both murdered by the Twins. (*Above*) The Blind Beggar scene of the Cornell murder.

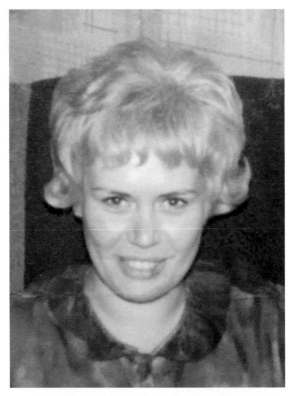

(*Above*) 'Blonde Carol' Skinner in whose flat Jack the Hat was murdered.
(*Below*) Frank Mitchell, 'the Mad Axeman'.

Ron Kray with his accusers – Ron, third from right, has dinner with two close associates who later betrayed him – on the left his cousin, Ronald Hart, and next to him the most successful con man in London, Leslie Payne. On the right is the old-time gangster, Sammy Lederman.

(*Above*) The spymaster from the USA Admiral John H. Hanly, head of the US Secret Service in Europe, who took on the Twins and caused more trouble than he bargained for.

(*Below*) 'The good guy' – arsonist Geoff Allen among his friends.

(*Above*) The stately home which the Twins said was theirs – Gedding Hall in Suffolk, now the home of former Rolling Stone Bill Wyman.

(*Below*) Retirement home – 'The Brooks' in the village of Bildestone in Suffolk, which the Twins owned at the time of their arrest.

Twins united.
The tombstone of Ron and Reg in 'Kray Corner' in Chingford cemetery.

idea that, whenever possible, a writer's life should have an element of mystery and adventure.

Ian would certainly have appreciated Gedding Hall – moat, black swans and all – but I'm not so sure about the lunch that followed. I was given the place of honour at the long oak dining table, with a twin on either side of me.

There was no comparison between the food served then and what Frank Taylor told me he had eaten. Instead, we all made do with tinned ham, corned beef and scotch eggs, washed down with a glass of lager.

Over lunch Reg explained that he and his brothers were anxious to have a book about them done as soon as possible. 'You see, John, we're thinking of retiring.' At this point I still naturally believed that Gedding Hall was theirs and took it for granted that they were figures of great wealth and power in the underworld. As I knew of several retired rich businessmen who had written their memoirs as an antidote to boredom I saw no reason why successful criminals shouldn't do the same.

'But how much can you tell me?' I remember asking.

'Enough,' Reg said. 'Of course we've friends we must protect, and we haven't been angels, but we ain't done nothing we're ashamed of.'

Unlike Reg, Ron wasn't one for casual conversation. But I remember one thing that he did say just before I left. 'So much rubbish gets written about our sort of people that what we want you to do is tell the truth about us.'

I was on the point of asking what if the truth included murder? But then I thought better of it and our meeting ended with this all-important question unresolved. Big Tom and the Mercedes got me back to London airport just in time to get the evening plane to Rome, and throughout the flight I sat there trying to decide whether to write this book or not. Only when I saw the lights of Rome twinkling below me and the thud of the undercarriage being lowered told me we were coming in to land did I realise that my mind had been made up for me already. If I chickened out, I knew the ghost of Ian Fleming was never going to forgive me.

So early next morning I rang through to Charlie Kray and suggested coming over the following weekend to discuss things further. I also asked him if he knew of somewhere I could stay in Bethnal Green where I could soak up something of the flavour of the old East End. Six days later I flew in from Rome on a wet Sunday evening and took a taxi from the airport all the way to Bethnal Green

Since I still believed that the Twins were the lords of Gedding Hall I imagined them, if not exactly basking in illicit splendour, at least inhabiting something like the Limehouse hideaway of my boyhood hero, the dreaded Fu Manchu, with its hidden entrance from the Thames and its misty views across the river. So I was disappointed when my taxi took a turning off Whitechapel High Street and dropped me slap outside the Blackwall Buildings.

The locals used to call this mouldering ruin with its minuscule apartments 'Barracks for the poor' and it had been declared 'unfit for human habitation'. But the Twins used one of the empty ground-floor flats as a punishment cell, and legend had it that anyone who needed to be taught a lesson was confined here for an hour or two with Ron's fierce Alsatian, Rex. Within The Firm the flat was known as 'the Dungeon'.

Little Tom was waiting in the pouring rain to let me in. Charlie Kray had taken me at my word with a vengeance. First the Ritz, now this.

I looked around me at the unmade bed and wondered who'd been using it before. Apart from a non-functioning TV, a sagging old armchair and a cracked sink with a dripping tap, there was no other furniture .

'Sorry about the décor,' Little Tom said cheerfully before he left. 'Reg said to tell you he'd be here to pick you up at eight.

He and Ron want you to meet some friends of theirs. So make yourself at home.' After I'd unpacked some books and a few possessions I sat there on the sagging chair, staring through the filthy window at the rain and waited for Reg.

When he did arrive I was in for yet another disappointment. No Rolls. No armour-plated Cadillac. Instead, a battered old Austin with a silent driver at the wheel. Luckily the journey to our destination didn't take us long. 'This is a favourite pub of ours,' said Reg. 'It's called the Old Horns and we thought you'd like to meet some friends of ours.' He pushed open the swing doors – and I found myself in Krayland.

This was to be the first of many evenings that I would spend with the Twins in a succession of East End pubs getting to know their friends and fellow criminals, but the Old Horns soon became my favourite too. Time could have stood still here since the days of Dickens. The Twins were at their best when they were surrounded by those they knew and trusted and the bar was crammed with assorted felons of all ages, shapes, and sizes. At the centre of them all was mad Ron, leaning on the bar and actually smiling as he listened to a tiny hunch-backed lady hammering away at an old piano and singing very loudy:

'I'll give you bluebirds in the spring . . .'

'It's me favourite song,' said Ron, leaning towards me. 'She always sings it specially for me.'

Then Reg introduced me to Teddy Berry, the landlord of the Old Horns, whose father had taught the Twins to box. Teddy limped because he had only one leg. Later I learned that Ron had shot the other leg off some years before, 'during a little misunderstanding' in a car park on the Kingston bypass.' Ron made it up to Teddy by giving him the pub. It was Ron's way of saying sorry.'

That night there were a lot of old East Enders the Twins had asked along to meet me and who had more or less retired from their lives of crime. Later I realised they had been carefully rehearsed for the occasion and had been told exactly what to say. There was tiny Sammy Lederman, former henchman of Jack Spot, and good-looking Moysha Blueboy, who had worked with the racecourse gangs of Derby Sabini long before the war.

Sammy was full of praise for the Twins. 'Take my word for it. After we're all dead and gone, someone will put a statue up to the Twins in Bethnal Green for all the good they've done.' Moysha nodded. 'Never a widow in Whitechapel went without her Christmas dinner, if the Twins had anything to do with it,' he said. 'And one thing you must mention in your book – whatever else they were, the Twins were gentlemen.'

Apart from the old-timers, the sheer range of shady characters on show that night bore witness to the Twins' influence and power.

There were several pickpockets, or 'dips' as they were known, who belonged to the notorious Hoxton whiz mob that worked the crowds at football matches. There were several burglars from King's Cross, along with a lot of hefty minders and enforcers from the clubs. There was a lesbian called Linda who was smoking a cigar. 'She's a nurse in an operating theatre in an 'ospital. She's a friend of ours, and 'elps me if I need a woman dealt with,' Ron told me. But she seemed a gentle soul, and while I was talking to her I felt something tugging at my trouser leg.

This was 'Little Legs' the dwarf, who worked in a circus and who the Twins had hired for the evening. Ron must have also told him what to say as well because he shouted up at me in a piping treble, 'If you don't write a good book about my friends Ron and Reg, I'll kill you.' Ron enjoyed that, and for the first time I heard him laugh.

The roll-call of infamy continued. There was old Harry from Stockwell who had made a living making counterfeit half-crowns, and Charlie with a squint who, according to Reg, was the most successful safe-blower in London. There was also Collins the getaway driver who, following a smash-and-grab raid on Mappin and Webb, drove a stolen Bentley the length of Bond Street in reverse with a police car in pursuit – and got away.

As we were leaving I could hear the quavering voice of another of the Twins' old guests. It was one of the forgotten stars from the vanishing East End music halls – Cavan O'Connor, 'Ireland's own Vagabond of Song', singing the refrain that years before had made him famous.

> 'I'm only a wandering vagabond,
> But goodnight, pretty ladies, goodnight.'

As I climbed aboard Geoff's battered Austin with the Twins, the words lingered on the evening air. They could have been Ron's own farewell to the East End that he would soon be leaving – except that Ron couldn't sing, and wasn't very keen on pretty ladies.

But the evening wasn't over and the Twins had something different to show me – the Astor Club off Berkeley Square. Although the Astor was one of the smartest nightclubs in Mayfair, during the 1960s in the early hours of the morning it became the unofficial showplace for the richest sector of the underworld. After the Old Horns, I was seeing something of the status that the Twins enjoyed in a wider world of crime than Bethnal Green.

I discovered later that, as the club's official 'minders', the Twins were drawing a 'pension' of £200 a week from the Astor. By now I'm sure that rumours of the McVitie killing must have got around the underworld, enhancing their authority even further.

I got some hint of the Twins' importance from the way that Sulky, the Astor's famous *maître d'*, treated them like royalty. 'Your usual table, gentlemen', he said.

It was said that Sulky, when he wasn't schmoozing important guests, had a key role in the world of crime as a go-between for both the underworld and the police. As for them themselves, I was left in little doubt of their importance from the two bottles of well-iced Dom Perignon that instantly arrived at our table 'with the compliments of the manager'.

Soon after we arrived Geoff Allen turned up with the Twins' good-looking cousin Ronnie Hart, an old cat burglar called Charlie Clarke and Dickie Morgan. They were followed by a steady stream of heavy men in suits who arrived throughout the evening to pay homage to the Twins. One of the few I remembered was their old ally – and soon to be co-defendant – the immaculate Freddy Foreman, looking more than ever like 'the managing director of British crime'.

I can't imagine what we found to talk about that evening but the conversation never seemed to falter. Reg appeared far more relaxed than at Gedding Hall and it was on this occasion that he became the first person I had ever seen demolish a bottle of Gordons in one sitting. But nor will I forget how, in the early hours of the morning, when bedtime in the dreaded dungeon beckoned and I bade the company goodnight, it was Reg who staggered after me and, blind drunk though he was, insisted on finding me a taxi and then paying the driver to take me back to Bethnal Green.

It didn't take me long to realise that, along with Frank Taylor, I had been adroitly conned by the Twins over their ownership of Gedding Hall – which, of course, belonged to Geoff Allen. The fact that they had taken so much time and trouble to convince us made me understand how desperate they were to have their story told so that their lives would never be forgotten.

It was only later that I discovered that fame and immortality were what really mattered to them now, but I do remember, how what time, I couldn't understand why they seemed to be much more concerned about my book and the film than about any threat from the police. I'd have been more puzzled still had I known that they had murdered Jack McVitie just a few weeks earlier.

This had to be because the mantle of invulnerability that the Goodman cover-up had thrown around them had protected them for more than three long years already and they were taking it for granted that they were still 'untouchable'. They must have also felt completely safe in Bethnal Green with their old familiar world around them.

In fact, at this very moment, Nipper Read together with a force of twenty-five detectives was working round the clock at Tintagel House, building up the case against them. At the same time, Admiral Hanly and the US Secret Service were also stepping up the pressure on Cooper to entrap them. In spite of this, to me at any rate the Twins seemed sublimely unconcerned about the dangers they were facing. Reg would occasionally ask me whether I'd heard any news from journalist friends about how the police inquiries against them were progressing. Apart from this the Twins appeared completely unaware of the hazards they were facing.

Much of their conversation with me seemed to be about the past. As well as discovering that Gedding Hall did not belong to them I also discovered that their home, which all their friends refered to as 'Fort Vallance', was actually a tiny terraced house in Vallance Road. I remember Reg taking me to see it on the morning after our visit to the Astor Club and making me realise how much it meant to him and Ron, from the sheer nostalgia with which he talked about their childhood there – how in the old days, none of the locals used to lock their doors, and how they had watched the old steam trains going back and forth across the bridge at the end of the road, to Liverpool Street station. Their uncle ran a cafe opposite, and Evans the Welsh dairyman kept his cow next door.

In Vallance Road they had always been surrounded by their family. It was their grandfather Lee who lived next door who gave Reg and Ron their earliest boxing lessons. The indomitable Auntie Rose lived one house away, and Auntie May lived next door to her.

Above all I remember how proudly Reg introduced me to his mother and how she obviously adored him. She showed no embarrassment when Reg showed me the coal shed in the backyard where his father used to hide when on the run from the police, nor did she seem at all concerned when recounting how, when Ron started shaving as a teenager, he copied his Mafia hero Al Capone, and like a true Italian gangster had the local Italian barber come each morning to the house to shave him. But when her sister May turned up for a cup of tea they were both at pains to emphasise how respectable their family had always been,

I was lucky to have seen all this. For, as I soon discovered, this cosy-seeming run-down little world of theirs was coming to an end. The whole of Vallance Road was due for demolition and already the Kray family were among the last survivors in the street. Old Cannonball and Grandma Lee would soon be moving into sheltered accommodation and the Twins' parents had been allocated a council flat on the ninth floor of a tower block a mile away in Bunhill Row.

More than ever now, relations between the Twins themselves were at the mercy of Ron's moods, which in turn depended on whether or not he'd taken his Stematol. His mood swings were becoming more pronounced and were starting to dominate their lives. When Ron was on a high he felt invulnerable and his thoughts would once more turn to murder. He was still talking to Cooper about Murder International and had started making lists of whom to kill.

Unlike Ron, Reg was in fact a terrible worrier and was also on tranquillisers, though these were not so strong as Ron's. At times, usually in the morning, when he was recovering from a hangover, Reg would talk to me about 'getting right away from all this fucking nonsense'. I remember discussing with him whether he could join the French Foreign Legion, or disappear to fight with the Americans in Vietnam. But these conversations always ended up with Reg saying, 'But then, of course, I never could leave Ron.'

And despite the fact that Reg was relatively sane, Ron could always make him join him in his madness. When Ron was driven by his demons he would dominate his weaker twin by resorting to the same tactics he had employed since childhood to survive. It was when this happened that the most sinister and dangerous aspect of their relationship appeared and, however briefly, the pair of them would become united. At such moments these two separate but discordant beings merged, becoming one person in the process, with the same genetic make-up and the same all-powerful mentality. And when this happened, this duplicated human being would become a homicidal madman. This had happened when they'd murdered Jack the Hat, but the killing of McVitie did more than bring the Twins inseparably together. By forcing Reg 'to do his one' and become a murderer, Ron had completed the process which had begun when he'd helped to wreck his marriage. When Frances died, Reg's hopes of ever having a 'normal' life away from Ron died too. Since the killing of Jack McVitie, less than ever were they ordinary twins. However much Reg might talk about 'getting right away from all this fucking nonsense' they were irrevocably locked together as twin murderers.

★

Reg had another way of trying to escape his fate and alleviate the guilt that he felt for Frances. Still in his early thirties, he was attractive to women as well as men, and a short time after Frances's death he met Carol Thompson, an attractive twenty-three-year-old receptionist, who fell in love with him. She told me once that what attracted her was that 'he seemed to be so desperately unhappy' and the hope of changing him became a challenge.

It turned out to be a predictably stormy affair. She told me that she soon felt that he was merely using her to get over Frances, and that they were hardly ever alone together. In spite of this he persuaded her to live with him but his drinking steadily increased and the rows got worse. At times he was violent but, as with Frances, he never hit her.

During this period the Twins could still surprise me. I remember an evening with them at the Carpenters' Arms, the other pub they 'owned', just round the corner from Vallance Road, when who should suddenly appear but the now seriously famous photographer David Bailey. I'd met him at the *Sunday Times* several years before at the start of his career when he was still one of the three young freelance photographers, who along with fellow East Enders Donovan and Duffy, earned a living from what cockney printers on the paper still called 'the smudge game' of press photography. Since then he'd become a huge success. Like Ron and Reg he was an East Ender, and they longed for fame like his. That very year Bailey had personally achieved their own greatest wish. The famous Italian director Antonioni had made a film called *Blow-up*, based on his life.

So it it was something of a tribute to the Twins' own status as celebrities that even at this late moment in their criminal career he was there because he had asked him to come to take pictures 'for our book' as he had now begun to call it. The Twins were particularly anxious to include pictures of themselves along with Read and Gerrard.

Here I should explain that Read and Gerrard were not the two detectives who at that very moment were working round the clock on the Twins' downfall but two pet pythons. Occasionally Ron still visited the Harrods pet department and had recently ordered two young snakes, one for himself and one for Reg. It was Ron's idea of a joke to name them after the two detectives, Superintendents Nipper Read and Gerrard.

Violet, ready as ever to indulge her boys, had even placed her spare bedroom at the snakes' disposal and it was there that I saw them several evenings later. Something about the snakes appealed to Ron who loved fondling them and playing games with them. What he particularly enjoyed was to place a live mouse at the far end of the room, at which point the Twins would bet on which snake got it first. One of the few times I saw Ron become genuinely excited was as he watched the mouse crouch petrified against the wainscot, then scuttle off beneath the table. Quick as lightning, both the snakes would dart off in pursuit. But somehow it was always Read who got the mouse.

Apart from taking pictures for the book of the Twins entwined with Read and Gerrard it was around this time that Bailey introduced them to his friend and agent David Puttnam. As well as having made themselves immortal as identical twin murderers, the Twins had now got themselves a film producer, a biographer, a famous photographer at their beck and call and an agent who would end up in the House of Lords.

Meanwhile Nipper Read, although still tucked away in conventlike secrecy in Tintagel House, had finally got lucky.

It was more than a year since the Twins had severed all connections with their one-time friend and patron Leslie Payne. But until Ron stupidly hired Jack the Hat to kill him, Payne had kept away from them and the last thing he would have done was to betray them. But when Ron began threatening not only him but also his family, the former infantry sergeant from Monte Cassino decided that he had had enough. When Inspector Hemingway approached him on behalf of Nipper Read and asked if he would help with his inquiries, he agreed to do so

During the first weeks of January, Nipper, methodical as ever, interviewed Leslie Payne every morning for several weeks in a room in a small hotel in Marylebone. Not only did Payne possess a remarkable memory but he had more detailed knowledge than anyone of what the Twins and members of The Firm had been up to during the last twelve years. From Payne's information Nipper compiled what he called his 'delightful index', a detailed list of more than thirty key accomplices of the Krays and their victims.

He and his team contacted every one of them and had little difficulty persuading them to talk. But Nipper knew that it would be a different matter persuading them to give evidence in court. As one potential witness said to him, 'I hate the sight of blood, particularly my own.'

To set their minds at rest he gave each one of them a written undertaking not to use their statements in evidence against the Twins until they were safely behind bars.

This meant that Nipper found himself in something of a Catch-22 situation. He was getting all the evidence he needed to put the Kray twins under lock and key but he couldn't use any of it until he'd got them there. Something had to happen that would break the deadlock.

Whenever the Twins were otherwise engaged they ordered their father, old Charlie, to show me round what remained of the traditional East End. I never met anyone who had a good word to say about this disreputable old cockney boozer but I found him fascinating company and finally got to like him, although it was obviously unwise to say so to the Twins. He was a great source of information, not only about the old villains he had known and drunk with but also about growing up in Hoxton after the first world war and how he had made a living as a rag-and-bone man. The poor man clearly had much to complain about at home, with everybody in the house against him, and it was hardly his fault that his maverick sperm had once decided to divide in Violet's womb and then turn into Ron and Reg

Thanks to the Twins I even got to meet Dot Brown, the wife of Tommy Brown, my one-time chauffeur. Dot's mad predictions had been having a dangerous influence on Ron. A big blonde woman who looked like a cockney Buddha, she was sharing a tiny flat over a betting shop in Walthamstow with her enormous husband and her crystal ball. The set-up was so absurdly cosy that it was strange to think of Ron coming here for consolation and advice. 'The thing about Ronnie is that he has a very strong spirit guide protecting him, and I tell him that no one can ever harm him or trick him. In any crisis his spirit guide will tell him what to do, and provided he listens no harm will befall him,' she told me.

Another member of the Kray entourage I met was Bobby Buckley, one-time jockey, former star croupier at Esmeralda's Barn and the only one of Ron's regiment of teenage lovers whom he might possibly have loved. 'If it'd been legal, I'd 'ave married 'im,' he told me. But as it wasn't legal, Ron married him off instead to his girlfriend Monica. Like Bobby, Monica was tiny and it might have been her doll-like appearance that appealed to Ron for he seems to have ended up in love with both of them. He told me that, apart from Violet, Monica was the only woman he had ever trusted. She seems to have brought out an unsuspected sentimental streak in him and he promised that he would always be her sugar daddy. 'Now tuck yourself up warm and make sure to look after yourself,' he used to tell her.

I also got to know most members of the so-called Firm, who

struck me as a fairly seedy lot, whose major role in life appeared to be to drink, collect the weekly 'pensions' from the local clubs and businesses and provide an appreciative audience for the Twins themselves.

It's interesting that the one member of The Firm who seemed a cut above the rest and whom the Twins obviously trusted was the one who would soon prove himself the greatest Judas of them all: their cousin, former pimp and merchant seaman, young good-looking Ronnie Hart whom I'd met that first night at the Astor. At the time, for Ron at any rate, Hart enjoyed the role of the Twins' honorary son and heir and, in accordance with the understanding I had reached with them, rather than tell me anything directly incriminating themselves, they relied on their cousin to do it for them, on the theory that anything he told me would be classed as 'hearsay'.

But since it was obviously important to the Twins that I should know something of the truth about them, cousin Hart was deputed to take me to the Blind Beggar and tell me what had happened. He did this very coolly, and as I got to know him better he hinted at other killings, including that of somebody he simply called 'The Hat'.

In a very different picture from the one he later gave in court, Ron Hart described living with the Twins as one great adventure, and for him everything about them was essentially heroic. 'The Twins are like Roman gladiators,' he said, 'and, like gladiators, they only kill their own.'

Ron Hart told me something else that stuck firmly in my mind. Recently Reg had told him that if anything happened to him and Ron he was to make sure they had the biggest funeral that the East End had ever seen.

Cousin Ron apart, the most fascinating character the Twins introduced me to was the former burglar turned criminal tycoon Billy Hill who was living in considerable style in his burglar-proof flat in Bayswater, opposite the Greek cathedral.

What I found so interesting about him was the fact that he was exactly the sort of rich, successful criminal that the Twins might well have been themselves if there hadn't been so many 'ifs' in their criminal career – *if* Ron and Reg had not been twins, *if* Ron had not been mad, and *if* they hadn't felt obliged to murder anyone.

Now approaching fifty, which in the 1960s seemed like terminal senility, Billy Hill had risen from a background of such poverty that it made the Twins' childhood in Bethnal Green sound like the lap of luxury. The eldest of twenty-three children of Irish parents – the father devoted to the bottle, the mother to the Virgin Mary – he told me how he started on his life of crime at the age of eight, stealing books from the stalls in Farringdon Market which he sold to other stallholders for a penny each.

But, unlike the Twins, he had completely cut himself off from his past.

'Not long ago I went back to King's Cross and saw some of the old friends I'd grown up with. All of them had been living decent, honest lives, and by the age that I am now almost all of them were burned out, done for, finished, whereas here am I enjoying the wages of sin. I have a new wife, a lovely house in southern Spain, and if people want to say that I'm responsible for the Hatton Garden *heist* or the London airport gold job, that's up to them.'

Billy Hill apart, my most significant encounter in the presence of the Twins around this time occurred one evening early in the New Year when the most unlikely couple I had seen in Whitechapel drove up in a brown and black Rolls-Royce and entered the saloon bar of the Old Horns, looking as if they owned it. The girl was ridiculously elegant in a pale designer coat and, although her companion was several inches shorter, he too was immaculately dressed in the sort of camel-hair overcoat that bandleaders were still wearing in the 1960s.

From their accents I took them for Americans in search of local colour who had wandered into the Old Horns by mistake. But to my surprise, instead of being promptly redirected to the door they seemed to know the Twins and I found myself being introduced to Alan Bruce Cooper, his wife Beverley and Sam, their Yorkshire terrier.

Each of the Twins reacted to the presence of the Coopers very differently. Before long, Reg turned his back on them, leaving me to talk to Beverley while her husband retreated to a corner for what was clearly an important talk with Ron. Later, when I asked Reg about them both, he changed the subject.

A week or so later the unlikely pair made a second visit to the Horns. This time they were accompanied by a weird young man who was as tall and silent as a stick of human celery. When I tried engaging him in conversation he looked desperately around him and seemed scared out of his wits.

Again I asked Reg about him afterwards, and he told me that the man's name was Elvey.

'What does he do for a living?' I inquired.

'He says he kills people,' Reg replied.

'And does he?' I asked.

Reg looked at me and shrugged.

21

Showdown in New York

O N THOSE TWO uncomfortable occasions when I met Alan Bruce Cooper and his attractive wife Beverley at the Old Horns in the presence of the Twins he struck me as a man with too much on his mind. But I had no notion of the problems he was facing, particularly on his second visit when he turned up with that pallid mystery man – and apparently potential murderer – Paul Elvey. Behind the scenes far more was going on than I suspected but it was not until much later that I understood the full importance of that most unlikely pair in the melodrama rapidly unfolding round the Twins, in what would prove to be their last remaining weeks of freedom.

It was a strange period, for during these climactic days I was not the only one completely in the dark over what was going on. Superintendent Leonard Read, for instance, knew even less than I did about what his boss Commander John du Rose was up to. Nipper had yet to meet Cooper in the flesh and had not the faintest notion of the relationship between him, Paul Elvey and that devious old detective.

Away from this uneasy situation, back in the relative sanity of Tintagel House, things were happening. Witness statements from a surprising range of victims of the Twins were mounting up. Leslie Payne in his morning sessions with Nipper in the Marylebone hotel was giving him a detailed run-down of everything he could remember from the past about the Twins and Nipper and his boys had now discovered that they had another murder on their hands – the so-far-corpseless death of Jack McVitie. But beyond all this they knew little more of what had really happened, and as things stood Nipper still had insufficient evidence to arrest the Twins and be sure of a conviction. Still less could he have secured the arrest of other members of the Firm who would undoubtedly have interfered with many of his witnesses. So the stalemate continued. Nipper and his men could only wait for something big enough to change the landscape of the whole investigation.

The one senior Scotland Yard detective who was perfectly aware of Nipper Read's frustration was, of course, his immediate superior, Commander John du Rose. But now was not the moment for du Rose to confront Nipper with the truth of what he had been up to. For more than ever now, what du Rose wanted was to be the old 'Four-Day Johnny' of the past, solving these unsolved murders with a sudden stroke of his former genius. Unlike Nipper, du Rose still believed that he held the secret that would break the stalemate, solve the case and leave the Twins wide open to arrest.

There was one further key development. On 8 March HM's Commissioner for Metropolitan Police Sir Joseph Simpson had his final heart attack. This meant that the Twins had lost their prime protector at the Yard. Simpson's successor, Sir John Waldron, was a very different character.

As for the Twins themselves, had they really wanted to avoid arrest and had they been prepared to stay contentedly in Bethnal Green, keeping a low profile and concentrating on their story and their film, they would have been immensely difficult to deal with. More importantly, had Reg not Ron been in command and made the key decisions they might still have rivalled Billy Hill in criminal longevity. But the murder of McVitie had left Ron more dangerously insane and powerful than ever.

★

During the last three years during which Lord Goodman's intervention in the Boothby scandal had rendered them 'untouchable' the Twins had not only got away with murder but with serial murder. As we have seen, their victims had included George Cornell, Frank Mitchell, Teddy Smith and now Jack McVitie. So it was not entirely surprising that, as long as Ron was on a high, he still believed he was invulnerable, particularly with psychic Dot around to reassure him that no harm could possibly befall him. The time was fast approaching when he couldn't wait to kill again.

Either way, believing he could count on Reg as his accomplice if it came to murder, Ron was becoming more dangerous by the day. But he also felt he needed Cooper if he was to deal with all the enemies around him. He had methodically started listing them. At the top of the list was Leslie Payne and he knew that Payne would shortly be appearing at the Old Bailey charged with fraud. This could provide an opportunity to kill him, and he automatically turned to Cooper for a foolproof way of doing so.

This was when Elvey made his first appearance on the scene. For amazingly, that frightened-looking white-faced character, that Cooper had brought along with him at our second meeting, was set to play a lethal role in the dangerous drama being acted out around him. I've no idea where Cooper found him. All that he ever told me was that Elvey was an unemployed electrician. He was also something of a fantasist and claimed to have seen active service with the SAS.

I never believed the talk about the SAS but Elvey was certainly a skilled technician, and during the short period when he worked as Cooper's assistant he showed himself prepared to use several deadly weapons for the Twins on Cooper's orders. Today, the first of these weapons has pride of place in the famous Black Museum at Scotland Yard, and on that one occasion when I met him at the pub with Cooper he and Cooper had arrived to give the Twins a demonstration of this sinister invention. From the start, Reg seemed bored with what was going on but Ron was obviously excited and couldn't wait to see what they had brought him. Whatever it was, Elvey had left it outside in the car and I discovered later that when they left the pub Cooper, Ron and Elvey drove straight back to Braithwaite House where they tried it out against one of Violet's sofas.

Elvey's secret weapon was a small suitcase containing a hypodermic filled with cyanide. Attached to the handle of the case was a small brass ring which, when pulled, made the needle of the hypodermic protrude through a small hole at the bottom of the case. When activated and then pushed against a human body in a crowd, the poison from the hypodermic would be instantly released into the victim's bloodstream and death would follow almost instantaneously. This was Elvey's murder weapon number one and he told the Twins that he was perfectly prepared to try it out on Leslie Payne if they wanted him to.

Despite the secrecy surrounding Nipper's meetings with Payne, word had got around of what was going on and Ron was now convinced that Payne was betraying them. He also knew that during the next few days Payne was going to appear in a fraud case at the Old Bailey. This would be Elvey's chance to prove himself and his secret weapon. For as Payne made his way through the crowded lobby of the Central Courts of Justice, Elvey – whom he didn't know – could get behind him with his suitcase, pull the ring, and thrust the hidden hypodermic into him. Apparently all of this had been arranged down to the last detail, and Cooper in his role as *agent provocateur* had also told du Rose of what would happen. Du Rose, in turn, had made arrangements for two plain-clothes officers to be waiting in the lobby at the Old Bailey, ready to arrest Elvey just before he struck.

But on the day when the murder should have taken place, Nipper had got the case against Leslie Payne postponed. This meant that, at the last minute, everything was called off but nobody told Elvey, who was left waiting with his suitcase in the crowded lobby of the Old Bailey for the would-be victim who never came.

For Ron this was a major disappointment. But as something of a consolation prize Cooper had already thought up one more way of killing Payne. On Cooper's instructions Elvey had found another secret weapon – a powerful crossbow which was normally used for hunting deer and planting anaesthetic darts in wild elephants in Africa. Elvey had calculated that the steel-tipped darts could kill a man at up to fifty yards and had presented a crossbow to the twins who tried it out on a cat in Epping Forest. This excited Ron, but Reg pointed out that it would impossible to use a crossbow in a public place and insisted on returning it to Elvey.

This made Ron more desperate than ever to lay hands on the two Thompson sub-machine guns that he'd been pestering Cooper about for months. In the film Bonnie and Clyde had used Thompson sub-machine guns in their final shoot-out with the FBI, and in his nightmares Ron could see himself with Reg beside him acting out the same scenario. It was on hearing this that Cooper nearly lost his nerve.

The role of an *agent provocateur* must be one of the most enviable jobs that any undercover agent can be given, and by encouraging Cooper to persuade a homicidal maniac like Ron to incriminate himself by murdering someone, the Admiral had placed him in a ghastly situation. For with Ron's bouts of homicidal madness steadily increasing, he was showing signs of getting out of all control. If anything, Cooper had actually been a little too successful. Elvey's weapons had excited Ron and he couldn't wait to use them.

Because of this, Cooper felt he had to stay in close contact with the Twins to be able to inform du Rose in advance about the next projected killing. But as Ron had by now told him how McVitie died, Cooper was under no illusions about the dangers he was facing. It was this that brought him close to panicking. Had he been on his own, self-preservation would have told him that the time had come to disappear and face the consequences. But he had a wife and child to think of, so he turned to John Du Rose instead.

Du Rose saw him, as he often did, in his office at the Yard, and calm as ever, puffed away at his cheroot, making sympathetic noises but there was not a great deal he could do to help him. Cooper was Admiral Hanly's man, not his. Over the last few months, the Admiral and the US Secret Service had invested large amounts of time and money running Cooper as an agent and John du Rose had no intention of poaching on the Admiral's territory. The Admiral was still very much in charge, and the truth was that John du Rose was wary of upsetting an organisation as powerful as the US Secret Service. It was only when Cooper told him he could not go on like this that Du Rose suggested that he went to Paris and discussed the situation with the Admiral.

Like du Rose, on seeing Cooper Admiral Hanly was extremely sympathetic, and finally produced a plan which he believed would solve the problem. The Admiral seemed to have a plan for everything and told Cooper that he didn't want to have his death on his conscience. Because of this he was determined to settle the whole case quickly now, before someone else was hurt: provided they were smart it should be possible to serve the interests of both the US Secret Service and Scotland Yard, and incriminate the Twins and their friends from the Mafia in a single operation. Just to prove to Cooper that the US Secret Service was behind him all the way, the Admiral told him that he himself would be directing operations from Paris.

★

As he had shown in the war, the Admiral was a man of action, and was eager for results. Obsessed as ever with establishing links between organised criminals in Europe and the USA he was hoping to set up a series of meetings between the Twins and old friends of theirs who were still important members of the Mafia. Their meetings and their phone calls could be monitored, their conversations recorded, and if he could only get them all together the results could be sensational, yielding information over a whole range of international criminal activities including narcotics, money laundering, lucrative gambling operations and even contract killings. The more the Admiral thought about it, the more exciting it appeared. With just a little luck, the Twins and their friends in the Mafia would incriminate themselves and arrests could follow on both sides of the Atlantic.

In fact the whole plan was wildly ambitious. If anyone should have known how deeply suspicious top members of the Mafia could be, it was Admiral Hanly. But the truth was that, having now invested so much Secret Service money in Cooper and the Twins, he wanted something positive to show for it to the folks back home in Washington. What was needed was a spot of action to reassure them that Admiral Hanly was still firmly on the ball.

Whatever Cooper may have thought of this, as usual he could only go along with what the Admiral was suggesting. And so what must surely count as one of the most bizarre episodes in the history of the US Secret Service started.

From the start Admiral Hanly's plan to bring together the Kray Twins with a group of top brass from the Mob faced one big problem. All those highly suspect characters that the Admiral was so interested in were in America, and since Ron, at any rate, was permanently banned from visiting the States such a meeting would take a lot of organising. A lesser man might well have quailed, but the word 'impossible' was not in Admiral Hanly's mental dictionary and he had always treated problems such as this as challenges. A visit to the USA by a pair of criminals as notorious as the Twins would certainly require official backing at the highest level, just as the logistics of arranging such a visit as he had in mind would be quite formidable and would need clearance by the FBI, the US Immigration Service and the directorate of the US Secret Service. All of which the Admiral must have had, since his plans for the Twins' visit to New York now went ahead.

As Ron's last trip to America three years earlier had ended with him being officially banned from entering the States, this must have needed quite a lot of doing. Certainly Admiral Hanly was one of the very few Americans who could have arranged for a criminal as notorious as Ron to be issued with a valid visa to enter the USA. As well as this there would need to be arrangements for airline tickets, and bookings in suitable hotels, in Paris and New York. Nothing could be left to chance and it was not until the last week of March that arrangements were in place for the Twins' visit to New York on which, apparently, so much depended.

Until now, Reg had reluctantly gone along with the idea of the trip. But at the last minute he refused to go. Why should they trust their lives to somebody like Cooper? How could Ron be certain that the whole thing wasn't just a trap?

There was a time when Ron would have listened to his brother and finally backed off. But now that he'd set his heart on going to America his voices told him that he was safe and he was determined to go through with it.

'You're just bein' babyish,' he said to Reg. 'An' if you're frightened of a cunt like Cooper I'm sorry for you. Any'ow I've never seen New York. I think it's time I did.'

★

On 5 April Alan Bruce Cooper collected Ron from Braithwaite House in the Rolls and drove him to Heathrow. Since Reg was still determined to stay out of this, Dickie Morgan, one of the Twins' oldest friends and a founder member of The Firm, took his place. None of what followed could have happened without the close cooperation of the US Secret Service, but because of the Admiral's status in the US Paris embassy everything went smoothly from the start. At Orly Airport they were waved through passport control and Customs, and outside a hired car was waiting to take them to the Hotel Frontenac in the heart of Paris.

'Ron, how d'you like being a VIP?' Cooper asked him. Ron muttered that he liked it very much.

For Ron at any rate his one-night stay in Paris was a great success. For some time Cooper had been spinning him a succession of elaborate fantasies of how the Firm could link up with the formidable Corsican Mafia, the *Union Corse*, and that afternoon he introduced him to the Corsican gangster who directed the Union's operations in Paris. In fact he wasn't really Corsican at all but a middle-aged Sicilian called Ricardo who had done time in San Quentin but since settling in France had earned a living as a supporting actor in a succession of French gangster movies. He had also helped the Admiral out on various occasions.

Whatever else he was, Ricardo was a famous talker. He spoke good English, Cooper had briefed him over what to say, and for the rest of the evening he kept Ron enthralled with his tales of violence and murder. He also talked of how Ron and his allies could cooperate with members of the *Union Corse*, with Corsican hit men flying in to London for the day to carry out a killing before taking the evening plane back to Corsica. Ron was enormously impressed.

Next morning, as soon as the US Consulate was open,

Cooper took Ron and Dickie Morgan along with their passports to be stamped with entry visas to the USA. Again there
were no problems and no questions asked, nor were there any
problems when Cooper took them on to a travel agent near the
embassy where return tickets to New York were waiting for
them in their names along with reservations on a midday flight.

Morgan asked how all this had happened so smoothly.

'Our Mafia friends are very powerful,' Cooper answered.

Later all three of them took a taxi back to Orly airport where
they boarded a midday flight to New York.

Once again everything went smoothly – possibly a bit too
smoothly, for Ron was hardly likely to forget his previous
reception by the US Immigration Service. But this time everything was so relaxed that, when they were safely in a taxi
heading for the centre of New York, Morgan turned to Ron
and asked, 'What's going on, Ron? I thought the Yanks hated
you.'

'Perhaps we've just got lucky,' Ron replied.

'Don't let it worry you,' said Cooper.

Once again everything was carefully arranged. Cooper had
booked three separate rooms in the downtown Warwick Hotel,
and next morning after breakfast he spent a lot of time with
Ron, helping him telephone all the top members of the Mafia
he knew. All three rooms in the Warwick had of course been
carefully bugged and every word they uttered was recorded.
Ron did his best to contact members of the Mob in Chicago
and Las Vegas, but all of them had clearly got the message and
nobody replied. The same thing happened when he rang Judy
Garland, using the number Reg had given him. But when he
gave his name the maid replied that Miss Garland was out of
town. It was the same when he rang Meyer Lansky in Las Vegas
to suggest a meeting. The only real meeting that he managed to
set up was with Frank Taylor who was somewhat mystified to
find Ron in the centre of New York but who told him of a lot

of interest in proposals for their film from Hollywood and that he had heard good reports of the progress of their book.

Cooper had foreseen this happening and was prepared for this eventuality. As in Paris, he had taken no chances and during a recent visit to New York had hired several actors to play the part of mafiosi and had spent some time while he was there rehearsing them.

Even so, for Cooper it must have been a nightmare keeping Ron occupied and happy and at the same time trying to arrange for him to meet high-ranking members of the Mafia. The only genuine gangsters within fifty miles were Crazy Joe Gallo and his bodyguard Frank Illiano, who out of bravado or curiosity put in a brief appearance at the Warwick just to check on what was happening.

Joe Gallo didn't stay around for long, but Frank Illiano was obviously intrigued by Ron and spent quite some time with him explaining how rival gangs were organised in New York and what lessons he could learn from them. Ron was impressed and to show his gratitude gave him his platinum and diamond ring as a keepsake. Cooper also managed to arrange for Ron to meet a retired member of the Mafia who claimed to be working as a bodyguard to the Mayor of New York and who talked for hours about Ron's hero, Al Capone, and the St.Valentine's massacre. This time Ron was so impressed that he gave him his gold Rolex.

But apart from them, Cooper clearly had his work cut out keeping Ron and Dickie Morgan happy and spent a lot of time showing them Brooklyn and Harlem and Skid Row, introducing them to various old time criminals he seemed to know. He also took them to Coney Island , which Ron enjoyed enormously, and met several of Cooper's actor friends who had specially briefed in advance. Between them they all put on a most convincing show, but it meant that instead of conferring with important members of the mafia, as the Admiral had intended, Ron was actually meeting a succession of washed up gangsters, dead beat con men and actors carefully rehearsed by Cooper to play the part of killers.

'Anyone else you'd like to meet while you're here?' Cooper asked him. 'Only that coloured boy behind the reception desk,' he answered.

By the fourth day of the trip Cooper was still trying hard to fix up something more impressive to satisfy the Secret Service, but Ron decided he had seen enough of little old New York and told him he was going back to London.

History does not relate how the Admiral subsequently explained this extraordinary business to his superiors in the Treasury Department back in Washington, although to have survived so long in the world of high intelligence he must have had a lot of practice dealing with disasters. In spite of this, by any estimation Ron Kray's New York City break should have a place as the most expensive fiasco ever staged around a homicidal madman in the history of the US Secret Service. But the strangest thing of all in this very strange affair is that in the end it brought results and through a succession of accidents and misunderstandings that followed led to a decisive moment in the downfall of the Twins by giving Nipper Read the lucky break he needed.

What happened was that while Cooper was making such desperate efforts to keep Ron occupied and happy by meeting all those deadbeat gangsters and criminal has-beens in New York, not to mention the actors he employed to play the part of mafiosi, Ron had been enormously impressed by what they told him. Just as he believed Ricardo's promises to fly in contract killers from Corsica, so he really took to heart the stories he was hearing about organised crime in America. What particularly excited him were Frank Illiano's stories of how in America criminals used car bombs and explosives to destroy their enemies. Once he was safely back with Reg, he couldn't wait to put these ideas into practice.

As du Rose had known all about the trip from the beginning I wondered why he didn't choose this moment to come clean with Nipper Read. But how could he make such a devastating revelation when all it did was end in failure? To have done so would have broken trust with Hanly and the US Secret Service. So Cooper was left to get on with the next episode in his life as an *agent provocateur*, with Ron even more excited and dangerous than ever.

Only a madman such as Ron could have appreciated lunacy on the scale of the New York tour that the US Secret Service specially arranged for him; and the ultimate irony of Ron's costly four-day visit there at the expense of the US Treasury Department was that all those conversations he had had with actors ad libbing the part of criminals and the interviews he had with deadbeat gangsters instructing him on how to organise a gangland murder had excited and inspired him as little ever had before. Far from feeling cheated by his trip, he returned excited and inspired by the boundless possibilities it offered him for killing people. He couldn't wait to tell Reg to get in touch with Ricardo in Paris, and he talked excitedly to Cooper of his plans for bringing death and terror to the streets of London.

What particularly excited him were the lethal possibilities of the latest weapon of the IRA and the Sicilian Mafia which Illiano had talked to him about – killing by car bomb. Here Elvey, as a skilled electrician, was in his element at last as he explained how a bomb could be wired into the ignition of a victim's car.

And yet, amazingly, there was yet more of this murderous make-believe to come. For after the fiasco in New York,

Cooper found himself being pressured more than ever from both sides – by the Admiral to get proof at all cost that could lead to an arrest and end his whole adventure with the Twins, and by Ron to get Elvey working on the car bombs which he was now excitedly imagining would blow up his enemies.

Ron was keener still on action, and had taken Cooper for a drive round Soho where he pointed out a man call Ed Caruana who he wanted murdered to impress another club owner called Silvers. He asked Cooper for the dynamite.

In the state that he was in Ron wouldn't take no for an answer and, under pressure from a now desperate Cooper, Du Rose went along with him and agreed that Elvey should be sent to Glasgow to collect the dynamite. After the fiasco of New York, this would be something they could really pin on Ron, though whether they intended to catch him just before he blew up Caruana or intended to wait until there were bodies littering the streets of London I was never able to discover.

At around this time, one of the Mills brothers who had recently become a reliable informant from The Firm reported back to Nipper, warning him that his life could be in danger since his name was on Ron Kray's list of people he was planning to destroy – along with Caruana – with one of the car bombs which Elvey was busily creating in his garden shed for Ron's big offensive.

Having informed du Rose what he was up to, Cooper sent Elvey off by plane to Edinburgh with instuctions to go on to Glasgow, collect the dynamite from a certain Gorbals gangster, and immediately then fly back with it to London.

By now Nipper had been given permission by the Home Office to tap systematically into the telephone conversations of the Twins and members of The Firm, which was how he heard that an associate of the Twins called Cooper was sending an emissary called Elvey by air to Glasgow to collect what was described as 'some dodgy gear' and bring it back to London. Knowing that there were close connections between the Krays and gangs in Glasgow, Nipper asked the local CID to put a tail on Elvey and report what happened. The result was more sensational than Nipper could ever have expected. Elvey was seen meeting a known Glasgow criminal outside a pub and returning to the airport with a holdall. He was followed and arrested as he was just about to board the plane to London. Inside the holdall were two dozen sticks of dynamite.

At last the the farce was over. Like two cars on a collision course, the two separate investigations to catch the Twins had finally collided.

Everything happened very quickly now. Nipper flew instantly to Scotland where he and his deputy Archie Hemingway grilled Elvey until he finally broke down and put the blame on Cooper. Then it was Cooper's turn to face the music. Back in London he was arrested and brought to Tintagel House but when Nipper repeated Elvey's allegations he angrily denied them.

'Fine,' said Nipper.' Then I'm charging you with conspiracy to murder.'

But Cooper's answer was hardly what Nipper Read expected.

'I want to see John du Rose,' he said

'What has Commander du Rose got to do with it?' said Nipper. To which Cooper delivered a reply which Nipper Read could not believe.

'If you contact John du Rose he will tell you that I have been working as his informant for the last two years and have been spying on the Krays.'

Nipper Read has never said what happened next when he confronted John du Rose and it was not until twenty-five years later that he so much as mentioned the incident in his memoirs. Nipper was always nobly discreet in his account of what he said to John du Rose and Scotland Yard was said to 'consume its own smoke in a crisis'. Certainly du Rose must have swallowed an awful lot of smoke in Nipper's office. Another cover-up occurred, and not a hint of what had really happened even faintly reached the press.

To those who didn't know the truth it was very much business as usual, with John du Rose still directing operations at Tintagel House and Nipper acting as his loyal deputy. But this was only done to keep up appearances. From now on John du Rose was only nominally in charge and Nipper Read was firmly in command of the battle with the Krays.

Whatever else this whole strange incident had done, it had broken the stalemate which had been hampering the investigation for far too long. Nipper had also learned a lot from Cooper since arresting him, including the plans for the car bombs and the fact that the Twins had access to a pair of Thompson sub-machine guns which, according to Cooper, Ron was 'itching to start using'. Clearly there was no time to lose, but the problem remained of getting clear-cut evidence against the Twins that would stand up in court.

This explains why Nipper now decided on a move that could have brought disaster. Ever since he arrested Cooper, he had had him under his control and had been careful not to let a word of what had happened to him reach the Twins. Instead he ordered Cooper to speak to them on the telephone and make an excuse that he'd been seriously ill with a bleeding stomach ulcer and was having to go into hospital. From now on all his telephone conversations were recorded.

Things moved fast. Nipper found Cooper a bed in a private London clinic and told him to wear pyjamas and act the part of a patient with a serious illness. The doctors were involved in the deception, the patient's room was bugged and he was told to keep in close contact with the Twins begging them to visit him.

The Twins themselves seemed genuinely upset and promised they would come. Nipper, of course, was hoping that by recording the subsequent conversation he would get some damaging confession, or at least some indication of their plans. But instead of the Twins it was little Tom Cowley who turned up. Cooper, although disappointed, kept up the farce, and Tom gave no sign that he suspected anything. But although he stayed a good half hour and they talked about a lot of things nothing incriminating was said. In fact Tom immediately reported back to the Twins that 'the fucking hospital is stiff with coppers.'

Two days later Little Tom took his wife off on a long holiday to Majorca.

Once Nipper realised his plan had failed he faced a difficult dilemma. After nine months his investigation had almost stalled. He still lacked much of the evidence he needed and he knew that, having failed to trick the Twins, he had actually given them a warning. But he also knew that if he hesitated much longer someone else would almost certainly be killed. Make-your-mind-up-time had come.

Late in the evening of 7 May, more than sixty specially chosen police officers were summoned to Tintagel House by Nipper Read. To ensure maximum security the doors were locked behind them and shortly after midnight they received their instructions.

At dawn the Kray Twins were to be arrested along with as many members of the Firm as possible in a carefully coordinated operation. Nipper explained that there were twenty-four separate addresses across London that had to be raided simultaneously. It was typical of Nipper's attention to detail that each member of the Firm had been covered with a file card bearing an address, a brief description and a photograph.

★

Throughout what was to be the Twins' last night of freedom unbeknownst to them they were under constant observation from the start by plain clothes police reporting back to Nipper Read by two-way radio. It was to be a long drawn-out evening for all concerned. It began at 9 pm with the Twins drinking as usual with their friends at the Old Horns pub in Bethnal Green. Shortly after midnight reports came through that they had just moved on to the Astor Club in Mayfair. Then the serious drinking evidently started, and it was not until after 5 am that they were reported to be back at their parents' flat in Braithwaite House.

Watches were synchronised at Tintagel House and the time for action had arrived. The mass arrest was set up for 7 am on the morning of 8 May, and every one of the police knew exactly who to arrests. When one of the raiding party asked Nipper who was going to get the Twins, he replied, 'that privilege is mine'.

In spite of their dreams of ending their days like Bonnie and Clyde and going down in a hail of bullets, nothing could have been more unromantic than the actual moment of the Twins' arrest. Violet and Charlie were away, and when Nipper and his men smashed in the front door of their flat Ron was in bed with a boy and Reg with a girl from Walthamstowe. Both twins were very much the worse for wear after a long night's heavy drinking and were barely awake when the handcuffs snapped around their wrists and they were dragged unceremoniously from their beds. There was no resistance.

22

Remand

THE TRUTH WAS that the unexpected nature of the accident which led to Elvey's freak arrest at Edinburgh airport had caught everybody by surprise, not least the Twins themselves, who had shown themselves unprepared for trouble – so unprepared that ten days later they had allowed themselves to be arrested in their beds, and were so hung over that, even if they'd wanted to, they couldn't have organised the grand finale to their lives that Ron had been dreaming of for years: with Reg beside him and both of them dying in a hail of gunfire, with their own machine guns blazing.

But Nipper also had his problems as he did his best to put together the prosecution case against the Twins and their followers in the sort of hurry and confusion that he hated. One of his problems was what to do about Commander John du Rose, for it would have been disastrous – particularly for du Rose but also for Nipper's hopes of dealing with the Twins – if the faintest hint of what had been going on between Cooper and du Rose over the last two years had ever reached the press. One could already see the headlines: 'Head of Murder Squad involved in Car Bomb Plot', followed by the sensational story of how the man in charge of Nipper's very own investigation had been working with Cooper all along without telling his second-in-command anything about it.

There had been far too much hushed-up scandal round the

Twins already without adding to it further, and had the truth of John du Rose's double-dealing been revealed, along with his relationship not just with Cooper but also with Admiral John H. Hanly, the all-powerful European head of the US Secret Service, it could have been disastrous at this stage in the inquiries. It would have inevitably diverted everyone's attention from the true crimes of the Twins at a time when Nipper's real investigation of their crimes had barely started.

Nipper was not a placid man by nature and was clearly furious at du Rose's behaviour. But he was also far too shrewd – and too loyal a policeman – to have plunged his own investigation into the chaos that would have followed had he rocked the boat about it now. So outwardly it was still very much business as usual. On the surface nothing had changed in Tintagel House and, in theory at any rate, Commander John du Rose was still in charge. After his retirement, he was still hailed occasionally as 'the man who caught the Krays'. But the truth was that from the moment when the Edinburgh police discovered the dynamite in Elvey's holdall Commander John du Rose's involvement in the case was over, and Nipper Read alone, took charge.

Similarly, two days later, when the Twins and their accomplices were brought from prison to the committal proceedings at Bow Street Magistrates' Court it was very much Nipper Read who placed his own inimitable mark on the proceedings and made it clear that this was no ordinary case – any more than the Twins were ordinary criminals.

One must remember that 1968 was the 'Year of Revolutions'. In Paris at this very moment students were ripping up paving stones and were building barricades, in Berlin the Red Brigades were forming, and in Italy the state itself was menaced by the double threat of urban terrorism and the Mafia. It was against this background that Nipper organised his own daily demonstration against the potential power of the Krays.

Until now, what had normally happened was that suspects on remand were transported without much fuss to court from prison in a Black Maria. But with the Twins and their followers things were different and each morning they were brought from prison to the Bow Street court in an impressive high-speed convoy of police vehicles complete with armed guards, blue lights flashing and a presidential-style motorcycle escort clearing a way for them through the morning traffic. Nipper insisted that this was necessary because of the danger, remote as it might seem, of an ambush on the way; but at times like this the message it conveyed was unmistakable. These were no ordinary criminals but potential urban terrorists.

Nipper Read clearly hoped that the message would not be lost on Mr Kenneth Barraclough, the Bow Street magistrate, for he was counting on Barraclough to deliver something only he could offer him at the moment: time. Time during which to continue his investigations, organise his witnesses, and above all to persuade them that it was safe to talk. For this to happen Nipper needed to convince the magistrate that the case against the Twins and their accomplices was serious enough to justify keeping them in prison while Nipper and his team got all the evidence they needed for their full-scale trial at the Old Bailey.

Nipper also knew that, at this delicate point in his investigation, apart from Leslie Payne the only witnesses he could so far count on to support a charge against the Twins for conspiracy to murder were Cooper and his henchman Paul Elvey. In Nipper's situation few policemen would have thought that this curious couple were reliable enough to have convinced anyone, let alone a cautious Bow Street magistrate. Nipper felt much the same, but he also knew that he had no alternative.

For at this stage in the game his case against the Twins had barely started. As yet he had no witnesses to the McVitie murder and nothing to connect the Twins with the disappearance of

Frank Mitchell. In addition, no bodies had been found in either case. As for the Cornell murder, the all-important witness Mrs X, the barmaid from the Blind Beggar, was sticking grimly by her statement that she couldn't recognise Ron Kray as Cornell's killer. Nipper could understood her feelings and her desperate fear of retribution from the Twins if they were ever released from prison, and he knew that it was up to him to make doubly sure they stayed in jail.

Nipper was not the only one who was hoping that the remand hearings went his way. So were the Twins, and no sooner did they find themselves in court than they did something absolutely unexpected. Three years earlier a total ban had been imposed on media reporting of remand proceedings, on the grounds that premature publicity concerning a defendant, before their innocence or guilt had been established, could prejudice their chances in a higher court. This ban could be lifted only when requested by a defendant. On their first day in court at Bow Street the Twins requested this to happen.

At the time this seemed so totally against the Twins' interests that I asked Reg why he did it. 'Because we wanted everyone to see the diabolical liberties the law was taking when they arrested us,' he said, but even then I knew there was more to it than that. Looking back on all that followed, I'm certain that they couldn't bear the thought of sitting there and suffering in silence while their actions were discussed in secret in a court of law – and missing out on the publicity.

Besides, even when they were desperate for publicity, bad as well as good, and since they were were aware that their celebrity status depended on their fame as criminals they knew that whatever happened in that crowded little Bow Street courtroom over the next two months would be of great importance in the creation of their legend.

★

Today the Bow Street Magistrates' Court has been replaced by a hotel, but in the Twins' day it was one of the oldest courts in London.

It was small and old and very business-like, with none of the ritual and theatricality of the Old Bailey. The presiding magistrate, Mr Kenneth Barraclough, was equally down to earth, a bespectacled figure with something of the elderly accountant about him. He was not distracted by a jury, for it was not his job to decide on the innocence or guilt of those before him. All he had to do was to decide whether the accused had a case to answer at the Central Criminal Court at the Old Bailey and, if they did, whether to keep them in prison or release them on bail.

For Nipper Read it was vital that the Twins and the members of the Firm were kept in prison on remand as long as possible. But at this early stage of the proceedings Nipper was having to rely on two extremely shaky witnesses – Alan Bruce Cooper and his strange assistant, the would-be assassin Paul Elvey.

Despite Cooper's obvious defects as a witness, Nipper had no alternative but to use him. For, like it or not – and Nipper didn't like it very much – the evidence that he'd recently obtained from interrogating him was exactly what he needed, particularly when backed up by the evidence of Paul Elvey. Here was undeniable evidence against the Twins of intent to murder. No magistrate, and certainly not Mr Barraclough, was going to ignore the presence of twenty sticks of dynamite in Elvey's luggage as he boarded the plane from Edinburgh to London, still less of evidence of plans to bring car bombs to the streets of the capital.

As we have seen, Cooper really *had* been working for the US Secret Service, otherwise he'd never have been able to get Ron and Dickie Morgan to New York and back with valid entry visas just a few weeks earlier. But, in a way, the truth about

Cooper and his stooge hardly mattered now. What was undeniable was the effect of their evidence on the court and its impact on the image of the Twins in the world outside.

Here Nipper Read was fortunate. From the moment they were on the witness stand almost everything about this shady pair appeared a touch ridiculous, so much so that when Cooper, under cross-examination, said quite truthfully that he'd been working for the US Secret Service nobody believed him. But as Cooper's cross-examination continued, the Twins' lawyers played into the prosecution's hands by revealing that they had no idea of what the US Secret Service really was. 'Did they give you a card to prove who you were?' one young lawyer asked Cooper brightly; and another lawyer, the bullying but not over-bright baronet Sir Lionel Thompson, thinking to catch the stuttering Cooper out for good, inquired, 'What branch of the Secret Service do you mean – the CIA, the FBI or the Drugs and Narcotics Bureau?'

When Cooper stuttered that he worked for *the* US Secret Service and offered to write down the name of his Secret Service contact for the magistrate it could have caused the prosecution – and Nipper Read – such awkward problems that I wasn't certain why the defence failed to pursue it. For had it ever been revealed, as it very nearly was, that through Cooper and Elvey the Kray Twins were being targeted by a senior agent from the US Secret Service who was in cahoots with an equally senior officer at Scotland Yard the case against the Twins, at this early stage of the investigation, might well have been in trouble.

Instead, Sir Lionel, confident that he'd made his point, asked the sort of question that lawyers throw at hostile witnesses when they feel they have them at a disadvantage.

'Mr Cooper, is it true that in the East End of London you're referred to by those who know you as "Silly Bollocks"?'

To be fair to Cooper, he took this rather well, smiling wanly at the ensuing laughter, and Reg followed with an interjection that reached the front pages of the evening papers – as, of course, he'd hoped it would.

'When are we going to hear from James Bond?' he shouted.

But although, as one reporter wrote, the atmosphere in court was 'getting like something from a high-grade thriller' and Cooper and Elvey were beginning to look like a pair of secret agents from a Whitehall farce, Nipper knew what he was doing. For this was the point at which he had arranged for the prosecution to produce two items he had found in Elvey's garage which were not a joke. From the moment they were put on show in front of the magistrate it was clear from the hush that fell across the court that, whatever happened next, the Twins had had it.

For Nipper knew that, when produced at the right moment in a trial, an exhibit can be more effective than a human witness. And there can't have been many previous occasions when a Bow Street magistrate had been confronted with an exhibit as lethal as Paul Elvey's suitcase, with its hypodermic ready to be filled with the contents of an accompanying small brown bottle.

Plump Kenneth Jones QC, the prosecuting counsel asked Elvey to show the court how the murder weapon worked. He did so, showing the court the hypodermic and the bottle of pale brown fluid, followed by a demonstration of how the suitcase operated. After this Jones produced the high-powered crossbow and Elvey once again explained how he had bought it for the Twins at a specialist sports shop, how it was sometimes used for hunting deer, and how the steel-tipped darts could wound or even kill a man at up to twenty-five yards.

But the most chilling testimony of all came not from Elvey nor from Cooper but from the expert witness who followed them – the Home Office pathologist, Sir Francis Camps, Professor of Forensic Medicine at London University.

A tall balding man, with horn-rimmed spectacles and a dashing red carnation in his buttonhole, Professor Camps was the *doyen* of expert witnesses who knew exactly how to play an audience in a case like this, answering the questions of the prosecuting counsel with all the authority of a famous medical consultant delivering an opinion.

'Professor Camps, would you please look at Exhibit One. The suitcase.'

'Yes. I've seen it before, and been present when experiments were carried out involving the positioning of the hypodermic in the suitcase.'

'And so you're also acquainted with the contents of the small brown bottle, labelled here "Exhibit Two".'

'I am. Exhibit Two consists of a quantity of hydrogen cyanide'

'And what, in your opinion, would be its effect if the contents of the bottle were placed in the hypodermic which was then used to inject the fluid into the body of someone brought in contact with it?'

'It would depend upon the volume and the strength of the solution. Two cubic centimetres of a two per cent solution would be fatal. In fact, something less than that would probably be fatal too.'

'And would you say that this mechanism of the suitcase used in conjunction with the hydrogen cyanide was a viable way of killing someone?'

'Most certainly.'

'And what would the victim know?'

'He wouldn't necessarily know anything, provided the needle were sharp enough.'

'And if this mechanism had been used, would the cyanide have been easily detected by a coroner upon examination?'

'In my opinion, no. It would probably have been accepted as death through natural causes.'

'Are you saying that at a post-mortem examination one could not necessarily detect a dose of hydrogen cyanide?'

'Only if you'd had a strong suspicion that it was there already. The rapidity with which cyanide works would make it more likely than most poisons to resemble a heart attack. And if someone suddenly dropped dead, that's what you'd probably suspect.'

As Professor Camps concluded his evidence, the silence in the court was palpable. Against evidence like this, little else really mattered – certainly not any questions of what Cooper had actually been up to with the Twins. His relationship with Admiral Hanly or with John du Rose receded into insignificance. If these were the sort of weapons that the Twins had had at their disposal, no magistrate on Earth – and certainly not one as careful as Mr Kenneth Barraclough – was going to turn them loose upon society.

In fact, the Bow Street hearings against the Twins and members of the Firm were far from over. Now that Nipper and the prosecution had the initiative they had no intention of surrendering it again, and there would be many more witnesses against the Twins brought before the Bow Street magistrate throughout that summer. But Cooper and Elvey had served their purpose, and for now at any rate the case against the Twins concluded with a neat display of very different evidence from a very different source – the man with the briefcase, Leslie 'The Brain' Payne.

After Professor Camps's chilling recitation of the possibilities of unsuspected death from cyanide, it was a relief for the court to be able to relax to Payne's unthreatening account of the complexities of the Twins' involvement in the European marketing of securities and so-called 'bearer bonds' on behalf of the American Mafia, who had stolen them from banks in Canada.

As was to be expected from that elegant fraudster, Payne was also a most convincing witness as he explained the operation of the bearer bonds, the size and the potential of the trade, and the code that the Twins and their partners in crime used to keep in touch with the Mafia in New York.

All this particularly impressed the Twins' prosecuting counsel, who in his summing-up talked of the Twins handling at least two million dollars' worth of bonds stolen by the Mafia and used the phrase that hit the headlines of next morning's press.

'Krays in worldwide plot, says QC.'

Ever since the Twins had lifted the restrictions on media reporting their interest value was growing by the day. First death by cyanide, then big-time financial operators with a worldwide clientele. And there would be a great deal more to come. For by the conclusion of the Bow Street hearings Nipper Read would have got exactly what he needed. By placing the Krays and accomplices on remand throughout the summer, Kenneth Barraclough had put them in the deep freeze, at least until October, leaving Nipper and the detectives from Tintagel House free from interference as they gathered their witnesses and put together what turned out to be the most elaborate criminal case ever heard at the Old Bailey.

23

The Trial of the Century

THE TRIAL HAD been carefully set up from the start, for with so much at stake it would have been irresponsible of any government to have left its outcome to anything as unreliable as chance.

Although it was getting on for five years since the Boothby scandal, most of the beneficiaries of Lord Goodman's cover-up were still very much in power. Boothby's 'Little Man', Harold Wilson, was now prime minister. His 'Mr Fixit', Arnold Goodman, who was now 'Lord Fixit', had grown larger and more indispensable than ever. Tom Driberg, since his marriage and promotion to the peerage as Lord Bradwell-Juxta-Mare, had given up 'cottaging' and was now the influential chairman of the Labour Party. And although the prime minister at the time of the scandal, Sir Alec Douglas-Home, had decided to resume his old identity as Lord Douglas-Home and had retired from politics, he still, as we shall see, retained an interest in the fate and future of the Twins.

But the responsibility for what ensued still rested largely with the original duo who had so efficiently suppressed that whole outrageous business back in 1964 – the Little Man and the Fat Man, Harold Wilson and Lord Goodman. Clearly it was they who still had most to lose if the faintest flicker of the truth were ever to emerge. In Harold Wilson's case, his time in office had increased the stresses on his anxious nature – leaving him more suspicious and more conspiratorial than ever.

For Wilson and for Goodman the prospect of the Kray Twins' trial must have been particularly disturbing. Hanging the Twins for murder would have solved their problems and guaranteed the Twin's silence most effectively. But since this was no longer possible, what they desired from the trial was the next-best thing – a chance to eradicate the Twins entirely with a lifelong prison sentence in maximum security and by so doing bring closure to the hushed-up scandal which still haunted the Establishment.

As the trial was rapidly approaching this called for careful preparations by the government, which at least partially explains the size and the sensational nature of the trial when it finally commenced at the Old Bailey on 7 January 1969. There was, for instance, the vexed problem of evidence. For over a year now Nipper had been assembling his cast of witnesses against the Twins. Early on, in discussions with lawyers from Scotland Yard and the Home Office, he had convinced them that the only way the Twins could ever be arrested was on 'villains' evidence' – most of it from other criminals who would have to be persuaded that it was either safe or profitable to betray them. 'If it's necessary to go down into the sewers to get them I'm perfectly prepared to do so,' he told them. Unlike most policeman, Nipper was good with lawyers and as a result of these discussions he was granted virtual *carte blanche* to offer even the guiltiest criminals immunity from prosecution if they would turn Queen's Evidence.

Such authority on such a scale would have had to have been sanctioned by someone at the highest level of government, which it clearly was, and the result was that promises of immunity from prosecution were granted on a scale unseen before in any major trial in England. The only modern parallels were in the big Mafia show trials currently being held in Italy, which depended almost entirely on the evidence of so-called *pentiti* – repentant ones – major criminals who were offered a degree of freedom if they would betray still greater criminals.

During the autumn of 1968, as Nipper and his team at Tintagel House worked busily away preparing for the mammoth trial to come, they soon discovered that the power of forgiveness could work wonders, and brought the most hardened accomplices of the Twins to see the errors of their ways. (Nipper had a well-developed sense of humour, and on one occasion he actually put on a dog collar and disguised himself as the prison chaplain to interview Big Albert Donoghue in Brixton Prison chapel thus ensuring that not a hint of what was happening reached the sharp ears of the Twins.)

One of the very few potential witnesses whose sense of loyalty was proof against Nipper Read's temptations was young Christopher Lambrianou whose involvement in McVitie's murder was fairly marginal and who had spent his time while Jack was being butchered sitting outside on the staircase, weeping. To be fair to Nipper, much as he wanted Lambrianou as a witness he was also anxious to prevent someone so young from being forced to spend a large period of his life in prison. He tried everything he could to convince him not to let this happen and was finally so exasperated that he almost hit him. But despite his tendency to tears Chrissie Lambrianou, unlike all the rest of the Twins' once faithful buddies, had his principles – and stuck to them. And in the end, of course, Nipper Read was proved right. Christopher Lambrianou, like his brother Tony, would serve fifteen years in prison for sticking by the Twins, without receiving so much as a subsequent thank-you for their loyalty.

Despite the so-called 'code of silence' which had ruled the old East End from time immemorial, important members of the Firm – who were far guiltier than the Lambrianous – felt no loyalty whatsoever to the Krays when it came to it, and it was estimated that by the time that Nipper and his team had finished work they had 'turned' something approaching twenty-five former friends, associates and perjured witnesses of the Twins in return for immunity from prosecution. Some were lifelong friends of the family like old Charlie's fellow deserter from the army Harry Hopwood, Ron's former bodyguard Bill Exley, and Lennie Dunne, the pornographic bookseller whose flat was used to conceal the Axeman after his release from Dartmoor. Some were long-term members of the Firm who had known the Twins from the beginning, colleagues like Dickie Morgan, Tom Berry's brother, Checker, and my one-time driver, Big Tommy Brown 'the Bear'.

Then there were the reluctant witnesses, like Lisa Prescott the hostess from Churchill's Club, who had slept with the unfortunate 'Mad Axeman' Frank Mitchell in Lennie Dunn's flat in Barking. More important still, Superintendent Mooney had employed his Irish charm to convince Mrs X, the still terrified barmaid from the Blind Beggar, that it was safe for her to come clean at last in court over what had really happened to George Cornell on that fateful evening in the pub. Along with Albert Donoghue, other major figures in the Firm who had been 'turned' by the offer of immunity included Scotch Jack Dixon, and Nipper's greatest catch of all: the Twins' own cousin, Ronald Hart. Such characters had been so deeply incriminated with the Twins that by betraying them they saved themselves from wasting their best remaining years of life in prison.

Something else that proved of great importance to the trial was the question of the judge. Normally High Court judges are appointed in strict rotation by the Lord Chief Justice. But this was not a normal trial and since its outcome was so crucial to so many people no one was terribly surprised when the choice fell on the toughest High Court judge of all, the sixty-seven-year-old Sir Aubrey Melford Stevenson.

A former vicar's son, Stevenson had made his mark and his money as a young man specialising in libel and divorce. But after switching to the criminal bar, hoping for promotion to the bench, he showed all the zeal of a convert to the cause of law and order. The one thing everyone remembered about him was the name he gave his country house in the old cinq port of Winchelsea – 'Truncheons'. More significant, as far as the forthcoming Kray trial was concerned, was the part that he had played as defence counsel to Ruth Ellis, the last woman in England to be hanged for murder. While defending her in court he had seemed too much at ease with the prosecution and afterwards was widely blamed for not disputing the judge's ruling against trying his client for the lesser crime of manslaughter, which would have automatically stopped her going to the gallows.

Clearly he was just the man to deal with the Twins and their accomplices. He would take no nonsense from them, nor from anybody else, nor would there be any danger of excessive leniency when he came to sentence them. Here again there'd been discussions over the maximum sentences he could give the Twins. Stevenson himself was firmly of the opinion that with such hardened criminals a life sentence should mean just that – for life – but it had been suggested that he might settle for a 'recommended' sentence of thirty years in high security. The home secretary of the day could always extend a judge's 'recommendation' if and when he thought it necessary, but a full life sentence might be thought excessive, even for the Twins if the case went to appeal.

Thanks to the Twins' own decision to lift reporting restrictions on the remand hearings at Bow Street and the sensational stories that had reached the media as a result – they arrived at the Old Bailey with an aura of unproven but sensational wickedness around them. Those stories had included blowing up their enemies with dynamite, murdering someone with a crossbow and a poisonous suitcase, running a million-dollar empire in stolen securities, and planning to kidnap the Pope. But rather than revive such way-out charges it was decided by the prosecution that the Twins and their accomplices should be charged with the most straightforward cases which would be easier to prove – the blatant murders of George Cornell and Jack McVitie, to be followed in a separate trial over the fate of Frank Mitchell after the Twins had had him freed from Dartmoor.

When the trial finally began at the Old Bailey on 7 January 1969, Nipper Read could not resist repeating the daily curtain-raiser he had used at Bow Street of whisking the Twins and their colleagues through London in a high-speed convoy with armed guards, flashing lights and a presidential-style escort of police motorcyclists around them. And the trial itself was taking place in that most grandiose theatre of the law – Number One Court at the Old Bailey in the presence of an elderly, frequently bad-tempered gentleman wearing a full-bottomed eighteenth-century wig and scarlet robes and with a symbolic sword of justice and the coat of arms of the City of London set high above him.

In fact, the two main charges facing the Twins turned out to be fairly run-of-the-murder-mill cases that you might have heard in any major court in England. But thanks to the notoriety of the Krays and the sheer scale of the immunity granted to so many self-confessed criminals in return for their testimony against them it was inevitable that their trial would rapidly become one of the great criminal spectaculars of the century.

In the first case, the Cornell murder, only two people standing in the dock were actually involved – Ron himself, who was charged with shooting George Cornell at the Blind Beggar, and Ian Barrie for firing the two shots into the ceiling to distract attention which had made him an accessory to the murder.

The other eight in the dock were all allegedly involved in one way or another in the murder of Jack McVitie: Reg (along with Ron) for killing him, the two Lambrianou brothers, Cornelius Whitehead and the owner of the Regency Club, Tony Barry, as accessories, and the Twins' older brother Charles together with a recent arrival on the Firm called Ronald Bender and the Twins' old friend and ally Freddie Foreman for disposing of the body.

With these ten men in the dock, all facing separate charges for two quite separate murders, there seemed to be an inevitable element of rough justice to the proceedings from the start. Before the trial began in earnest its legality was disputed by Ron's counsel, the schoolmasterly John Platts-Mills QC, who was briskly overruled by Melford Stevenson. Then, adding insult to injury, the judge introduced a further novelty of his own by ordering everyone in the dock to wear a cardboard number round his neck 'to help members of the jury to identify them'.

This produced an angry clash of wills between the judge and the nine accused when they quietly refused and ended by tearing up the numbers and throwing them into the body of the court. This produced an instant show of temper from the judge and his angry exit from the court brought a temporary end to the proceedings.

But after half an hour spent cooling down in the judge's room, Sir Aubrey must have realised that not even he could force nine grown men to wear large cardboard numbers round their necks if they didn't want to. So he finally returned, made no further reference to the incident and the court resumed its business. But there was now a sense of genuine antagonism in the air, and a feeling that the judge would get his own back by the time the trial was over.

The trial began in earnest with the leading counsel for the prosecution, Kenneth Jones QC, reminding me of a Welsh methodist preacher as he outlined the prosecution case in singing tones. Gone were the days of the murder trials in this very court when silver-tongued barristers used all their skill in cases such as this with the life or death of the accused depending on their barrister's eloquence. Plump Kenneth Jones did not possess a silver tongue but he did his best to make the case against the Twins as clear as possible. 'On a Wednesday evening on the ninth of March a man called George Cornell went out for a drink at a pub in the East End called the Blind Beggar. As he was sitting in a corner of the bar he looked up and saw a man holding a pistol. A shot was fired, and Cornell crashed to the ground, mortally wounded in the head.

'Twenty months later on a Saturday evening in October, another man by name Jack McVitie, went to have a drink at a club in Stoke Newington. From there he went on to a party, where waiting for him was another gunman armed with a pistol which failed to fire. Then the gunman attacked him with a knife, while his brother held McVitie and urged him on until McVitie lay on the ground, murdered by the two brothers. The case for the prosecution is that the gunman who made the first attack was Ronald Kray, and that in the second attack the would-be gunman was Reginald Kray, urged on by his brother Ronald.'

Such were the accusations, and Kenneth Jones would spend the next two days going into a detailed account of both the killings. This was fairly heavy going and it was not until the first of the witnesses entered the witness box that the trial took off and became totally absorbing. Listening to it was like being present at a cross between an extraordinarily bloodthirsty grand opera, and an ongoing version of *EastEnders*, with ordinary people recounting the dramas and the horrors they had lived through. Some of the descriptions were harrowing in the extreme, and some of the witnesses were clearly lying, which made the drama more interesting. But one thing that struck me from the start was that the most impressive witnesses of all were women. Just as it was the womenfolk who were the real victims of the brutalised world of East End villainy so, as they now recounted their stories to the court, they all emerged as the trial's unsung heroines.

The first of them to enter the witness box was Mrs X, the barmaid from the Blind Beggar. She was a mousy little woman and was clearly terrified at first by this whole ordeal. As principal witness to the shooting of Cornell her evidence was crucial but she was also highly vulnerable, having previously sworn on oath at Cornell's inquest that she hadn't recognised Ron Kray as the killer on the night Cornell was murdered.

Ron's defence rested on an out-and-out denial that he'd been there at all. This had been backed up by an alibi from Scotch Jack Dixon that he and Ron had been together at another pub in Bethnal Green on the night Cornell was shot. Since then Scotch Jack had joined the happy band of penitents who, in return for their freedom, had turned against the Twins. He was now claiming he had lied about the alibi and was finally prepared to tell the truth – that he had actually driven Ron from the Blind Beggar back to Vallance Road after the shooting of George Cornell.

But since Dixon was obviously a 'tainted' witness everything depended now on Mrs X's supporting evidence. Platts-Mills made every effort he could muster to discredit her and break her down.

Since she admitted to having lied on oath, how could any jury believe her now?

'I think you're just making all this up, aren't you?' he said.

He should have known better, for her whole demeanour changed as she stood up against him; and as she spoke, one heard the voice of countless East End women who had suffered and kept quiet in the past.

'You're calling me a liar but I'm not one. If you'd had the nightmares I'd had afterwards, you'd understand why I acted as I did. I was frightened for myself and for my children.' More accusations from Platts followed but Mrs X stood her ground, and by the time she concluded her evidence Ron's so-called alibi was in tatters and it was obvious that he was guilty. So was the young, heedless Gorbals gangster Ian Barrie who had been stupid enough to go along with him. After this the court was free to turn its full attention to the killing of Jack McVitie.

Throughout the trial Nipper Read was constantly in court like an anxious stage director, and I guessed that, as usual, he knew exactly what he was up to when he decided who should be the first witness in the case of the murder of McVitie. But to begin with nothing could have seemed less threatening to the Twins that this waiflike woman standing so nervously before the court in a pale blue dress. She was addressed as 'Sylvie', although she was actually McVitie's widow. At first she seemed to have nothing very much to say, apart from nervously explaining how Jack had told her that he was meeting the Twins for a drink and how he never came back, although she looked everywhere to find him. Then she paused and stared for a moment in silence at the figures in the dock before she screamed out, her voice echoing around the court: 'You murdering bastards. It was my husband that you killed.' Then she burst into tears.

Until this moment Jack the Hat had been a faceless, feckless character whose importance lay in his having been murdered by the Twins. But suddenly Jack was there before us, the husband of a wife who missed him and who had loved him, and who was never going to forgive the bastards who had killed him.

There would be far worse accounts than this to come but in its way Sylvie's evidence remained the most electrifying moment in the trial. Even the judge was momentarily at a loss for words as Sylvie was led, weeping, from the witness box. And it was now that the trial itself appeared to change. No longer were the barristers simply scoring points off one another, but they too seemed suddenly involved in this killing of another human being and the suffering that had followed.

It was now that another female witness, Blonde Carol Skinner – who had been living in the flat where Jack was murdered – also came into her own in the witness box. She was no longer the unimportant creature whom the Twins had entirely ignored in the aftermath of Jack McVitie's murder. As she spoke, she conveyed the sense of outrage of a woman whose home had been turned into a slaughterhouse and communicated vividly the horror of knowing that McVitie's bleeding body had been wrapped in her own bedspread, then dumped on the bed beside her sleeping children.

None of the male witnesses achieved anything like the women's sense of authenticity in their evidence, but then, each one of them was only standing in the witness box to save his own skin. Never before in the history of the old East End can so many villains have betrayed each other in a court of law. There was Ron's former bodyguard, Billy Exley, barely recovered from a major heart attack, who entered the court in a wheelchair to testify against the Twins. There was their father's oldest friend and fellow deserter from the army, Harry Hopwood, explaining how he had looked after the Twins after they had murdered Jack by disposing of their bloodstained clothing and throwing the jammed .32 automatic into the canal. And there was 'Big Albert' Donoghue, as large as life, explaining in detail how he got rid of all traces of McVitie's blood from Blonde Carol's flat. If any of them felt any shame at betraying their former friends to gain their freedom they certainly didn't show it.

At times like this, it was as if all the villains from the past were on trial with the Twins as their former followers turned against them. So much for the first commandment of the Old East End – 'thou shalt not grass'. So much too for the sense of solidarity that had once bound East Enders to their local criminals, as rebels against an unjust society.

But the greatest betrayer of them all was still to come – the Twins' own cousin, Ronald Hart. I'd been seeing quite a lot of him when working on *The Profession of Violence* before the Twins' arrest and was surprised to hear that he too had 'gone over to the other side'; but nothing had prepared me for the sight of the tall, good-looking figure in the pale blue suit, standing up in court with a bible in his hand and promising to tell the truth, the whole truth and nothing but the truth, while knowing as he did that every word he spoke was saving him from at least twenty years in prison.

Inevitably it was his description of McVitie's murder that dominated the proceedings. It has remained in my memory ever since as the most nightmarish first-hand account I've ever heard of cruelty inflicted for its own sake by one human being on another.

Presumably Hart felt obliged to describe every detail of the Twins' behaviour to justify betraying them. By the time he'd finished, he'd left nothing to the court's imagination; Jack's screams for mercy, Ron's frantic encouragement to his twin to kill him, and the way Reg thrust the knife not once but twice through McVitie's throat, leaving him pinioned to the floor and flailing in his death throes like a dying animal.

By describing the murder in such horrendous detail Hart was doing something more than just providing evidence against his cousins. He was also acting out in court a gripping tableau of sadistic wickedness and it was now that the image of the Twins as exceptionally evil murderers was born.

Evidence like this was a hard act to follow and by 30 January, the seventeenth day of the trial, the plodding voice of Kenneth Jones QC summed up for the prosecution, and the case against the Twins and their accomplices was over. It was time for the defence, but the truth was that by now, after so much drama from the witness box, there wasn't a great deal left to defend.

There a certain black humour in the fact that the only person the defence could find to go into the witness box and speak in the Twins' favour was the last man in England who had had the cat-o'-nine-tails for assaulting a prison officer and who was at the time in prison with other members of the Richardson gang – 'Mad' Frankie Fraser.

After Mad Frankie, since no one else would speak in the Twins' defence, Ron Kray decided he would do so.

He had had his Stematol and he had probably heard his voices for he was clearly on a high. That very morning he had noticed one of his heroes the American film-star Charlton Heston was in court. He had never forgotten Heston's performance in the 1966 film *Khartoum* about another of his heroes, General Gordon, and was determined now to face his enemies as Gordon had faced the Mahdi and his men.

Ron was, of course, completely mad – and like many psychopaths and paranoid schizophrenics he was devoid of any sense of guilt or remorse for anything he'd done. When Kenneth Jones tried to cross-examine him, Ron denied everything and was probably convinced that every word he spoke was true. For him, the real victims in this case were neither McVitie nor Cornell, but he and his family because of the way the police had treated them and made their friends betray them.

As Ron continued what did come over was the importance he attached to the Twins' self-image. Betrayal plays a part in many legends and soon he was saying how everyone had turned against them, and how in spite of all the lies being told in court about them, he and his brother Reg were public benefactors who had spent thousands on the poor of Bethnal Green and had been honoured with the friendship of the great and famous.

'I took Joe Louis up to Newcastle, and Rocky Marciano and Sonny Liston to the Repton Club.' And he couldn't resist adding, 'If I wasn't here I could be having tea with Judy Garland, or having a drink with Lord Boothby.' Quick as a flash this brought an instant reprimand from the judge – and one saw that just by mentioning the name of Boothby, Ron was venturing into forbidden territory.

Apart from this, what seemed to interest Ron was no longer the outcome of the trial but the number of celebrities who came to see them. I had a letter from him at around this time informing me that he and Reg had had fifty-four visitors while they'd been in prison, including Cliff Richard and Diana Dors. What pleased him most of all was when Francis Wyndham brought along the young actor James Fox to see him and discuss a film that Mick Jagger was planning to make on the subject of a famous celebrity who became a criminal. The criminal was to be based on the Krays and the script was being written by David Litvinoff.

Unlike Ron, Reg seemed to have completely lost the plot by now as he sat in court and rarely spoke. The only time he did was when Kenneth Jones made a passing reference to the brother of his dead wife, Frances. He suddenly broke down and tearfully shouted out 'you fat slob' at the lawyer. In contrast with his swift reaction to Ron's reference to Lord Boothby the judge let this pass.

By this point I can remember thinking that in the absence of any credible defence the Twins really had no alternative to changing their plea to guilty with a serious plea in mitigation. For throughout the trial certain things had puzzled me, particularly the way that in spite of all the witnesses against them the Twins themselves had remained such enigmatic figures; and how so much about them had been left unsaid. During the whole trial no one had spoken of the fact that they were identical twins. Still less had anyone mentioned that Ron was once certified insane and diagnosed as a paranoid schizophrenic. And of course, there was no reference at all to the way that the cover-up of the Boothby case had made them virtually 'untouchable' as far as the police were concerned, which had effectively given them a three-year licence to kill.

But instead of pleading guilty, with their lawyers arguing what could have been a fascinating case in mitigation, the Twins continued to deny all the charges against them to the last. Afterwards, when I visited them in prison, and asked them why they'd acted as they did they always changed the subject; and it was not until many years later that I learned the answer.

Although he was in his sixties at the time of the trial Ron's counsel, the indomitable John Platts-Mills, had gone on practising the law until well into his nineties, and not long before he died in 1999 I chanced to meet him in his chambers in the Middle Temple. We talked about the trial and I finally inquired about the weakness of the Twins' defence. Why was it never mentioned that Ron had been a certified paranoid schizophrenic and that when Reg killed McVitie, not only was he on the edge of a nervous breakdown following his wife's suicide, but he was also dominated by his homicidal twin brother? And why did no one in court even mention the fact that they were identical twins?

'Oh, but we wanted to' replied Platts-Mills. 'Before the trial started, Wrightson (Paul Wrightson QC, who defended Reg) and I had both decided it was the obvious line for their defence. It would have been difficult arguing a case like that before old Melford, who wasn't the most liberal of judges, but the facts were there and they were undeniable. As Ron had been certified insane in the past he would have been sent to Broadmoor. And as for Reg, any sentence he received would have been considerably reduced on the grounds of diminished responsibility. *Folie a deux* between identical twins, with one of them a homicidal madman; it would have made a fascinating case. Certainly I'd never heard of anything remotely like it, which is why Wrightson and I were both so keen to argue it out in court.'

'So why didn't you?'

'Why do you think? Because of the Twins, of course. They wouldn't hear of it.'

'Why not?' I asked.

'Their reputation. They thought that once we said that Ron was mad, it would destroy their credibility as criminal celebrities and along with it their precious legend. Besides, Reg believed that it would be a terrible betrayal of his brother to condemn him to a mental institution, which of course is where he finally ended up anyway. To be fair to Ron, to my certain knowledge, on several occasions during the trial he urged Reg to do so. 'Save yourself, Reg' he said in my very hearing. But Reg wouldn't listen. I've always admired Reg for that, but he paid a very heavy price.

He paused. 'More than thirty years in prison, and he's still there today with little hope of freedom. It's a dreadful story.'

So there it was, and Platts–Mills was right: in its way it *was* a dreadful story. But at least it partially explained why the twins decided they would rather spend the rest of their lives in prison as criminal celebrities than have Ron consigned to Broadmoor.

On the day the Twins were sentenced Sir Alec Douglas-Home, the Conservative Prime Minister at the time of the Boothby scandal, was in court to hear the words of Melford Stevenson.

'Ronald Kray, I am not wasting any words on you. The sentence upon you is life imprisonment. In my view society has earned a rest from your activities, and I recommend that you be detained for no less than thirty years. Put him down.'

The same sentence was pronounced on Reg. Ian Barrie received twenty years, the Lambrianou Brothers both received fifteen, Charles Kray and Frederick Foreman were awarded ten, and Cornelius Whitehead seven. Anthony Barry, owner of the Regency Club, was acquitted.

A few days later, a second trial would begin before Judge

Lawton in which the Twins and Foreman were accused of murdering Frank Mitchell. The principal evidence against them came from Big Albert Donoghue, and the trial concluded when Judge Lawton ruled that since he was a 'tainted witness' his entire testimony was inadmissable. Whether Sir Melford Stevenson would have concurred is debatable. Probably not. The decision made no difference to the Twins, who were already sentenced to thirty years in prison, but it must have brought immense relief to Foreman and Charlie Kray, who would otherwise have faced a similar sentence.

But in one respect the Mitchell trial had done the Twins a favour – by adding the truth about that whole strange story to the other tales of villainy and murder which had formed around them.

On that April day in 1969 when the Mitchell trial ended, as I watched them being led off to the cells, I realised that in a weird way they had got what they had always wanted. When Ron succeeded in persuading Reg to murder Jack McVitie the Twins finally became what they'd never been before – identical twin murderers. Since then, those two murders, senseless and sadistic though they seemed, had been elevated out of all proportion by this interminable trial which had also established the legend that would bring the Twins their immortality. Thus the greatest murder trial of the Sixties had reinforced that fatal bond between the Twins and made them more notorious than ever.

It had also given them what they'd always longed for and were willing to sacrifice their freedom to attain – enduring fame and the certainty that they were special. Provided they had this, and were respected by their fellow criminals for what they were, they were perfectly prepared to face the future.

24

End Game

WHEN THE TWINS were sentenced in 1969 they were thirty-four years old and their days of violence and murder lay behind them. Ron would serve twenty-six more years of his thirty-year sentence before he died of a heart attack in March 1995; Reg served thirty-one, and was released thirty-five days before he died of cancer on 1 October 2000. As I have described this period in depth in my book *The Cult of Violence* I won't go over it here again.

But during these years one thing still obsessed the Twins – preserving the precious image of themselves as twin criminal celebrities which they had so cruelly established on the day they murdered Jack McVitie.

As we have seen, they had already made their preparations for a film about themselves to be coupled with my biography before they were arrested, and during their early days in prison their plans showed every sign of working.

The prison authorities had decided that after they'd been sentenced the Twins would not only be separated but also sent as far away from each other as possible – Reg to the maximum-security unit at Parkhurst on the Isle of Wight and Ron to the even more forbidding maximum-security unit in Durham Jail. This unit was actually a reinforced small prison within a prison which somebody described as like 'living in a submarine'. According to the sociologists Cohen and Taylor, who wrote about the Durham unit at around the time that Ron arrived, its effect on long-term prisoners was usually 'withdrawal and complete capitulation to the system', which was presumably what Melford Stevenson had in mind when he'd sentenced the Twins to thirty years in top security.

But Ron and Reg had no intention of surrendering to anyone if they could help it, least of all to Melford Stevenson. They thought they already knew everything there was to know about life in prison; and they also thought that they could use their fame as criminal celebrities to beat the system. Amazingly, both of these assumptions would ultimately prove to be correct, but only after they had spent more than a dozen years in close confinement.

Not that there could have been any question over their role as the country's top criminal celebrities by the time their trial ended. For more than a year the sometimes shocking exploits of the Twins had been making headlines in the press, and the trial had ended by making them utterly notorious. This meant that when the Twins arrived in prison they were treated with considerable respect, not only by the other prisoners but by the prison staff as well.

Throughout the months to come the Twins were fortunate to have Violet always there to help them. In many ways this was to be their mother's finest hour. Far from despairing at the shame the Twins had brought upon the family, she saw her boys as victims rather than as murderers. As always she was proud of them and did everything she could to help them. She was a great organiser and when she wasn't on the telephone persuading somebody to visit them she'd be searching for something that they'd asked for, then sending old Charlie trotting off to Durham or the Isle of Wight to deliver it. It was thanks entirely to Violet that the Twins lacked for few of life's necessities like boxer shorts, Brylcreme for their hair and cigarettes.

But since prison regulations banned them from seeing anyone with a criminal record from outside prison there were problems finding friends to visit them, which curbed the Twins' social life considerably. But thanks again to Violet, a handful of non-criminal acquaintances, and even the occasional celebrity, would go and see them, which added to the Twins' reputation.

During these early days in prison the Twins faced one big disappointment: Frank Taylor had been having problems finding backers for his film about them and had finally opted out. But even this didn't worry them for long, thanks to a sudden upsurge of interest in the Krays in the British film industry.

Until now, all the Twins' old favourite gangster movies had been modelled on the American mafia, but already the first British gangster films were in production inspired directly by the Twins. The first of them, which was screened in 1971, was actually entitled *Villain* and starred Richard Burton as Vic Dakin, a sadistic gang leader clearly based on Ron. The same year saw another very British gangster movie, although not so obviously modelled on either of the Twins: the exuberant *Get Carter*, starring Michael Caine.

Then in 1972 came the most unusual British film of all to be touched with the mystique of the Twins. This was the cult film *Performance*, made by several of those members of the celebrated Chelsea 'Popocracy' who had been so gripped by the legend of the Krays in the days of Esmeralda's Barn. It had even been scripted by Ron's one-time devotee and flatmate David Litvinoff and directed by rich young Donald Cammell, the former painter who had also been besotted with the Twins. James Fox, the promising young actor who had visited them in Brixton Prison, played the part of an escaping criminal who took refuge in the house of an androgynous, drug-crazed pop-star played by none other than Mick Jagger. With its mesmerising vision of the floating world of homosexuality and drugs and violent crime, this film has long been seen by many as a classic British movie of the sixties. The British Film Institute historian Colin McCabe goes further actually claiming, rightly or wrongly, that 'it was through *Performance* that the image of the Krays became imposed upon the national consciousness as the dominant image of the violent criminal.'

Any publicity was encouraging for the Twins, but they and the family were still in need of money. Geoff Allen had helped them out as usual, but most of their other 'bankers' who had been 'minding' quite large sums of money for them at the time of their arrest had mysteriously disappeared. The Twins were not entirely surprised at this, but were still anxious to keep their house in Suffolk, largely for Violet's sake, and 'so as we 'ave something to look forward to when we come out,' as Ron said with a hollow laugh.

Since I lived by writing books I also needed money, and the revelations of their trial meant that I could now write the uncensored biography that would have been impossible had they still been free. We came to an agreement: I would pay their share of the royalties on the book to Violet and in return would be free to write about them as I pleased. This suited me and meant that over the next few months I could talk to almost everyone I needed, including the Twins themselves, members of the 'Firm', their victims and the police.

By the end of 1971 my book was all but finished. Jonathan Cape, who published my biography of Ian Fleming, liked it and the *Observer* newspaper was offering me £20,000 for the serial rights on publication. Then came trouble, and like so much that the Twins became involved in, it all related back to Robert Boothby.

I had interviewed Boothby earlier that year, and it was then that he told me that it had been Harold Wilson who had personally persuaded Arnold Goodman to represent him when the scandal burst in 1964. He seemed remarkably untroubled by it all, and when I mentioned Ron telling me about having dinner with him at the House of Lords he cheerfully admitted that as well. 'Well, bless my soul, I think you're right. So I did' he said.

Soon afterwards I saw two personal letters he had sent to Ron which made it all too clear that, as I thought, there had been more to their relationship than those 'three occasions at my flat to discuss business matters,' which Boothby had mentioned in his famous letter to *The Times*. But it was not until Ron himself told Violet to give me a small brown suitcase containing 'a few things that might come in useful for the book' that I realised the friendship between Ron and Boothby was even closer than I thought. Inside the little suitcase was a personally inscribed copy of Boothby's memoirs along with photographs of him with Ron at the flat in Eaton Square and also at a dinner party at the Society restaurant. There were also a number of typewritten notes from Boothby to Ron on crested paper, sent between the autumn of 1963 and May 1964.

Although I didn't understand it at the time, this was in fact a cache of evidence that Ron had been entrusting to Violet in case he needed it in future. It was not in any way salacious. There was no mention in it of Litvinoff and the rent boys or the rough-trade parties at the flat in Ashburn Gardens. Ron, like Reg, would never talk about any of this for fear of rumours of it getting back to Violet. This had always been the Twins' one great fear about the scandal, and I didn't learn the full truth about it all until much later. But the real reason why Ron had so carefully retained the contents of the suitcase was itself quite interesting. The truth was that, unlike Reg, Ron had always secretly admired the English upper classes. He didn't particularly like them but, as he told me once, he was convinced that 'when things go wrong, the upper classes always save their own', which was why he'd been so anxious to get in with Boothby. It was also the reason why he had kept the letters and the photographs of himself with Boothby, not necessarily for blackmail but to prove his friendship with one of the most important politicians in the land. One never knew when friendships such as this might come in useful.

When Violet gave me the suitcase I still had no idea of the way that Arnold Goodman had covered-up the scandal. Still less did I envisage the political explosion that would have certainly followed had the truth about it been revealed. All that I could see from the letters and the otherwise completely harmless photographs of Boothby and Ron Kray together was that there *had* been a genuine, if unlikely, friendship between them, and that Boothby had been less than honest on the subject. Since this was clearly of importance to my story I decided to include the gist of it in my book, mentioning Boothby's visits to Esmeralda's Barn, his meals with Ron at the House of Lords and the Society restaurant, and how he met Vi Kray at Vallance Road. And that was all.

Even so, I had what should have been a warning of trouble when I went away on holiday and returned to discover that my study had been turned over and several things were missing, including the letters from Boothby to Ron and a copy of the manuscript of my book. (Fortunately I had already deposited duplicates of the letters and the manuscript in my bank, before I went away.) Then Deborah Rogers, my agent, informed me that her office in Warren Street had also been broken into and her files on my book were also missing.

We'll never know who did it, although we had our suspicions at the time. Cape had read my book and were pleased with it, the artwork for the jacket was complete and the *Observer* was deciding when to run my three part serialisation. Then suddenly my world collapsed around me.

It began with one of those 'I think that you should know' telephone calls from Lord Goodman in person. 'I think that you should know that I've read parts of the manuscript of your book that contain highly libellous allegations against Lord Boothby,' he informed me, but when I asked him to explain what libellous allegations he was refering to, he refused to say and then rang off.

Shortly afterwards I received a call from Deborah telling me that Lord Goodman had also been in touch with my publishers. As a result, Cape were rejecting my book immediately on the grounds of libel.

Then next day came the final blow when the *Observer* followed suit. (I hadn't realised that among his other influential appointments, Lord Goodman was also the Chairman of the *Observer Trust*.) So in one day I had lost my publisher, my publisher's advance and the promise of being serialised in a leading Sunday newspaper.

My instincts were to fight it out on the grounds that I stood by every word I'd written. But every lawyer I consulted advised firmly against taking on the establishment. 'Up against these people you will never win,' they told me. As it was, they had broken me financially and I was left with no choice but to sell my house.

About six months later, the publisher George Weidenfeld came to my rescue by taking my book over and publishing it late in 1972 under the title *The Profession of Violence*; but all references to the Boothby case had had to be removed. From the start the book was a success. Sales were good, and the reviews were excellent. The Twins hated it of course. Violet positively loathed it and told a reporter from the *Daily Telegraph* that I'd 'betrayed her boys and told a lot of lies about them'. She never spoke to me again, which was a pity as I liked her; but I've discovered that this often happens to biographers, and one gets used to it.

Then the unexpected happened. While telling the story of the Twins I had intended it to be a dire warning over the danger of organised crime in Britain. But the Twins rapidly discovered that far from damaging their reputation, my book was giving it the boost it needed. And not only did it bring in fame to them in prison, it was soon producing an extraordinary range of dedicated fans outside. So much for warning Middle England of the perils of people like the Krays. My book had made them more popular than ever, particularly among the new punk generation, and *Time Out* magazine was hailing it as 'a cult book among the young', many whom were actually regarding the Twins as heroes.

Nor was this all. It's always hard to find how fashions start, but it's often claimed that *The Profession of Violence* started a whole new genre of so-called true crime books. It certainly became the one reliable source of information on the Twins and the whole Kray family, and started off a cottage industry of people writing books about them. At the last count there were more than thirty of such books, and the Krays now have a special section of their own in the 'True Crime' section in most bookshops. More important to the Twins, the book had suddenly inspired both Adam Faith and Bill Curbishley, the influential manager of the pop group The Who, to start thinking about making a major film about them.

But although the Twins' status as criminal celebrities was flourishing and adding to the fame they'd always wanted, it did little to offset the stifling regime of maximum security, which after their first few years in prison was beginning to destroy them.

Not that they did anything to help themselves on the one occasion when, thanks again to Violet, they had a genuine chance to improve their quality of life. Violet had been in touch with Tom Driberg and had begged him, as an old friend of the Twins, to use his influence to get them reunited. It was thanks to him that they were finally permitted to share a cell in maximum security in Parkhurst.

This lasted for several months, until a half-witted fellow prisoner began to irritate them unbearably and finally they lost their temper. The killer streak within them suddenly ignited and they set about him with a broken bottle. If a posse of warders hadn't dragged them off they would probably have killed him. As it was, their victim needed more than a hundred stitches to save what remained of his face, and the Twins were once again separated. From now on they would have to cope with the deadening routine of maximum security without each other.

Their reputation as celebrities did little to alleviate their troubles, and by the late seventies both of them were showing signs of going off their heads and becoming institutionalised. The curse of Melford Stevenson was upon them, and it looked as if their dreams of finding fame and immortality through crime were over.

It was Ron who buckled first. By 1979 he was back on massive doses of stematol and was in a very bad way, having lost five stone in weight.

It was around this time that I received a letter from Ron saying that he'd decided to follow the advice of the prison doctors to get himself re-certified insane and go to Broadmoor as the lawyers at his trial suggested.

In his letter Ron said that he knew his life would be much better in Broadmoor than in maximum security: he wouldn't need to wear a prison uniform and seemed to think that he would be able to more or less please himself over anything he did. He was obviously excited by the thought that in Broadmoor he could have all the sex he wanted. Only one thing worried him: the thought that once in Broadmoor he was in for life.

In fact something a great deal more important than Ron Kray's sex life was going to depend upon his move to Broadmoor. As time would show, his transfer to this famous 'hospital for the criminally insane' would bring a total transformation in the lives of both the Twins and help to magnify their legend as Britain's best-remembered criminal celebrities.

★

In the bad old days, as Britain's major institution for the criminal insane, Broadmoor was run on the lines of an ordinary prison. But after the war, when the Ministry of Health took over, it started to resemble a normal hospital, and thanks to a whole new range of drugs to restrain the mentally deranged, its inmates could be treated more as patients than as prisoners. Security remained all-important, but otherwise the 'patients' had much the same rights as non-criminal patients would enjoy in any other hospital. There were no restrictions on visitors, they could even speak to journalists if they wished, they could wear more or less what they liked and, within reason, they could buy anything from the world outside that they could afford. On the day Ron Kray entered Broadmoor, following ten years in maximum security, he must have felt as if he'd entered Heaven.

With so many specialists in mental illness on the staff of Broadmoor there was no problem getting his medication reassessed, and his health rapidly improved. When I visited him there a few months later he was looking more like an opulent psychiatrist himself than the ghostly presence I remembered from the year before. Violet had brought him in several of his old Savile Row suits and still did his laundry for him every week, just as she'd done all those years before in Vallance Road. Thanks to her, his white shirts were as immaculate as ever and his solid gold Rolex watch shone brightly on his wrist. As we sat down in the big reception hall at Broadmoor and drank an alcohol-free lager I asked how things were going.

'Well, John, they could be worse' he said, smiling at a young male nurse he fancied.

For Ron one of the most important things about being at Broadmoor was the right to see virtually any visitors he wanted, even those who had a criminal record. This meant that, apart from his mother, one of his earliest visitors was his brother

Charlie, who by this point had been released, having served eight of the ten years awarded him by Melford Stevenson. Nor was there any problem when Freddy Foreman, also recently released from prison, arrived to see him and before long most of the leading members of the London underworld were traipsing out to Broadmoor to offer their respects to Ron.

Reg, meanwhile, was still enduring the maximum security regime at Parkhurst, and growing increasingly despondent. Things grew worse when in early 1982 he was suddenly transferred to Long Lartin, a modern top security prison near Birmingham. From the moment he arrived he hated it, and a few weeks later he tried to slash his wrists. When Violet heard of this she rushed to Birmingham to see him, and was so shocked by what she saw that the moment she was back in London she went directly to the Home Office in Whitehall and demanded to see the Home Secretary.

Unsurprisingly the Home Secretary was unavailable but Violet did meet an under-secretary with whom she pleaded for a 'more humane treatment for my boy, Reggie. He is now a broken man, and I don't want him to lose his reason.' The under-secretary promised he would try to help but, apart from moving Reg back to Parkhurst, nothing happened.

For more than a year now Violet had been suffering from cancer; she and Charlie had hidden the truth from the Twins, but it was getting worse and she got weaker. All she could think about was how the Twins would cope without her. She need not have worried so much because when she died, quite suddenly in August 1972, her funeral became the most valuable legacy she could have left them.

Of course they were both shattered by her death and instantly applied for permission to attend the funeral. Although the Home Secretary was concerned that the funeral 'could become some sort of circus', he couldn't possibly have refused; and the funeral of Violet Kray at Chingford parish church became something far more important to the legend of the Twins than a mere circus.

This was their first public appearance after thirteen years of total exclusion from the outside world. Attempting to make them look ridiculous, the prison authorities had ordered them to be handcuffed to the two tallest warders in the prison service. But from the moment that the Twins appeared it was not them, but the pair of gangling warders, who looked ridiculous. If Violet's funeral proved anything it was that here in the East End 'her boys' were still celebrities. Prayer book in hand and swathed in black, the East End's very own film star Diana Dors led the mourners; and as Ron and Reg and brother Charlie entered the church together people started clapping. The reporter Paul Callan, writing on the front page of the following day's *Express*, described 'men with hands as large as babies' heads grabbing at the passing brothers and hugging them with a wild East End passion.'

At the committal poor old Charlie inevitably got drunk and fell into his wife's grave. For the Twins this was their father's final, unforgivable disgrace, and when he himself died of grief a few months later neither of the Twins applied for permission to attend *his* funeral.

Once again the Twins' had their photographs in all the papers. They now knew for certain that they were not forgotten, and it wasn't long before they started to create one of the most successful and outrageous publicity campaigns ever mounted by a pair of murderers in captivity.

From the start they realised that, whatever happened, they needed to stay firmly in the public eye. At that moment there was little that Reg could do about this from his cell in Parkhurst, but for Ron the situation was completely different and in Broadmoor, with unrestricted access to the press, he was in his element. He enjoyed talking to journalists and made it clear that he expected to be paid for interviews, which brought him in extremely useful sums of money. By early 1983 Ron had started a press campaign to reinvent himself and Reg as East End heroes. He did this by shifting all the blame for their murders onto their victims. He told a reporter from the *Daily Star* that 'George Cornell had just been vermin. He was less than nothing, and I reckon that we did society and the East End in particular a favour by getting rid of him.' Similarly, Jack the Hat was 'nothing more than a drunken slag and a danger to decent women'.

Then Reg joined in to spread the word that, apart from doing a public service by killing characters like Jack the Hat, the Twins genuinely had hearts of gold. In the press he'd read about a fourteen-year-old boy in Liverpool who was fighting for his life against a rare brain disease, and Reg started his own campaign to spread the message by publicly sending money to children he had read about in the newspapers who were sick or dying. He would also include a personal note of encouragement with their cheque, and welcomed the subsequent publicity.

Then Reg realised that there was yet another way to keep the Kray name in the news. Many convicted murderers attract fan mail from lonely women, and Ron and Reg were no exception, often receiving more than twenty letters in a week. Their stories of romance in prison always appealed to the press. For the sake of publicity, Reg became engaged twice, but Ron decided to take this one step further. He would actually get married in Broadmoor. For some time he had been receiving the most romantic letters from a lonely divorced mother of two called Elaine Mildener. He proposed to her and she accepted. In fact Ron had already made a deal with a reporter for the exclusive rights to the story of his Broadmoor marriage for £6,000.

But the new Mrs Kray rapidly discovered that, far from offering her any of the normal joys of marriage, her chief job was to take the place of Violet, washing his shirts, bringing in food and drink from Harrods and becoming his general dogsbody.

This meant that, as well as earning Ron a lot of money, marriage brought a considerable improvement to his quality of life in Broadmoor. According to one journalist, 'tonight Ron Kray will have smoked salmon for his supper, together with thinly sliced brown bread and his favourite Normandy butter, all delivered specially from Harrods, the top peoples' store.'

The truth was that by now the Twins' days of crime were really over. Instead they had become professional criminal celebrities whose lives were now completely dedicated to exploiting the apparently endless public interest in themselves and the utterly engrossing story of their lives.

At the same time, outside prison their brother Charlie had spotted the business opportunities offered by the name of Kray and founded a company called Krayleigh which sold Kray T-shirts nationwide at £7.50 each. With the Kray name still behind him he of course had the market to himself and would-be competitors were soon warned off

On one visit Charlie brought in a friend of his Wilf Pine, recently returned from America, to visit Ron. It was unbelievable that no one at Broadmoor seemed to know that this charming fellow with a beard knew almost every leading member of the American Mafia.

This of course impressed Ron enormously, and he grew to respect Wilf for many reasons, not least for his connections with the Mafia. At the same time, Wilf summed up Ron as ' the smartest madman I have ever met' and a close and very profitable friendship followed.

Nobody objected when Wilf started visiting Ron in Broadmoor almost every day, and the man from the Mafia effectively became his business manager. The two of them realised that a lot of money could be made, not only in fees from journalists, but by effectively franchising the name of Kray throughout the country. In return for a hefty fee, security firms and gaming clubs would once again be protected by the name of Kray. For the first time since they were sent to prison the Twins started to become seriously rich.

But throughout the eighties the Twins' most ambitious financial coup of all continued to elude them – that all-important film about their lives which, when they had murdered Jack the Hat, they thought would bring them immortality.

At one stage the pop star Roger Daltry was apparently planning a £4 million film about the Twins, and just before Richard Burton died he too visited Ron in Broadmoor to discuss yet another film.

But in the end it was Wilf Pine, the Englishman from the Mafia, who would put a deal together with a small company called Parkway Films to make a film about the Twins starring Martin and Gary Kemp, two members of the pop group known as Spandau Ballet. And although the film went on to gross over £10 million, the Twins and Charlie had to share £750,000. Inevitably a family row followed when brother Charlie somehow got the lion's share, and they didn't speak to one another for several years.

When compared with the real story of the Twins, the film was deeply disappointing, but for the Twins it did two things: it made them even richer than before and it glamorised them more than ever.

With so much going on and, having by now divorced Elaine, Ron could not resist the excitement of marrying once more. He was determined not to make the same mistakes twice and this time chose someone the exact opposite of Elaine to be his bride.

When he met Kate Howerd at Broadmoor he knew at once that she was more his type. She was a pretty, fun-loving former kiss-a-gram and at their very first meeting he asked her to marry him. In spite of the fact that Ron made it clear from the start that sex was not included in the deal, Kate accepted his proposal. This was another wedding aimed at increasing the Twins' publicity still further. To start with, Kate went along with everything very happily. She bought herself a lovely dress and, at Ron's request, ordered the wedding breakfast from Harrods. Since Lord Snowdon had refused the honour of taking the bride's wedding portrait, Kate made do with the Queen's cousin Lord Lichfield instead. Ron hired a white Rolls Royce driven by a Broadmoor nurse wearing a peaked cap as her chauffeur, to bring Kate to the wedding in the Broadmoor chapel, where Reg had been brought across from Parkhurst to act as his best man. Ron had also promised Kate several things, including a house in the country, which never materialised, and before long, like the first Mrs Ron she discovered that her marital duties consisted largely of shopping and running errands for her husband. Luckily for Kate she had a good sense of humour, which she was going to need before the marriage ended.

Meanwhile life was getting easier all the time for Reg. Not only was he now allowed to visit Ron once a month, but he was finally moved to the more tolerant atmosphere of Maidstone Prison, where he soon became the most indulged and privileged high security prisoner in the country.

Their biggest asset would always be the name of Kray, but now it was backed up with endless money and wall-to-wall publicity. From the moment Reg arrived at Maidstone the other prisoners were in awe of him. A new governor had been recently appointed to replace the harsh prison discipline of the past with a more liberal regime, and since Reg made no trouble, and made sure that those around him made no trouble either, everyone including the Governor was happy. And with all his money Reg had no difficulty persuading members of the prison staff to get him almost anything he wanted, including the most attractive fellow prisoner to share his cell. During his time in prison, Reg had already had several male lovers but it was in Maidstone that he met the last male lover in his life who would be there for him until he died. This was a willowy, handsome would-be gangster called Bradley Allardyce, whose speciality was robbing post-offices

Only the Twins could have ever got away with what they did. The skill and the effrontery with which both of them had bucked the system reminded me in a way of those eighteen months in the early 1950s when, as young conscripts, they took the British army for a ride during their so-called military service with the Royal Fusiliers, and Ron had had his first experience of acting like a madman.

But by this point time and cigarettes were catching up with Ron. Lively Kate had made it clear that, unlike the first Mrs Ronald Kray, she had no intention of accepting too much nonsense and she was getting bored with running non-stop errands back and forth to Broadmoor. The press was now on to everything they did or said, and when Kate published a book about their marriage, Ron was deeply upset and felt that he was being victimised and made to look a fool.

It was now that Ron took offence one morning when another patient smiled at him at breakfast and tried to strangle him. Luckily the nurses stopped him, but the incident left Ron more depressed than ever. Then Kate said she wanted a divorce.

By now Ron was pushing sixty and in a state of almost permanent depression, and the life suddenly appeared to go out of him. The man who was once the most feared criminal in the whole of London actually complained to Wilf Pine that two of the male nurses were bullying him. Taking things into his own hands, Wilf ambushed the two nurses outside the local pub where they used to drink and threatened them with bloody murder if they didn't treat Ron with respect. The bullying ceased, but it was not long after this that Ron was taken ill and rushed by ambulance to Wexham Hospital near Broadmoor. There he died of a sudden heart attack on 16 March 1995.

It is said that when he heard the news Reg went crazy. No one in Maidstone could control him and the governor ordered his entire landing to be locked up to stop the violence spreading. By now Reg's lover, Bradley Allardyce, had been shifted to another prison, and one gets some idea of the power Reg Kray wielded inside the prison from the fact that Bradley was instantly transferred back to Maidstone as he was the only person who could console him.

Calm now that he had Bradley with him, Reg realised what he had to do. He was now sole keeper of the the legend that he and Ron had spent so much of their lives creating, and it was his duty to give Ron a worthy send-off.

When he had organised Frances's funeral all those years before he had been desperate to make it 'the East End's funeral of the year.' Now he was even more desperate to turn Ron's departure into the East End's funeral to end all funerals.

I've often wondered how Reg put together such a complex operation from inside prison. Certainly only someone in his privileged position could have managed it. He modelled it partly on the traditional Mafia funerals he'd read so much about, and also on the state funeral of Ron's old hero, Winston Churchill. Above all, it must also be an East End funeral with the traditional black plumed horses to pull the hearse, several hundred dedicated minders in black overcoats to line the route and twenty-five gleaming limousines for those who mourned.

Among the wreaths, there were two from America. One was from the Twins' only serious contender in the celebrity stakes for murder, the U.S. Mafia don John Gotti, who was also in prison; and the other was from Wilf Pine's friends, the Pagano crime family of New York. But the wreath that everyone noticed was the one from Reg. Spelled out in a huge arrangement of blood red roses on a background of white chrysanthemums and fixed to Ron's coffin was an inscription that said it all: 'TO RON, MY OTHER HALF'.

Now that the lifelong battle for supremacy between the Twins was over Reg became more of a conscious celebrity than ever, and their legend now depended entirely on him.

He had long ago given up denying his sexuality and now admitted that he was bisexual. Like some doting father he had married Bradley off to a pretty girl called Donna Baker. Reg had chosen her from one of the many girls who visited him regularly in Prison, and this suited him because he too was set on marriage.

His bride to be was Roberta Jones a thirty-six year-old English graduate from Southport Manchester. Reg had come into contact with her when her company was making a video of Ron's funeral. Their marriage took place in Maidstone Prison on 14 July 1997. Bradley Allardyce was his best man. But unlike Ron's last marriage, this was a much more low-key ceremony and although it hit the headlines in the next day's newspapers he was not allowed to make any money, even from selling the wedding photographs to the press.

Unlike any other Mrs Kray, Roberta was utterly devoted to Reg and since he had nearly served the full thirty years that Melford Stevenson had reccomended, she campaigned tirelessly for his parole. Had Reg been an ordinary murderer convicted of a gangland killing he would almost certainly have been released long ago by now. The unofficial 'tariff' for murder at the time was twelve-and-a-half years in prison. But by making himself the country's top criminal celebrity, Reg had made himself too hot for any Home Secretary to handle and no politically conscious politician, like the current Home Secretary Jack Straw, could ever have recommended the most notorious murderer in the country for release.

★

Then in April 2000 Charlie died. He had been caught in what looked like a fairly obvious police trap for allegedly dealing in £2 million worth of cocaine. He had served out his last days in Parkhurst and his final wish was to be buried in peace with a minimum of fuss. But Charlie was more useful to his brother Reg dead than alive, and although Charlie was the least important of the three Kray brothers, his funeral gave Reg the chance to stage the greatest full-scale celebration of the ever-growing legend of the Twins with Reg himself now firmly in the centre.

Some said that there were twenty thousand people in Whitechapel High Street on that March morning, but I would guess that it was twice that number. With police everywhere and their helicopters circling overhead, the old East End had never seen the like of it before.

When the unmarked van bringing Reg from Bellmarsh Prison drew up outside English's funeral parlour and Reg stepped out, handcuffed this time to a female warder, there was a huge roar of applause from the crowds outside, many of whom had not even been born when the Twins were arrested, and fewer still had ever met them.

This was to be Reg's last public appearance and in its strange way it was a profoundly emotional occasion. Although he didn't know it yet, Reg too was dying and he could never have expected such a heartfelt demonstration of warmth and affection as he received that day. It ended in Chingford cemetery where, after kissing Frances's tombstone, he stood alone by Charlie's grave while Freddy Foreman called for three cheers for Reggie Kray. Then in the silence that followed the last of the Krays stepped into the unmarked van that would drive him back to Wayland Prison outside Norwich.

It was unfortunate for Reg that the only one of these three epic funerals that he was unable to appreciate was his own. For the last two years he'd been complaining of painful indigestion and the prison doctors had told him there was nothing wrong and insisted on giving him Milk of Magnesia. In fact he was suffering from advanced stomach cancer and the disease had spread. In spite of an operation in which the surgeons removed a large growth from his stomach, they could not save him. But it was only when the doctors could assure Jack Straw that Reg was safely on the point of dying that the Home Secretary granted him his last few days of freedom.

Reg and Roberta spent their last few weeks together in freedom in the honeymoon suite in a small hotel with a view across the river. It had been paid for by Reg's old friend Bill Curbishley and, as Reg lay dying, Bradley and Roberta shared the death-bed vigil.

But to the very last Reg's thoughts were on his precious legend. As a thank you to Curbishley, Reg had given him the TV rights to a final deathbed interview. Reg was close to death by now and looked like it, but the interviewer, Aubrey Powell, said that he had one last question that he really wanted Reg to answer.

'Do you regret killing Jack the Hat?' he asked him. Reg shook his head.

'Then why did you kill him ?' Powell insisted.

Reg paused a while before he answered.

'I killed him because he was a vexation to the Spirit,' he whispered.

Reg died a few days later, but even in death there was no escaping from the bond that had always tied him to his twin, and his coffin was placed next to Ron's in the double grave in Kray Corner, with Frances in her grave beside them.

But the Twins' true memorial was their precious legend, which they had killed for and suffered for and which, with Reg's death, was even more alive than ever.

Appendix

During the year between the Twins' arrest in 1968 and the conclusion of their Old Bailey trial a year later Ron wrote me many letters from prison. Some were about the progress of the biography I was writing with him and Reg, some about his hopes for the future and others about the celebrities who came to visit him in prison.

In reproducing a few of these letter here one gets some idea of the way he wrote and spelled and because on re-reading them myself they kept an echo across the years of his inimitable voice.

EIL

In replying to this letter, please write on the envelope:—

Number 058110 Name KRAY RON

H.M. PRISON, BRIXTON,
LONDON, S.W.2.

57 FEB 1968

Dear John
THANK you FOR your letter,
JoHN IT IS now up to your
SOLISITOR TO GET THINGS
SETLED AND TO PUT THINGS
RIGHT FOR my mother.

John I am Glad I
am going GRAY, I LIKE
IT.
John I WANT you TO Keep
your word. ABOUT NOT
SAYING ANY THING BAD
ABOUT THE RITCHISONS
comeing FROM me or
Reg AS THEY HAVE
Been very nice
TO us they ofered to
GIVE EVIDENCE FOR us.

Dont LISTEN TO much
FROM DICK Morgan

No. 243 30141 8-2-68

AS He is not allways
alright about
the Crime

You should go and
see Jim HAGRIS.

AND PiP THE HEAD WAITER
AT. THE STORIC. CLUB,

ALLSO EDDIE FRANKS
we used to work For
HIM IN A GLASS FACTORY,

You should HAVE A
TALK WITH my
FATHER ABOUT Some
of the old timers
LiKE JiM SPiNX
AND CHARLY. BARTWICK
THEY, ARE BOTH
DEAD. ALLSO
DOFER MULLINS

He is DEAD AS well
you met DOGGO iN
the Crown Pub
WITH US,

I HAVE GiVEN You
A LETEGI For
FRANCES. BACON
BUT REMEMBER
I DON'T KNOW
Him very
well,

RON,

XL5

In replying to this letter, please write on the envelope:—

Number. 058710 Name. KRAY Ron

35 MA 1969

H.M. PRISON, BRIXTON, LONDON, S.W.2.

Dear John

I Hope you are well,
well AS you Know me
Got 30 YEARS AND CHARLY
10 YEARS
well we are all Smokeing
TOBACO AND TRYING To
MAKE IT LAST,
I would Be Pleased if
you were to see my
mother as often as
you could.
Have you seen JIM HARRIS
YET, LET me Know who
you Have Seen.
Please write soon
John if I DONT ALL WAYS
ANSwere your letters
it is only Because
I will only Be getting one
letter a week now,
Reg and CHARLY SEND
THEIR BEST
To you.

R.T.O

No. 243   (21442—3-11-42)

Dont Forget keep in
touch with my
Mother and Father,
And you can come on
to see one or oc

Visit,
Some of the things they
have said in the news
papers about Grey
and his dead wife
are Disgusting and
all lyes as he really
treated her well.
He thought the world
of her.
I thank you for Being
so understanding
about the Photo Business.
You should go to
see Joe williams
again. and Charly
Clark,
write soon,

I am going to Bed now
and Try to have
some nice Dreams.

God Bless

your Freind

Ron,

In replying to this letter, please write on the envelope :—

Number O.8110   Name KRAY

OL
27/7
27/7

H. M. PRISON,
OLD ELVET,
DURHAM.

DEAR JOHN
now the APPEALS HAVE
FINISHED we only get one
letter a week, SO IF I
DONT write Verry OFTEN
I AM SURE you will
UNDERSTAND. I HAVE now
GOT A CANNERY BIRD. So
when I GO TO the EXERZIZE
YARD I take THE BIRD
IN ITS KAGE AND let IT
GET SOME FRESH AIR. IT
DOSE THE TWIST IN THE
MORNING TO the RADIO.
HAHA, THE TOUGHTEST MAN I
HAVE EVER met IS my
FREIND PUNCHY WHO
I MET IN BROOKLYN.
AND HE WAS A verry NICE
MAN. AND A REAL
CHARACTER.
I HAVE JUST Been
LISTENING TO SOPHIE
TUCKER   P.TO

ON MY RECORD PLAYER.
SHE HAD THE BEST PERSONALITY
OF ANY ONE I HAVE EVER
MET.

JOHN WOULD YOU DO ME
A FAVOUR AND PHONE
FRANCES BACON. UP AND
ASK HIM IF HE WOULD
ACEPT A PAINTING OFF
of me. IF I DONE HIM
of one, WOULD YOU
write and say

me know what
HE SAYS.

I HOPE YOU WILL GO
AND SEE PEGGY AND
he will BE ABLE to
Help you a lot.

I WOULD Like to
SEE YOU again
IF YOU CAN FIND
the TIME.

Do write to me
when you CAN.

AND Let me
KNOW WHO
YOU HAVE SEEN
of LATE.

DID YOU see
JENNY LYNCH.
Or WINIFRED ATWELL

well John thats
all for now

GooD LUCK
your FREIND

Ron

NO DOUBT YOU HAVE
NOT GOT AS MUCH
TIME AS me. HAHA.

In replying to this letter, please write on the envelope :—

Number 058110   Name KRAY   Ronald

H. M. PRISON,
OLD ELVET,
DURHAM.

DEAR JOHN
I Hope you are well.
I Hope Reg likes it AT
PARKHURST AS much AS I
like it Hear. I wrote to Reg
a few DAYS AGO SO I should
Be getting a letter FROM
Him soon.
their are 7 of us in the
wing 6 are CONVICTED For
murder the other is one
of the GREAT TRAIN
ROBBERS.
I CANT Help Feeling a
GREAT COMPASSION For
my Fellow PRISONERS.
to me they are all
GENTLEMEN who I am WITH,
AND I am Glad that they
Have ASSEPTED me.
like they Have.

Please write Soon.

No. 243   (28150—3-10-62)

P.T.O

I AM STARTING WEIGHT
TRAINING THIS comeing
week,
 I will like that,
     Do try to get to
see me one
          DAY,
     Reg will more
        than likely
write to you.

     God Bless

          Your friend

                    Ron
   JOHN I THINK
   You SHOULD put
   IN THE BOOK
   THAT I AM
     BYSEXSuel

H. M. PRISON,
JEBB AVENUE,
BRIXTON,
LONDON, S.W.2.

DEAR JOHN
THANKS FOR your
letter.
YOU ASK WHAT I THINK
ABOUT when the
TRIAL IS going
on.
well some times
I GO A SLEEP.
I DONT LISTEN TO WHAT
IS BEING SAID
I LIKE TO THINK I AM
A PEBLE IN A STREAM
AND THE WORDS ARE
WATER Running over
me.
I CANT BE BOTHERED
LISTENING TO THE
LYES AND RUBISH.

THE WITNESES REMIND
me of when you SEE

P.T.O

No. 243   (28150—3-10-62)

People at the Zoo
THROWING STONES
AT THE ANIMALS
TO HAVE THEIR
SPIGHT out,

still it will
soon Be over
and we will
Be able to
HAVE A BIT of
PEACE

I Hope to Hear
FROM
you soon,

Good luck
Ron,
LET me Know
who you see
IF ANY one,,

Ron

In replying to this letter, please write on the envelope:—

Number 058110   Name KRAY RON

BRIXTON Prison

23-4- 1969

DEAR JOHN

THANK YOU FOR COMEING INTO
SEE me TODAY,
IT WAS NICE TO see you,
REG GOT YOUR LETTER to NIGHT
HE ASK me to thank you,
I ASK my mother to get
you a RECORD that I
Heard on the RADIO.

we Have GOT our RADIOS
NOW, IT PASES THE time
LISTENING to them,
I will Be Glad when
I can HAVE my RECORD
PLAYER, So I CAN HAVE Some
of my Records sent IN,

I Hope you liked my
HAIRCUT HAHA,

yes John you should
GO AND see CHARLY
CLARK AGAIN,
AND CHECKER, I like

No. 24A 21440-3 11-42,

P.T.O

them Both a lot.
John GET my old MAN
to TAKE you to ree
Bill TUCKER AND
Some more of the
old TIMERS.

well John I Hope
to Hear From
you Soon.
Do POP IN TO ree
me AGAIN Soon.
all the Best
of Luck. your
FREIND.

Ron

TED SMITH
IS A REAL
NICE FELOW
HE WHENT TO ABAVAN IN WALES
when IT WAS HIT By DISASTER AND
HELPED DIG THE CHILDREN OUT.